THE ALLAN SCHORE

Eva Rass, a leading expert on the work of Allan Schore, presents a collection that provides an overview of his core ideas and makes accessible the evolution of his thought. Including interviews and original papers, as well as integrating his ideas with research in psychoanalysis, developmental psychology, biology and developmental psychopathology, this book provides an in-depth introduction to Schore's theories.

The Allan Schore Reader: Setting the Course of Development represents a major contribution to the understanding of Schore's often dense and complex work. The choice of papers, interviews and subject matter is structured and instructive, while the content captures both the depth and breadth of Schore's ideas, including important extensions into other fields, like paediatrics, social work, and family law. Schore's contribution to the advancing knowledge base – pioneering the paradigm shift in researchers' focus in psychopathogenesis from the cognitive verbal left brain to the affective, preverbal right brain – is here made accessible to a far greater readership.

The book will be of interest to all practitioners, researchers, educators, and policy makers dealing with the critically important and broad field of mental health service delivery and prevention of mental illness for those "at risk", particularly psychoanalysts, psychoanalytic psychotherapists, and counselors.

Eva Rass is an analyst in private practice with over 35 years of experience working with children and adolescents. She is Professor at the University of Applied Sciences in Mannheim, Germany, and lecturer and supervisor at several psychoanalytic institutes. Her work covers several areas including developmental psychology, attachment theory, clinical learning disabilities, affect regulation theory, psychodynamic psychotherapy, and analytic self-psychology.

THE ALLAN SCHORE READER

Setting the Course of Development

Edited by Eva Rass
With a Preface by Sir Richard Bowlby

Routledge
Taylor & Francis Group

LONDON AND NEW YORK

First published 2018
by Routledge
2 Park Square, Milton Park, Abingdon, Oxon OX14 4RN

and by Routledge
711 Third Avenue, New York, NY 10017

Routledge is an imprint of the Taylor & Francis Group, an informa business

Originally published in German as *Allan Schore: Schaltstellen der Entwicklung: Eine Einführung in die Theorie der Affektregulation mit seinen zentralen Texten* by Klett-Cotta, 2012.

© 2018 Introduction, selection and editorial matter, Eva Rass, all other material, the contributors.

The right of Eva Rass to be identified as the author of the introductory and editorial material has been asserted in accordance with sections 77 and 78 of the Copyright, Designs and Patents Act 1988.

British Library Cataloguing-in-Publication Data
A catalogue record for this book is available from the British Library

Library of Congress Cataloguing-in-Publication Data
A catalogue record for this book has been requested

ISBN: 978-1-138-21464-4 (hbk)
ISBN: 978-1-138-21465-1 (pbk)
ISBN: 978-1-315-44556-4 (ebk)

Typeset in Bembo
by Apex CoVantage, LLC

Printed and bound by CPI Group (UK) Ltd, Croydon, CR0 4YY

CONTENTS

PERMISSIONS

Schore, A. (1991), Early Superego Development: The Emergence of Shame and Narcissistic Affect Regulatoin in the Practicing Period. In A. N. Schore (Ed.), *Affect Regulation and the Repair of the Self*, 151–186. New York, London: Norton.

Schore, A. (2003), Dysregulation of the Right Brain: A Fundamental Mechanism of Traumatic Attachment and the Psychopathogenesis of Posttraumatic Stress Disorders. In A. N. Schore (Ed.), *Affect Dysregulation and Disorders of the Self*, 234–265. New York, London: Norton.

Schore, A. (2014), Looking Back and Forward: Our Professional and Personal Journey in *Neuropsychotherapist*, issue 7 October 2014, Queensland Australia: Dahlia Media, pp. 8–17.

PREFACE

I first met Allan Schore on 16th July 1998. There was to be a conference at the Tavistock Clinic the following weekend and I had been asked to collect the speaker and his wife from Heathrow and to provide them with a few nights' accommodation at our house nearby in Hampstead; Allan and Judy have been dear friends ever since. The only conversation that I can recall on the car journey back from the airport was when I asked Allan "What kind of a guy are you?" His reply was illuminating. "It's odd; I find that if I read something that is personally meaningful, even science, I'm able to not only precisely remember where I've read it, but how it links into related information. And I read a lot."

My first understanding of Allan's profound commitment to my father's work on attachment theory was that weekend when I had asked him if he would like to see round my father's study (we live in the house next door). My father had died eight years earlier in 1990 and his study had been taken over by our daughter Sophie as her art studio, but the room still had his original writing desk, his file cabinets and much of his library. Allan's physical response to being in John Bowlby's study was intense – I could see that he was deeply moved.

Eighteen months earlier I had videotaped an interview with Alan Sroufe about his Minnesota study and his thoughts on attachment theory, and so I decided to ask Allan Schore if I could record an interview with him about his views on neuroscience and attachment theory, which he agreed to do. At the time of the interview my knowledge of attachment theory was sketchy at best, but my knowledge of neuroscience was next to zero. The result was that my questions were so naïve as to be practically incoherent. But that meant that I had stumbled on the perfect combination: Allan's passion to explain his new understanding of the neurobiology of attachment theory to me – John Bowlby's son – combined with my obviously limited grasp of the subject had forced Allan to use the simplest of terms to describe the most complex of concepts so that I might be able to understand what he was saying. The resulting interview is unique, and after I retired in 1999 I edited the recording and incorporated much of it into a training tape (DVD) on attachment theory, extracts of which have made their way onto YouTube.

Over time I was to learn that by the early 1980s Allan was already an accomplished attachment scholar, and that he spent ten years immersed in the study of the latest neurobiological findings, exploring the fit between attachment theory and neuroscience. Allan's return to being a full time student was only made possible by what he called "The Judith Schore Foundation." They switched income responsibilities so that Judy's and to a lesser extent Allan's psychotherapy incomes supported a household and two young children! Judy continues to play a crucial part in Allan's work in a similar way that I saw my own mother supporting my father in his work. The outcome of this intensely creative period of Allan's life was the publication in 1994, the onset of "the decade of the brain," of his groundbreaking book, *Affect Regulation and the Origin of the Self.*

In my present role as a lay ambassador for attachment theory, it brings me much reassurance to know that there are people such as Allan who are able to explain and integrate the complexity of the multiple specialties of neuroscience, of attachment theory and of psychotherapy. I believe that the ability to make the crossover between such specialties is the key to the synthesis of new conceptual frameworks, and that there is no substitute for having a single mind which is able to hold the mass of information needed to distil out new insights.

I am confident in believing that of all the many advances in attachment theory since my father's death, he would have selected the link between attachment theory and neuroscience as being the most significant. I think that Allan's contribution to the understanding and dissemination of attachment theory – the science of family love – has been profound. There is now a broad understanding within society that early childhood experiences have a physical impact on the developing brain. This general acceptance fundamentally changes attitudes to the vital importance of the early years, an acceptance that attachment theory alone has struggled to achieve. The weight that the "hard science" of neurobiology has added to the "soft science" of psychology has lifted attachment theory to a new level.

All human achievement is built on the shoulders of giants, and just as John Bowlby and Allan Schore have stood on giant's shoulders, so future generations of scientists will in turn be standing on their shoulders. In his books he has integrated a vast array of scientific advances and organized it in an overarching way that deserves the deepest acknowledgement and gratitude.

Sir Richard Bowlby
London, May 2012

INTRODUCTION

Since the publication of his first book *Affect Regulation and the Origin of the Self* in 1994 Allan Schore has become one of the leading authorities in the field of developmental neurobiology and early child development. The following chapters of this volume provide a detailed insight into his creation of a new field of scientific research: the concept of affect regulation and its relationship to emotional development, first introduced by Allan Schore. His research integrates findings that draw from various scientific disciplines, such as attachment theory, affective neuroscience, developmental psychology, and psychodynamic psychotherapy. Over the course of more than 30 years he has tirelessly and continually attempted to deepen our understanding of how early relational affective interactions with the social environment may fundamentally influence all later stages of life. In his continuous research he rarely misses publications in the biological, psychological, social, medical, or cognitive disciplines that address this problem, the central focus of his regulation theory. Due to the complexity of his multidisciplinary approach, his writings may seem arduous and challenging as he combines various scientific fields and multidisciplinary backgrounds.

Over this time period Schore describes a paradigm shift from the primacy of behavior, cognition, and content to the primacy of emotion, relationship, and context. In parallel to these psychological changes the neurosciences have shifted the emphasis of their empirical research from the later maturing left hemisphere which is involved in conscious, verbal and cognitive processes to the earlier maturing right hemisphere which is engaged in preverbal, unconscious and emotional processes. Schore's synthesis of the literatures of various scientific fields has been a major contributor to the now accepted idea that developmental processes represent psychobiological phenomena, progressions in both psyche and body. Indeed, humanistic and biological scientists are currently using a common approach in order to achieve an overarching conceptualization of early human development.

In the introduction of the German translation (2007) of *Affect Regulation and the Repair of the Self* (2003) I emphasized the courage of Schore in offering an integration of the growing body of scientific research over the last three decades in developmental psychology and developmental biology. Moreover, I pointed out that comprehending Schore's writings places a heavy demand on the reader. Although his work has gained positive critical resonance and outstanding acknowledgement, readers have expressed difficulties in understanding the complexity of his work and have been daunted in struggling with the texts. This issue made the German publisher Klett-Cotta reach out to me to write an introduction for Schore's work, especially after I had translated *Affect Regulation and the Repair of the Self*. As I have written, his accomplishments and findings are of extreme importance for all those who are working in the field of mental health and early education.

To make this access more comfortable a gradual approach to five original Schore papers and one lecture is presented. But first I begin with some book reviews of different Schore volumes, chosen to accentuate specific issues. These reviews also contain summaries of the rich content of these books, as well as an overarching perspective of his work at different points in time. Following this I offer four interviews with Allan Schore, in order to give not only a more informal presention of his theories, but also a more personal glimpse into his motivations and his creativity.

With this introduction to Schore and to the reception and impact of his work, the reader will be prepared to read a sample of original articles and addresses. I start with the *Preface* and the *Introduction* of Schore's first volume *Affect Regulation and the Origin of the Self* (1994) in which he outlines his original hypotheses about the general nature of development, and in particular human social-emotional development. In less than ten pages Schore describes his provocative model not of cognitive but of socioemotional development, and simultaneously suggests a scientific continent that has to be explored. Here he develops his concept of affect regulation that runs throughout all his work. Then we have to go back three years – to 1991 – the year of the first publication "Early Superego Development: the Emergence of Shame and Narcisstic Affect Regulation in the Practicing Period." In this seminal and far-reaching paper Schore has elaborated on an interdisciplinary conceptualization involving observations from various fields that were beginning to offer studies of socioemotional development – psychoanalysis, infant research, developmental psychology, and neurobiology. This overarching model of early regulation attempted to elucidate specifically how psychological experiences influence the maturing structures of the developing brain and how these evolving structures sustain more complex psychological functions. This paper was written before the "decade of the brain" and it highlights the primacy of emotion – at a time when psychodynamic theory did not yet have a theory of affect. Furthermore he investigates developmental lines in the preverbal period, i.e., during the developmental phases in which the key issue of psychoanalysis, the Oedipus complex, does not play a role. Schore also explores the basic functional mechanisms of shame which have an earlier developmental origin than the emotion of guilt. He also introduces his models of psychopathogenesis, wherein states of neglect and emotional failure in the mother-infant relationship can lead to pathological coping mechanisms in the early developing right hemisphere. His focus is on events in the latter parts of the first and into the second year, describing the interpersonal neurobiology of the research of the developmental psychoanalyst Margaret Mahler's practicing period of separation-individuation and rapprochement crises.

Following chronologically, the essay written in 2000, "Attachment and the Regulation of the Right Brain", documents the enormous advances in the field of attachment research since 1969, and Schore's profound acknowledgement of the work of John Bowlby. He refers to the growing body of studies indicating the critical importance of the development of attachment that supports the emergence of affect regulation, of the sensitivity and availability of the mother in responding to her baby's cues, and of the amount and interpersonal nature of their emotional interactions. Utilizing an interdisciplinary perspective Schore demonstrates that the infant's stress coping capacities are shaped by the primordial relationship with a mature adult, the primary attachment object. These processes indelibly influence the earliest stages of the development of the brain and mind. Differences in humans in regulating inner tension states and in developing synchronized interactions are the result of the transgenerational transmission of psychobiological attunement and not primarily a result of genetics. Both the development of successful adaptability or deficient capacities occur in the caretaking environment which influences the promotion or the failure in the maturation of right hemispheric regulatory circuits. Schore suggests that Bowlby reminds us that Freud also had attempted to integrate neurobiology and psychology in order to create a theory of the development of unconscious processes that is grounded in a "natural science." For almost 30 years now, Schore has been following this same path of integrating brain research and clinical psychoanalytic models.

The essay "Dysregulation of the Right Brain: a Fundamental Mechanism of Traumatic Attachment and the Psychopathogenesis of Posttraumatic Stress Disorder" was published in (2002) in the *Australian and New Zealand Journal of Psychiatry* and was awarded the accolade of best scientific paper of the year. In this complex work Schore integrates developmental psychology and psychiatry in order to describe the neurobiological consequences of relational trauma with its severe disturbances and pathogenic phenomena. In great detail he sets out the consequent negative repercussions of chronic relational stress on developing right brain subcortical and cortical circuits. Microanalytically he sheds light on the nature of the protoconversation which is embedded in the attachment dialogue. Frequent unrepaired missattunements lead to enduring and intense states of affect dysregulation, causing enduring deficits in stress coping mechanism over the life span which may result in damage to physical, mental, emotional, and cognitive systems. Schore emphasizes attachment research and its importance for mental health workers in the area of infant and developmental psychology. Education via intervention and prevention programs is vital for the crucial mother-infant dyad in order to improve the quality of many lives throughout all stages of human development.

In March (2014) at the UCLA Interpersonal Neurobiology Conference Schore gave a very personal talk *Looking Back and Looking Forward: Our Professional and Personal Journey* in which he described the arc of his professional career with all the challenges and "downfalls" bringing along disappointments in the beginning, followed by continuous "ups" that lead to satisfaction and personal pride. In this speech he expressed deep affection and thankfulness to his wife Judy who has supported and accompanied him in this "tremendously exciting quiet life", being an eye-to-eye, shoulder-to-shoulder partner, and thereby not just a great woman *behind* but *beside* him.

In (2001) Allan Schore was invited to present the Seventh Annual John Bowlby Memorial Lecture and the consequent essay "Minds in the Making: Attachment, the Self-Organizing Brain, and Developmentally- Oriented Psychoanalytic Psychotherapy" was published in (2001) in the *British Journal of Psychotherapy*. In (2010) he elaborated on this concept and it was published under the title "The Right Brain Implicit Self: A Central Mechanism of Psychotherapy Change Process" in the book "*Knowing, Not-Knowing and Sort of Knowing*" (Ed. Petrucelli). In these papers Schore wanted to present some recent interdisciplinary advances that are forging tighter links between the common goals of classical analysis and attachment theory. He emphasized that the new developments that are re-coupling Freud and Bowlby come from neuroscience. Schore suggested that an integration of current findings in the neurobiological and developmental sciences can offer a deeper understanding of the origins and dynamic mechanisms of the system that represents the core of psychoanalysis, the system unconscious. In these papers he described a number of psychoneurobiological mechanisms by which attachment experiences specifically impact the experience-dependent maturation of the right hemisphere. Further he suggested that regulation theory describes the mechanisms by which the patient forms an attachment, that is a working alliance with the therapist. The major contribution of attachment theory to clinical models is thus its elucidation of the nonconscious dyadic affected transacting mechanisms that mediate a positive therapeutic working alliance between the patient and the empathic therapist. Complementing this, the neurobiological aspects of attachment theory allow for a deeper understanding of how an affect-focused developmentally oriented treatment can alter internal structure within the patient's brain/mind/body system. This approach supports Bowlby's assertion in his last writings that "clearly the best therapy is done by a therapist who is naturally intuitive and also guided by the appropriate theory".

In his workshop at the 107th Conference of the German Pediatricians 2011 in Bielefeld, *Using Modern Attachment Theory to Guide Assessments of Early Attachment Relationships,* Schore refers mainly to the previously mentioned (2002) essay as well as to diverse other scientific findings since the first elaboration in 2002. Similar to the first publication in (1991), he defines a well-structured field of developmental neuropsychology in which new scientific findings supported his regulation theory. Furthermore, a vignette is offered to demonstrate the approach of regulation theory. In his keynote presentation at the conference, *Developmental Origin of Health and Disease,* he clearly pointed out the relevance of the pediatrician as being the first professional to get insight into and pragmatic understanding of the early interactions between a particular caregiver and her baby. Via primary clinical observations, paediatricians may function as mediators recognizing early problems in developing parent-child relationships and therefore the first professional who can refer families to sustaining intervention programs. In the human sciences there is now strong support for the idea that the origin of illness in adulthood can often be found in developmental impairments which have occurred during the first years of life. The rapid increases in knowledge about attachment transactions, nonverbal communication, and interactive regulation that lay at the core of the mother-infant relationship allows the clinician to more deeply understand this psychobiological realm. This is of especial importance for dyads with a high-risk status that may predict later pathological dysfunctions as well as psychosomatic illness. A body of clinical research now shows that timely therapeutic interventions in phases of high developmental vulnerability have enduring positive effects. At the end of this section I offer my own thoughts about the application of Schore's work to day care and early childhood education.

In the final chapters of this book, more fields of application are demonstrated for regulation theory. In addition to the previously described significance of affect regulation theory for the developmental and clinical disciplines, this work has important implications both within and beyond the field of mental health. Indeed, the theory can not only increase our understanding of patients but also generate more effective models of treatment. This is articulated in Judith Schore's and Allan Schore's essay (2008) "Modern Attachment Theory: The Central Role of Affect Regulation in Development and Treatment" published in the *Clinical Social Work Journal*. The importance of regulation theory for decisions of the family court can be seen in the publication "Family Law and the Neuroscience of Attachment" (2011) published in the *Family Court Review* (together with J. Macintosh), as recent psychological knowledge about human relationships, attachment needs, and affect regulation can also influence legal decisions based on the best interests of the child. Furthermore, the vast realm of education and learning should be grounded upon this knowledge. The current Zeitgeist overly emphasizes left brain language capacities, cognitive flexibility, and executive functioning skills. But the field of early childhood should combine cognitive-linguistic enrichment with greater attention to emotional process and affect regulation in order to prevent significant adverse effects on the early developing right brain.

In addition, affect regulation theory offers explanatory developmental models of behavioral distrurbances and cultural effects beyond the human species. The destruction of early developing attachment structures can have long-lasting and enduring detrimental influences on the physiology, behavior, and transgenerational social culture of not only human but also animals. In the journal *Nature* (2005), as well as in *Ethology* (2007), findings in the fields of behavioral biology were published in order to explain "elephant breakdown" – a social trauma that results from human-induced early disruption of attachment bonds. In the future, interdisciplinary research may further develop trans-species concepts of development of brain and behavior.

In 2015 (November, Santa Fe) and 2016 (October, Chicago) Schore offered presentations on the topic of the gender's influence and the developing brain. He described in detail the differences in brain development of both sexes. Neglecting these differences and resulting needs can be dangerous.

This book offers the reader an entry and overview as well as a deeper look into Allan Schore's critical research, as well as the mind that created it. For those of you new to his work understanding its complexity may be challenging at first. But stay with it – it may open new horizons, and I would say, unimagined dimensions of knowledge and self-awareness.

I thank Allan Schore for agreeing with the concept of bringing him and his work closer to the field of mental health care workers, and for his interest and support during this evolving process.

References

Bradshaw, G. A., & Schore, A. N. (2007). How elephants are opening doors: Developmental neuroethology, attachment and social context. *Ethology*, 113, 426–436.

Bradshaw, G. A., Schore, A. N., Brown, J. L., Poole, J. H., & Moss, C. J. (2005). Elephant breakdown. *Nature*, 433, 807.

Petrucelli, J. (2010). *Knowing, not-knowing and sort-of-knowing: Psychoanalyis and the experience of uncertainty*, 177–202. London: Karnac.

Schore, A. N. (1991). Early superego development: The emergence of shame and narcissistic affect regulation in the practicing period. *Psychoanalysis and Contemporary Thought*, 14, 187–250.

Schore, A. N. (1994). *Affect regulation and the origin of the self: The neurobiology of emotional development*. Mahwah, NJ: Erlbaum.

Schore, A. N. (2000). Attachment and the regulation of the right brain. *Attachment & Human Development*, 2, 23–47.

Schore, A. N. (2001). Minds in the making: Attachment, the self organizing brain, and developmentally oriented psychoanalytic psychotherapy. *British Journal of Psychotherapy*, 17, 299–328.

Schore, A. N. (2002). Dysregulation of the right brain: A fundamental mechanism of traumatic attachment and the psychopathogenesis of posttraumatic stress disorder. *Australian and New Zealand Journal of Psychiatry*, 36, 9–30.

Schore, A. N. (2003). *Affect regulation and the repair of the self*. New York, London: Norton. (dtsch.: Affektregulation und die Reorganisation des Selbst. Übersetzt von E. Rass. Stuttgart: Klett-Cotta 2007).

Schore, A. N. (2010). The right brain implicit self: A central mechanism of the psychotherapy change process. In J. Petrucelli (Ed.) (2010), *Knowing, not-knowing and sort-of-knowing: Psychoanalyis and the experience of uncertainty*, 177–202. London: Karnac.

Schore, A. N. (2014). Looking back and looking forward: Our profesional and personal journey. *Neuropsychotherapist*, 10, 8–17.

Schore, A. N., & McIntosh, J. (2011). Family law and the neuroscience of attachment, Part 1. *Family Court Review*, 49, 501–512.

Schore, J. R., & Schore, A. N. (2008). Modern attachment theory: The central role of affect regulation in development and treatment. *Clinical Social Work*, 36, 9–20.

1

ALLAN SCHORE THROUGH THE LENS OF BOOK REVIEWS

With his (1991) essay "Early Superego Development: The Emergence of Shame and Narcissistic Affect Regulation" Allan Schore entered with a "beat of a kettledrum" into the scientific community. Since then his creativity, mental power and ability to approach new research with unusual openness for interdisciplinary thinking seems inexhaustible. This early essay contains, comparable with an overture of an opera, all the important and essential elements which he has worked through in the last 25 years. Three years later in 1994, this small but extraordinary creek became a mighty stream, developing into a powerfully flowing river that is continuously growing. With the publication of his first book *Affect Regulation and the Origin of the Self: The Neurobiology of the Emotional Development* (1994) a sequence of publications and presentations took a nearly incomparable course. In 2003, a double volume was published in which a selection of significant essays were collected – "Affect Dysregulation and Disorders of the Self" (2003b) and "Affect Regulation and the Repair of the Self" (2003a). The latter was translated soon after into a variety of languages including German, French, Italian, and Turkish, indicating the importance of his detailed work and the volume of his outstanding knowledge. In 2012 a fourth volume was published expanding his theories, *The Science of the Art of Psychotherapy,* which includes various and more recent essays. Worldwide, Schore is invited to present workshops as well as various lectures – in North and South America, Europe, Asia, and Australia. The acceptance and recognition of his work has been recognized with important honors, including an Award for Outstanding Contributions to Practice in Trauma Psychology from the Division of Trauma Psychology and the Scientific Award from the Division of Psychoanalysis of the American Psychological Association, Honorary Membership of the American Psychoanalytic Association, and the Reiss-Davis Child Study Center Award for outstanding contributions to Child and Adolescent Mental Health. In (2016), in testimony to the enduring recognition and influence of his seminal book, this publisher reprinted

Affect Regulation and the Origin of the Self as part of the Routledge Classic Editions Series.

Allan Schore is a clinical psychologist and neuropsychologist and has been working since 1971 in private practice as a psychoanalytic psychotherapist. He is member of a number of psychological, neuroscientific and psychoanalytic associations. He is editor, co-editor and member of the editorial board of more than 45 scientific journals in the Anglo-American language area. He has consulting and teaching functions in many clinical, teaching, and research institutes. As of the beginning of 2017 his works have been cited in over 15,000 references in Google Scholar.

The publications of his volumes has led to a variety of book reviews such as M. Solms (1997); J. Issroff (2006); D. L. Thiselton (2004); M. Richlin (2005); M. H. Spero (1996); V. Kraft (2008); Naumann-Lenzen (2008) and M. Stark (2015). All writers have emphasized unisono that Schore has investigated human development from the early beginnings in an outstanding depth and wide range by summarizing and integrating the growing body of literature in the fields of developmental neurobiology, infant and attachment research, and related disciplines relevant to the function of affect regulation. The resulting conceptualizations explicate in detail the precise mechanisms by which the infant's brain might internalize and structuralize the affect regulatory functions of the mother, which can be observed primarily in circumscribed neuronal tissues. These findings describe an essential finding in epigenetical history (Solms, 1997).

The abundance of evidence he presents to support the theses in his books has been characterized as "exorbitant." In *Affect Regulation and the Origin of the Self* more than 2300 publications were used and cited (Spero, 1996). In *Affect Regulation and the Repair of the Self*, Kraft (2008) has described the scale of the references as an "independent chapter." Schore follows his train of thought free from dogmatic limits and is therefore able to integrate a vast array of information which is organized in an overarching way. Due to its complexity most of the book reviewers noticed that a good range of theoretical expertise is required in order to understand the broad spectrum of neurological research, and that the book cannot be read "by the way" or casually. Some themes are repeated in different contexts for different purposes so that unavoidable redundancies occur. On the other hand this recursive nature may facilitate revisitation and familiarization of the complex approach and findings. In his review, M. Solms proposes that Schore has not integrated Freud's drive concept into the core of his affect theory and has therefore underestimated the relevance of mainstream Freudian psychoanalysis for modern neuroscience. Partly in response, in 1997 Schore wrote the essay "A Century After Freud's Project: Is the Rapprochement between Psychoanalysis and Neurobiology at Hand?" in the *Journal of the American Psychoanalytic Association*. There he traced affect research from Freud to the contemporaneous decade of brain research and pointed out that despite updated conceptualizations such as psychoanalytic self-psychology, Freud's concept of drive has not been ignored but transformed.

All book reviewers emphasized Schore's detailed and complex elaboration of his central theses that it is the mother-infant dyadic system which regulates the infant's psychobiological states and that interactive affect regulating events act as a mechanism for the social constructions of the human brain. This central theme is first outlined in his first book, where he offers interdisciplinary data in order to explain the neurobiology of emotional development, i.e., the discovery of the right brain neurobiological base of attachment. The quality of the mother-infant affective dialogue imprints itself upon a complicated neurological network and acts as a growth-facilitating environment for the postnatal maturation of a corticolimbic control system in the right prefrontal cortex that mediates regulatory, homeostatic, and attachment functions. This intricate wiring of the circuits in critical periods of the infant's developing brain is responsible for the future socioemotional development of the individual. Certain areas in the brain that are specific for each developmental phase pass through growth spurts. This conceptualization made it possible to integrate the previous conceptual gap between "nature versus nurture.".

With the first 1994 "voluminous opus magnum" (Naumann-Lenzen, 2008, p. 299 ff) Schore laid down a visionary and broad fundamental basis for his future research. The interdisciplinary perspective that integrated biology and psychology, as well as his creative and novel synthesis of various scientific disciplines in this and all of his later writings has given him the reputation of an "American Bowlby" as well as a comparison with Einstein (Issroff, 2006, p. 685).

In both of his volumes published in 2003, Schore scrutinized the clinical models of major twentieth century psychoanalysts, and utilized his interdisciplinary perspective to cast a modern neuroscientific view of the concepts of Sigmund Freud, Melanie Klein, Heinz Kohut, and John Bowlby, specifically on their thoughts concerning development, trauma, and restoration. More and more he focused on not only severe developmental trauma such as neglect, maltreatment and abuse, what he termed cummulative "relational" trauma, but also on the unavailability of a responsive attachment figure to comfort and regulate stress after more benign misattunements that are a daily part of the young child's experience. Furthermore he applied regulation theory and interpersonal neurobiology to the treatment of patients with a history of attachment trauma. Extrapolating the advances in mother–infant research, Schore offered the reader a clinical model of the affect regulating therapeutic relationship in which the patient undergoes a body-mind reorganization as he/she re-experiences in the patient-therapist transference-countertransference relationship his/her trauma and developmental arrests. With a focus on the expression and regulation of the patient's emotional (more so than cognitive) states and on the socioemotional communication and protoconversation between therapist and patient, developmentally oriented psychotherapy shifts from the talking cure to the communicative cure. Schore also emphasized that both Bowlby's attachment theory and Kohut's analytic self-psychology have contributed to this crucial paradigm shift in psychoanalysis.

Three years after the appearance of his next volume, *The Science of the Art of Psychotherapy*, in (2012) Martha Stark from the Harvard Medical School published a book review in which she emphasized that Schore, by dint of his meticulous research and giftedness as integrative thinker, has earned the well-deserved distinction of being at the forefront of the affective neuroscience movement:

> He manages to bring together the incisiveness and clarity of his analytical left brain with the creativity and synthetic ability of his intuitive right brain in the interest of capturing the beauty of something that few have dared to try and fewer still have been able to accomplish – to offer a compelling explanation for how exactly a psychotherapy works and what exactly its scientific underpinnings are.
>
> *(2015, p. 228)*

Stark observes that Schore is highlighting a structural and functional difference between the two hemispheres and is appreciating their complex interdependence, complementarity, and synergy. His conviction, which is amply supported by exhaustive research, is that cognitive exchanges (a left brain function) between therapist and patient may well be necessary but rarely enough to effect enduring psychotherapeutic change. An affectively attuned psychotherapy will afford the patient an opportunity to rework relational trauma that had once been overwhelming but that can now, with enough affective support from the therapist, be processed, integrated, and adapted. Furthermore, Stark suggests that Schore goes to great lengths to stress the primacy of interactive regulation by both therapist and patient in the interest of creating transformative moments that will advance the therapeutic endeavor.

In Stark's view, Schore has made a masterful attempt to capture with words the essence of phenomena that are without words but she felt that his efforts to bring the clinical moment alive is only partially satisfying. She thought that the volume would have benefitted from the inclusion of more clinical examples that would have captured not just a moment in time but movement over the time. Finally, as others have mentioned earlier she described Schore's material as a bit redundant – although she personally found, as others do too, the repetitiveness to be reinforcing of his central ideas. To conclude, she emphasized that *The Science of the Art of Psychotherapy* is a must-read for health professionals and interested persons alike because "it is ultimately a book about what it means to be human and how it is that we can deeply and meaningfully connect to others" (p. 233).

To summarize these book reviewers, amongst many others, the description of Allan Schore as an unusual and creative scientist has been made repeatedly. He indeed has become a pioneer who has brought integrative psychodynamic psychotherapy into the 21st century. Convincingly, he has elaborated that the development of the self is a core issue of neuroscience and that the development of the self-structure is grounded in the caretaking affect regulation during the first year of life. The developing infant is existentially dependent on a maternal self object who unconsciously and right hemispherically "reads" the needs of the baby in order to regulate his emerging emotional states, which in turn allows for the imprinting of brain circuits that underlie the development of adaptive coping mechanisms. The major task of the maternal figure consists of vitalizing and soothing the infants in appropriate quantities in heightened moments of emotional arousal. The optimal maturation of the right hemisphere, which in the early developmental stages moves through an enormous growth spurt, requires the adaptive and "good-enough" functioning of a consistent and reliable caretaker. The structuralization and differentiation of the self, and that of the brain also, can only occur when it is embedded in a regulated attachment relationship, i.e., in a right-brain-to-right-brain communication. This conceptualization also mirrors Freud's concept of the development of the unconscious mind (located in the early maturing right hemisphere) before the conscious mind (located in the later maturing left hemisphere).

In order to convey Schore's complex theory to the reader, both scientists and clinicians who have reviewed his books have discussed their impressions and assessments regarding his ability to offer models that integrate psychological and biological concepts. In essence, his theory focuses on the early developing right hemisphere which can also be seen as a psychobiological substrate of Freud's unconscious mind, as well as on its continuing development over the life span.

References

Issroff, J. (2006). Affect dysregulation and disorders of the self. By Allan N. Schore, New York & London: W. W. Norton, 2003, 403 and affect regulation and the repair of the self, New York & London: W. W. Norton, 2003, 363. *Contemporary Psychoanalysis*, 42 (4), 681–685.

Kraft, V. (2008). Allan N. Schore (2003): Affektregulation und die Reorganisation des Selbst. Stuttgart, Klett-Cotta, 2007. *Psyche*, 62, 718–722.

Naumann-Lenzen, M. (2008). Allan N. Schore (2003): Affektregulation und die Reorganisation des Selbst. Stuttgart, Klett-Cotta, 2007. *Analytische Kinder-und Jugendlichenpsychotherapie: Zeitschrift für Theorie und Praxis der Kinder-und Jugendlichen-Psychoanalyse und der tiefenpsychologisch fundierten Psychotherapie*, 39 (2), 299–303.

Richlin, M. (2005). Affect regulation and the repair of the self (2006). *The Permanente Journal*, 9 (2), 109–110.

Schore, A. N. (1991). Early superego development: The emergence of shame and narcissistic affect regulation in the practicing period. *Psychoanalysis and Contemporary Thought*, 14, 187–250.

Schore, A. N. (1994). *Affect regulation and the origin of the self: The neurobiology of emotional development*. Mahwah, NJ: Erlbaum.

Schore, A. N. (1997). A century after Freud's project is a rapprochement between psychoanalysis and neurobiology at hand? *Journal of the American Psychoanalytic Association*, 45, 807–840.

Schore, A. N. (2003a). *Affect regulation and the repair of the self*. New York/London: Norton.

Schore, A. N. (2003b). *Affect dysregulation and the disorder of the self*. New York/London: Norton.

Schore, A. N. (2012). *The science of the art of psychotherapy*. New York/London: Norton.

Schore, A. N. (2016). *Affect regulation and the origin of the self: The neurobiology of emotional development: Routledge classic editions*. Routledge: New York and London.

Solms, M. (1997). Affect regulation and the origin of the self: The neurobiology of emotional development. By Allan N. Schore. Hillsdale, NJ: Erlbaum Associates, 1994, 670. J. Frosch et al. (Eds.) (1997). *Journal of the American Psychoanalytic Association*, 45, 964–969.

Spero, M. H. (1996). Affect regulation and the origin of the self: The neurobiology of emotional development. By Allan N. Schore. Hillsdale, NJ: Erlbaum Associates, 1994, 670. *The Psychoanalytic Quarterly*, 65, 395–398.

Stark, M. (2015). The science of the art of psychotherapy. By Allan N. Schore, New York, NY: W. W. Norton & Co., 2012, 458 pp. *Psychoanalytic Psychology, 215*, 32 (1), 228–234.

Thiselton, D. L. (2004). Affect regulation and the origin of the self: The neurobiology of emotional development. By Allan N. Schore. Hillsdale, NJ: Erlbaum Associates, 1994, 670. *Psychological Medicine*, 34, 1590–1592.

2

INTERVIEWS WITH ALLAN SCHORE

The acceptance of Schore's Affect Regulation Theory and its dissemination via writings and lectures gave rise to opportunities for interviewers to approach him in conversation. Therefore, many scientists, clinicans, and journalists have met with him over the years, with the results being published in specialist journals, the Internet, newspapers, magazines, radio, and television. Due to the importance of his work to so many fields of life the interview partners came from different areas of interest. The four interviews described in this chapter represent only a small account of these many dialogues, which Schore has himself has selected for this book. The question–answer formats cover a wide variety of themes, and also give a more personal glimpse into Allan Schore's mind and personality.

2.1 Bowlby's genius: integration across disciplines. Excerpts from Schore's interview with Roz Carroll (2001)

One of the main topics in the interview between Schore and Carroll was the recognition of John Bowlby's elevated position in both the developmental and psychiatric sciences. Schore sees him as one of the three or four major psychological theoreticians of the 20th century. Bowlby was intensely interested in the process of development and the connection between infant and mother, proposing that the formation of an emotional attachment bond is critical to all later aspects of the personality. He also persuasively argued that the mechanism of this crucial attachment bond occurs not only within humans but across the entire animal kingdom. He also stressed the specific relevance of the nonverbal communication between mother and infant via facial mimic, gestures, and prosody.

Bowlby was trained as a physician, as a psychoanalyst, as well as a child psychiatrist. His medical training brought him into contact with the problems of stress and coping and their effects on the body. His psychoanalytic training allowed him to enter a door leading into the world of the infant's developing unconscious. Finally, psychiatry raised the questions about early predispositions to psychopathology. In order to ground attachment as a theory of psychological science, Bowlby integrated findings from various disciplines, including developmental psychology, ethology (the biology of behavior), psychoanalysis, and psychiatry. He stressed the importance of the early years of development but was equally interested in the expression of the attachment process over the life span. Carroll describes Schore's work also as the integration of multiple disciplines. The biological emphasis in his work is seen in his understanding of Bowlby's attachment as regulation, and in his use of developmental affective neuroscience and complex dynamic systems theory in order to offer holistic models of the organism which generate adaptive changes to environmental social stresses.

Indeed, Schore's research demonstrates that the concepts of interactive regulation and self-regulation are now being used as an organizing principle in all of the physical sciences as well as in developmental psychology. Attachment is conceptualized as dyadic regulation, the interactive regulation of emotion. Social experience directly impacts the development of the regulatory systems in the brain that regulate all forms of affect, cognitions, and behavior. The attempt to regulate affect in order to minimize unpleasant feelings and to maximize pleasant ones is a driving force in human motivation.

Bowlby – like Freud – believed that the mother is the regulator of distressed states. Schore advances these ideas by proposing that a child in distress reaches out to its mother so that she can act as a regulator of his right brain generated negative affective states. But Schore also adds that the attachment relationship also regulates the infant's burgeoning positive states, such as joy and excitement. Developmental neuroscience now indicates that play experiences, which start at the end of the second month after birth, are also associated with right brain functions. Attachment to the mother therefore not only minimizes negative states but also maximizes positive states. In support of Schore's expansion of Bowlby's ideas, in the last two decades molecular biology and affective and social neuroscience have generated large bodies of new information about infancy. Additionally, Schore has moved Bowlby's focus of the onset of attachment from six months back to initial date of birth and even prematurely – and at the same time over the entire life span. The idea of developmental stages has been superseded by the more precise concept of sensitive periods. In these critical periods of brain growth the infant needs certain types of social and emotional experience.

In the latter part of the interview, Carroll posed the question of whether these new findings may have relevance to psychotherapy. Schore pointed out that there is a movement in all psychotherapies on early social and emotional development, on the importance of experiencing and regulating specific emotions during the intervention with the therapist, and on altering attachment styles and internal working models of attachment. Another common trend is on not only the patient's mind but body, and the patient's felt experiences of his own body. He also suggested that psychotherapy, which is still geared toward the removal of symptoms and negative emotions, must also focus on the expansion of positive states. Research on the mother's role as an amplifier and regulator of joy has to be digested fully in updated models of psychotherapy.

At the end of the interview, trends in the early care of infants are discussed and Schore expressed his deep concern that in the US, which lacks a national parental leave policy, mothers return to work only six weeks after giving birth, the very time when cortical areas of the infant's brain begin to mature, and when face-to-face joyful interaction begins. Parents face a terrible dilemma of how to address this problem without any cultural or political support. The level of day care is on average sub-optimal and professional caretakers are not trained enough and paid poorly. Schore used the words "shame" and a "scandal" because the US culture and politicians pay little attention to their responsibilities to future generations.

2.2 The scientific career path against the background of the personal life: excerpts from a conversation with George Halasz (2009)

In this talk with the Australian child psychiatrist George Halasz, Allan Schore described himself as a clinician-scientist rather than as a scientist-clinician. In a very real sense, all of his enquires about the deeper mechanisms of the human condition arose out of both his personal life – his intimate relationships as a son, a husband, and as father of two children, and as a friend – as well as out of his professional life – his relational experiences with his patients as a psychotherapist. All these experiences have led him into to the question of why the early interpersonal and emotional events of life have such an inordinate influence on literally everything that follows.

After his training in clinical psychology in the 1960s he felt that psychodynamic approaches were more effective with a wider variety of patients than behavioral techniques. His own therapeutic explorations deepened his appreciation of a psychodynamic perspective. After finishing his studies and internship in clinical neuropsychology at an interdisciplinary training hospital he took a position in the Psychiatry Department of Kaiser Permanente in Los Angeles, where for the next ten years he practiced his craft of psychotherapy, seeing a wide variety of psychiatric outpatients and patients, and training the department's staff in neuropsychological assessments. At the same he set up a private practice in order to work more deeply with long-term patients.

In 1980, after working for ten years, he left his position and decided to continue yet cut back his clinical hours and began what would be a ten-year period of intense independent study. Moving beyond the fields in which he was trained he became particularly interested in the points of contact between disciplines such as psychiatry, neurology, and pediatrics, as well as the physical sciences. For the next decade he spent one day every weekend roaming the stacks at a local California State University library, xeroxing copies of a large numbers of articles in various fields and pored over them in his home office. In this "homemade ivory tower" he switched family roles and income responsibilities with his wife Judith. He also became the parent who was at home when their two children returned each day from school. And so for ten years his wife earned the bulk of the family income through her private practice, allowing for his studies to continue on a so-called "Judy Schore fellowship."

By the end of this decade he had familiarized himself with a vast amount of research data across disiplines, and was convinced that an integration of these various fields could produce powerful theoretical models. Intuitively, he knew that it was now time to formulate a model of early emotional development grounded in what had become a psychoneurobiological perspective. With this approach he moved past the predominant concepts which described the child's development beginning with the oedipal phase and generated hypotheses about preoedipal experiences, including the early development of the unconscious mind. This was a move back from the verbal to the nonverbal, from the development of the conscious to the unconscious, and the cognitive to the emotional realms.

In the 1960s, behavioral psychology was the dominant force in psychology. In the 1970s and 80s there was a paradigm shift into cognitive psychology. In 1983, Judith Schore wrote her dissertation on the topic: *The Study of the Superego: The Relative Proneness to Shame of Guilt as Related to Psychobiological Masculinity and Femininity in Women*. In the following years Allan's clinical work also became very focused on early forming shame – at the time an unexplored field. In the late 1980s, Allan and Judith Schore were thus both applying their research to early stages of the shame dynamic and to the treatment of narcissistic personality disorders. More and more, Allan's clinical work explored the early interpersonal origins of shame affect which plays out nonverbally, beneath the words, in all relationships and developmental stages. After a decade of exploring emotional processes in a period of solitary and independent study, he decided to end the 80s internal journey and to convert it into an external journey in the form of writing, discussions with other therapists, and clinical presentations. And so the Schores wrote an article about shame and development. They submitted it to the *Journal of the American Psychoanalytic Association* but it was not accepted. In this paper they were questioning a cardinal tenet of psychoanalysis and were discussing the primacy of emotion at the time when psychoanalysis had no theory of affect. This rejection had powerful emotional and motivational effects. Schore allowed himself to experience this rejection to its fullest, but then became even more motivated to find the right home for this revolutionary paper.

With this learning experience in body and mind, Schore's professional career became energized and focused. Weaving together different disciplines, Schore created his conceptualization of affect regulation, providing a heuristic model of how attachment relationships directly influence the evolution of psychic structure. This concept allowed him to describe how early psychological events impact the maturing structure of the brain and how this more complex biological structure now supports more complex psychological function. He submitted his next essay "Early Superego Development: Emergence of Shame and Narcissistic Affect Regulation in the Practicing Period" to the journal *Psychoanalysis and Contemporary Thought* and it was accepted immediately.

In his interview, Halasz observed that this single article alone preceded the publication of Schore's first book, *Affect Regulation and the Origin of the Self: Neurobiology of Emotional Development*. In that work, after the ten years immersion period in reading across so many disciplines, Schore described how the concept of regulation, central to chemistry, physics, biology and medicine, could also be applied to the problem of early emotional development. In his synthetic developmental models, Schore came to conceptualize specifically how nature and nurture interact. He reminded the interviewer that, at this time, the field was plagued with what appeared to be unresolvable dichotomies – biology vs. psychology, nature vs. nurture, brain vs. mind, mind vs. body. He sent the book proposal to a psychoanalytic publisher and they immediately accepted the book. But they had severe reservations that the book would not sell well because they feared that people who were interested in biology would not be interested in psychology, psychiatrists would not care about neuroscience, and so on. Halasz stressed that it was absolutely unusual that a first book following a single published article should become the conceptual platform for the following decades of Schore's work, and that this in itself was a monumental achievement.

From the start, the book received a very warm reception in the form of a large number of appreciative personal letters from scientists and clinicans in various fields, as well as very positive journal reviews. The book was the generator of a great number of invitations to lecture nationally and internationally and it created deep friendships with many new-found colleagues. A number of faculty members at UCLA who were studying how neuroscience could be integrated into psychiatry, psychology, and linguistics invited him to join a study group, in which he spent an entire year on the *Affect Regulation* book. The book was written in 1993–1994, before what was to become known as "the decade of the brain." But by the late 90s, there was an explosion of not only neuroscience but also in an appreciation of the value of interdisciplinary research and theortical models. Over the following years and as a result of invitations from editors of prestigious journals, Schore continued to develop regulation theory towards new problems and directions. These subsequent writings were incorporated into his next two books, published in 2003.

In the interview Halasz moved to this double publishing of *Affect Regulation and the Repair of the Self* and *Affect Dysregulation and Disorders of the Self*. The first volume focused more on scientific research, the second more on clinical themes. Schore stressed that he sees his three books as a three-volume set where the seminal ideas of the earlier book were expanded and propelled into the next decade. The theory of regulation thus generated new hypotheses that could be tested experimentally, as well as new clinical applications, especially to the treatment of trauma and personality disorders. These books included a large body of new research, especially neuroimaging research. The numerous dialogues with other scientists provided him with a feedback system. So by the end of the 1990s the

UCLA attachment conference – in part organized by Schore – brought him in direct contact with the trauma field, including Bessel van der Kolk and others. He started to re-think the whole problem of trauma as early attachment or relational trauma. At the time there was little work on disorganized-disoriented insecure "type D" attachments. So he began to really think about the more disturbed attachments, and about how early abuse and neglect would effect brain development. This open space allowed him to expend the trauma model. He felt honored when the article "Dysregulation of the Right Brain: A Fundamental Mechanism of Traumatic Attachment and The Psychopathogenesis of Posttraumatic Stress Disorders" was chosen as the most outstanding article of 2002 in the *Australian and New Zealand Journal of Psychiatry*. At the same time, he was seeing pateints with a history of early attachment trauma in his psychotherapy practice. These clinical experiences revealed the importance of remaining intersubjectively emotionally connected to the patient's bodily state in order to interactively regulate the traumatic state. Halasz described it as a "radical movement" when he read together the two words "relational trauma", and asked Schore if he could recall the origin of this synthesis.

Schore explained that this expression was first introduced by him in (2001), in his article "The Effects of Relational Trauma, Right Brain Development, Affect Regulation, and Infant Mental Health" which appeared in the *Infant Mental Health Journal*. The concept of relational trauma bridges psychology and biology and therefore he had to reformulate his work on the psychobiology of attachment theory. The central question then became – what if the trauma comes from the primary caregiver, the heaven of safety *per se*? He described the mechanisms by which the mother in a highly dysregulated, traumatized state would negatively imprint the infant's early developing right brain. In the 2002 article he further expanded regulation theory to tie together relational attachment trauma and the origins of predisposition for posttraumatic stress disorder (PTSD).

Furthermore, Halasz referred to Schore's keynote speech earlier in 2009 at the American Psychological Association, *The Paradigm Shift: The Right Brain and the Relational Unconscious*. In order to expain this shift Schore asserted that in the 1960s and 70s psychology was essentially observing behavior and therefore it was a period of the dominance of behavioral psychology. The brain, the body, and the unconscious were placed in an opaque "black box" that was not opened. In psychoanalysis, drives and motivational states were downgraded and relegated to the realms of metapsychology. In the 1970s and 80s science was beginning to study not just external behavior, but internal cognitive processes (memory, attention, etc.). This led to a period of dominance of cognitive psychology, and this too impacted models of psychotherapy. But by the end of the century, scientific research entered into the current period where rapidly forming bodily-based emotions and psychobiological states came into the foreground. Because the brain's emotion processing is fast acting and occurs beneath levels of awareness, this has also shifted scientific observation from explicit to implicit phenomena. This paradigm shift from behavior to cognition to emotions allows an integration of psychology and biology and therefore a forging of strong connections between the disciplines of psychology, psychiatry and neuroscience. Neuroscience is moving from predominantly observations of left brain language-based cognitive processes and voluntary motor functions into studies of the right-lateralized emotion processing limbic system and stress regulating hypothalamic–pituitary adrenorcortical (HPA)-axes. In their letter of invitation, the APA asked Schore to consider not using the term "paradigm shift" and instead wanted him to use the more palatable and watered-down term "the emotional revolution." Schore declined. In the plenary he argued that science was now supporting the primacy of affect, including unconscious affect in the human experience. Integrating psychology, psychoanalysis and neuroscience he described the central role of affect and affect regulation in models of development, psychopathogenesis, and the change process of psychotherapy. It is now clear that psychotherapeutic change in just cognition without changes in emotion processing are limited.

In his APA plenary he also argued that the paradigm shift from cognition to emotion is paralleled by a shift from the left hemisphere to the right hemisphere. The brain can no longer be thought of as two halves of a single entity. Rather, these two lateralized systems process different types of information in very different ways. The right and left human brain hemispheres differ in macrostructure, ultrastructure, physiology, chemistry, and control of behavior. The left hemisphere is specialized for the control of well-established patterns of behavior under ordinary and familiar circumstances. The right hemisphere is the primary seat of emotional arousal. There is agreement that verbal, conscious, rational and social information processing takes place in the left hemisphere, while unconscious, nonverbal and emotional information processing takes place in the right. Schore asserted that the right brain is the biological substrate of the human unconscious.

In the final phase of the interview Halasz asked a set of questions centered on the implications of the paradigm shift for the mental health professions in the broadest terms – health, education, curricula, the legal world, and wider culture. Schore suggested that the biopsychosocial perspective of regulation theory and its focus on adaptive and maladaptive emotional processes can serve as the basis for new integrative psychiatric and psychological treatments of mind and body. He quoted Richard Lane (2008): "The physiology of emotion is arguably the cornerstone of psychosomatic medicine . . . aversive emotional states are associated with adverse health outcomes." On the matter of training of psychiatrists, psychologists, social workers, counselors – all need to be informed about the interpersonal neurobiology of attachment, not only in early development, but also how these dynamics are playing out in the patient's psychopathology and in the relationship between the patient and the therapist. This information is relevant to more people than just the psychotherapists. The relationship between the medical doctor and patient is now being addressed not only in psychiatry but in internal medicine journals. These findings challenge the recent trend of psychiatry training models that focus exclusively on psychopharmacology, and devalue psychotherapy. This trend has been particularly alarming in child psychiatry. In fact, recent research indicates that long-term psychodynamic psychotherapy is effective in the treatment of patients with personality disorders and chronic mental disorders.

As a final theme Halasz asked the question of whether current cultural trends are ambivalent about delving more deeply into those fundamental problems of the human experience. Schore answered in the affirmative. Depth psychologies have long described intrapsychic defenses against pain existing in individuals. Defenses such as repression and even dissociation are collectively used by the culture to avoid confronting more directly the serious stressors that many individuals face in today's world. Schore spoke of his work in a recent book, *The Impact of Early Live Trauma on Health and Disease: The Hidden Epidemic* and *Human Nature and the Environment of Evolutionary Adaptiveness* (Lanius, Vermetten, & Pain 2010). This volume reveals a number of serious psychological and social problems that lie behind our cultural blind spots.

In summarizing, Schore stated that from the very beginning of his work, indeed the first page of his 1994 book, he has stressed that the understanding of early development is one of the fundamental objectives in science. The beginnings of living systems set the stage for every aspect of an organism's internal or external functioning throughout the life span. This principle is now accepted, and it refers not only to the predispositions or resilience to mental disorders, but also to pre- and postnatal precursors of physical disease.

2.3 On the same wavelength: how our emotional brain is shaped by human relationships. Excerpts from the interview with Daniela F. Sieff (2012)

In the beginning of this conversation Schore and Sieff discussed the now accepted proposition that our earliest relationships structure our emotional brain in ways that have long-lasting consequences for our emotional well-being. If we are nurtured by our caregivers, our right brain develops in such a way as to allow us to become comfortable with own emotions and to respond to our social environment healthily. We can deeply experience joy and its associated sensations as well as access coping mechanisms (regulatory strategies) that help us through the stressful moments of life. This implicit self-knowledge is at the root of the feeling of security. However, if we grow up in an environment that does not nurture our burgeoning emotional self, then the development of the emotional brain can be compromised. As a consequence, we might not to be able to learn how to regulate our emotions in a healthy fashion, and could too frequently be easily overwhelmed by them. Being emotionally overloaded for extensive periods of time can cause not only long-enduring states of stress, but also chronic dissociation from our true emotions and needs in order to prevent overwhelming emotions from reaching consciousness. If we have to revert to dissociation often enough, what initially began as a defense mechanism that has become engrained in our neurological circuits becomes part of our character. We are trapped in a rigid way of being. We cannot cope with emotional stress, cannot grow emotionally, and cannot attain an emotional security.

At the beginning of his converstion with Sieff, Schore emphasized that his scientific and clinical thinking has focused on three questions:

- How do some children develop emotional security?
- What prevents other children from developing emotional security, and what are the consequences of that?
- What is required of therapy if it is to help those who failed to develop emotional security as children, to develop it later in life?

Schore does not just look at these questions psychologically; a fundamental principle of his work is that no theory of emotional development can be restricted to a description of psychological processes, but must also be consonant with what we now know about the biological structure of the brain. When we are born our emotions are relatively crude – we are content or we are stressed. As we develop, our emotions become increasingly differentiated, shaped and refined, yet also integrated. We learn to create blends of different emotions simultaneously. We begin life with a very small window of tolerance for intense emotions, therefore the tolerance of intense emotions has to be expanded. We need to acquire the ability to differentiate what is happening outside us from what is happening inside. As children we are not able to do so and we have to learn which emotions are internally present and what we receive externally from another person, such as the primary caregiver, and how to regulate the perceived emotions.

Sieff asked the question about what features of the brain are most relevant to understand emotional regulation. Schore answered that there are crucial differences between the right hemisphere of the brain and the left. The left brain is the thinking brain as it is highly verbal and analytical. It operates as a conscious emotion regulation system that can modulate low to medium arousal. It is the domain of cognitive strategies as it processes highly verbal emotions such as guilt and worrisome anxiety. In contrast, the right hemisphere is the emotional brain. It processes all of our intense emotions, regardless of whether they are negative, such as rage, fear, terror, disgust, shame and hopeless despair, or positive such as excitement, surprise, and joy. When our level of emotional arousal escalates the left hemisphere goes off-line and the right hemisphere dominates. Our right brain enables us to read the subjective state of others through its appraisal of subtle facial (visual and auditory) expressions and other forms of nonverbal communication. The right hemisphere is more holistic than the left, holding many different possibilities simultaneously. Dreams, music, poetry, art, metaphor and other creative processes originate in the right hemisphere.

The first critical period of development of the right brain begins during the third trimester of pregnancy and this growth spurt continues into the second year of life. It is primarily the right brain which is shaped by our early relational environment and which is crucial for the development of emotional security. Around two months after birth the right anterior cingulate comes on-line, meaning that it allows for more complex processing of social-emotional information than the earlier maturing amygdala. It is responsible for developing attachment behavior.

Starting from about tenth months after birth, the highest level of the emotional brain, the right orbitofrontal cortex, becomes active. It continues developing for the next twenty years and remains exceptionally plastic throughout our entire life span. During the second year of life the right orbitofrontal cortex establishes strong, bidirectional connections with the rest of the limbic system. Once these connections are established it then monitors, refines, and regulates amygdala-driven responses. It is the healthy development of the right orbitofrontal cortex and its links to the amygdala that enables us to have a wide window of tolerance for intense emotions and to respond flexibly and adaptively to our interpersonal world.

Next, Sieff asked how the relationship between an infant and its caregiver shape the development of the emotional right brain. Schore answered that genes code for when the various components of the emotional brain come on-line, but how each area develops depends on the infant's epigenetically shaped emotional experiences with his primary caregiver. Those experiences, as John Bowlby first described, are circumscribed by the infant's innate drive to become emotionally bonded to his or her primary caregiver. The infant's experiences with his caregiver are internalized through changes in his rapidly developing brain. Typically, an attuned caregiver will minimize the infant's discomfort, fear and pain, and, as importantly, creates opportunities for the child to feel joy and excitement. The caregiver will also mediate the transition between these emotional states. Mirroring by the attuned caretaker amplifies the infant's emotional state. In physics, when two systems match it creates what is called "resonance," whereby the amplitude of each system is increased, comparable to face-to-face play between an infant and an attuned caretaker who creates emotional resonance and amplifies joy. Together, infant and mother move from low arousal to high positive arousal which helps the infant to extend his window of tolerance for intense positive emotions, a key developmental task.

At other times the emotional intensity becomes more than the infant can tolerate, and he will avert his gaze. When this happens, an attuned mother intuitively disengages from the infant and reduces her stimulation. Then she waits for her baby to signal his readiness to re-engage. The more the mother tunes her activity level to the infant during periods of engagement and the more she allows him to recover quietly in periods of disengagement, and the more she responses to his signals for re-engagement, the more synchronized are their actions. At times, emotional mirroring between mother and infant can be synchronized within milliseconds. "On the same-wavelength" becomes more than a metaphor, the intersubjective internal state of both mother and infant converge, and the infant's emotionally reality is both validated and held safely through his mother's ability to be with his feelings. During this process a mother inevitably makes mistakes, and then the interaction becomes asynchronous. However, when asynchrony arises, a good-enough mother is quick to shift her state so that she can then help to re-regulate her infant, who is likely to be stressed and upset by their mismatch. Indeed, relational moments of rupture and repair allow the child to tolerate negative affect.

Additionally, Sieff asked Schore to talk about internal models that are created as a result of interactions between mother and infant. Schore explained that in response to their caregivers, infants create unconscious working models of strategies of affect regulation in order to cope with relational stressors in the attachment relationship. These models are then generalized and applied not only to a mother but also to other people. For instance, if a caregiver is mostly attuned to the infant's basic needs and is emotionally available, the infant creates an implicit expectation of being matched by, and is more likely able to match another human's states. The child is likely to form a secure attachment. Similarly, moments of misattunement, if repaired in a sensitive and timely manner, lead the infant to implicitly believe that caring others will calm him when he is upset. This is the first step towards developing a sense of agency. The timely repair of misattunement also teaches an infant that instances of discourse and negative emotions are tolerable. Emotional resilience is thus key to creating an inner feeling of security and trust.

On the other hand, if caregivers are chronically not attuned, an infant will create an internal model which dictates that other people are not trustworthy, that when stressed he cannot really emotionally stay connected to them, and that he is unworthy of being loved. This way of seeing the world is typical of insecure attachments and these unconscious emotional biases will guide overt behavior, especially under relational stress. What is more, the infant of a misattuned mother will frequently be presented with an aggressive expression on his mother's face, implying he is a threat, or with an expression of fear-terror, implying that he is the source of alarm. Images of his mother's aggressive and/or fearful face, and the resultant chaotic alterations in her bodily state, are internalized, meaning they are imprinted in his developing right brain limbic circuits as an implicit memory, below levels of consciousness. Although out of awareness, they can plague him and his relationships for his entire life unless he finds a way to bring them into conscious awareness and work with them.

Furthermore, when the caregiver is attuned in her early interactions, her more mature nervous system is regulating the infant's neurochemistry and homeostasis. This, in turn, has a profound influence on the structural organization of the developing brain. Conversely emotional trauma will negatively impact the parts of the brain which are developing at the time of trauma. For example, if high levels of stress hormones are circulating in a pregnant mother, it up-regulates the fetus' developing stress response – making the child, and future adult hypersensitive to stress. Relational trauma that occurs around the time of birth has a negative impact on both the developing micro-architecture of the amygdala itself, and the amygdala's connection to the HPA axis, as well as to other parts of the limbic system. Thus high levels of early unrepaired interpersonal stress have a profoundly harmful effect on the ability to form social bonds, and on temperament. Suffering unrepaired and frequent emotional stress after about ten months interferes with the experience-dependent maturation of the highest level regulatory systems in the right orbitofrontal cortex. This opens the door to an impaired emotional regulation system, a limited facilitation for empathy, and problems in distinguishing present reality from irrelevant memories. In the long-term there is an increased risk of developing future psychopathologies and personality disorders.

As opposed to secure attachments, organized forms of insecure attachments reflect inefficient strategies for coping with attachment emotional stress. In cases of avoidant attachment the mother may be averse to physical contact and block her child's attempt to get close to her. She may be intensely ambivalent about being a mother. Her avoidance of the infant is more than behavioral – psychological harm can occur through the mother who is emotionally unavailable when her infant is distressed, even if she remains in physical contact with her child. In parallel, due to the lack of interactive regulation, the child learns how to disengage from the mother under stress, as well as from his own emotional responses to her rejection. To avoid this, the stressed infant will signal his need to disengage by looking away. On the other hand unpredictable and intrusive mothering often leads to ambivalent-anxious attachment where infants can only cope with a certain limited intensity of emotional arousal before they move beyond their window of tolerance into a state of stressful emotional dysregulation. These infants are overly dependent on the attachment figure (presumably desperately seeking interactive regulation) but also angry with the caregiver's unpredictable regulation.

In the most unfortunate situation, the infant/toddler is exposed to the most intense social stressors, such as physical and/or emotional abuse. This also includes neglect, which is proving to be the most serious threat to the development of the emotional brain. The most severe forms of attachment trauma, both abuse and neglect, create "disorganized-disoriented attachment." It occurs when an infant has no strategy that will help him to cope with his caregiver, causing the infant to be profoundly confused, physically aroused, yet emotionally paralyzed. This context thus generates dissociation, "the escape when there is no escape." An infant typically seeks his parents when alarmed, so when a parent actually causes alarm the infant is in an unsolvable situation in which it can neither approach or avoid. Neurobiologically this represents a simultaneous and uncoupled hyperactivation of the sympathetic and the parasympathetic circuits. This is subjectively experienced as a sudden transition into emotional chaos.

Sieff asked what might cause a mother to behave in such a harmful way with her baby. Schore answered that this is not a conscious voluntary but an unconscious involuntary response, and that typically women who cannot mother their child in an attuned way are suffering from the consequences of their own unresolved early emotional trauma. The experience of a female infant with her mother influences how she will mother her own infants. Thus if early childhood trauma remains unconscious and unresolved it will inevitably be passed down the generations.

Additionally, Sieff asked what role the father plays in a child's emotional development. Schore explained that children form a second attachment relationship to the father especially during the second year. The quality of the attachment to the father is independent of that to his mother. At eighteen months there are two separate attachment dynamics in operation. It also appears that the father is critically involved in the development of a toddler's regulation of aggression. This is true of both sexes, but particularly of boys who are born with a greater aggressive endowment than girls.

Afterwards, a long discussion followed where Schore highlighted the damaging effects of long bouts of unregulated shame for the toddler, the differences between shame and guilt, and the enduring consequences of early chronic shame. Schore emphasized that when the caregiver is unable to help the child to regulate either a specific emotion or intense emotions in general, or − worse − that she exacerbates the dysregulation, the child will start to go into a state of hypoaroused dissociation as soon as a threat of dysregulation arises. This temporaily reduces conscious emotional pain in the child living with chronic trauma, but those who characterologically use the emotion-deadening defense of dissociation to cope with stressful interpersonal events subsequently dissociate to defend against both daily stresses, and the stress caused when implicitly held memories of trauma are triggered. In the developing brain, repeated neurological states become traits, so dissociative defense mechanisms are embedded into the core structure of the evolving personality, and become a part of who a person is, rather than what a person does. Dissociation, which appears in the first month of life, seems to be a last resort survival strategy. It represents detachment from an unbearable situation. The infant withdraws into an inner world, avoids eye contact and stares into space. Dissociation triggered by a hypoaroused state results in a constricted state of consciousness, and a void of subjectivity. Being cut off from our emotions impacts our sense of who we are as a person. Our subjective sense of self derives from our unconscious experience of bodily-based emotions and is neurologically constructed in the right brain. If we cannot connect to our bodily emotions then our sense of self is built on fragile foundations. Many who suffered early relational trauma have a disturbed sense of their bodies and of what is happening within them physiologically as well as emotionally.

The interview moved along to the topic of how we can possibly master these adverse and potentially damaging relational experiences. Schore replied by explaining that the human brain remains plastic and capable of learning throughout the entire life span, and that with the right therapeutic help and intervention we can move beyond dissociation as our primary defense mechanism, and begin to regulate our emotions more appropriately. When the relationship between the therapist and the client develops enough safety, the therapeutic alliance can act as a growth-facilitating environment that offers a corrective emotional experience via "rewiring" the right brain and associated neurocircuits. This is predicated on the formation of a trusting relationship between the patient and therapist, who must be sensitive enough to receive the patient's underlying negative state, and implicitly empathically resonate with what is going on within the client's right brain and within his body. All therapeutic techniques sit on top of the therapist's ability to access the implicit realm via right-brain-to-right-brain communications. A strong therapeutic alliance depends on the therapist's knowledge about the patient from the inside out, rather than from the top down. The patient's emotional growth depends on the therapist's ability to move, and to be moved by, those that come to him for help. The therapist has to help patients to learn how to regulate feeling associated with trauma so that the patient can integrate them into his emotional life, rather than having to dissociate when they arise.

When a patient is catapulted into a hyperaroused state and subjectively experiences the therapist through the lens of the previous insecure internal working models, this is the expression of "negative transference." For a patient who is in the midst of a negative transference the therapeutic alliance is severely ruptured, and the therapist is seen as an analogue of the early misattuned other and is experienced as source of dysregulation rather than interactive regulation. However, if the therapist can maintain an attuned connection to the client, then the door opens to working with what was laid down early in the patient's life and reorganization becomes a possibility. A problem may arise if the therapist cannot contain the negative emotions created in negative transference and in projective identification. There is an old adage in therapy that no patient can achieve a greater level of healing than the therapist has achieved. With modern scientific knowledge we can be more specific: the patient's unconscious right brain can develop only as far as the therapist's right brain can take them. For a therapist to stay with a dissociating patient who is projecting his trauma onto her takes a good deal of clinical experience. More importantly, the therapist needs to have worked deeply with her own early life experiences, and has to actively work with it throughout the life span. A successful therapeutic relation precipitates emotional growth not only in the patient but also in the therapist.

Sieff refered to the fact that short-term cognitive behavioral therapy (CBT) is currently very popular and widely used. Can it help with healing relational trauma? Schore answered that CBT is grounded in cognitive psychology, and its research base is grounded cognitive processes such as explicit memory, rational thought, language, and effortful conscious control. Cognitively based therapy's basic theoretical assumption is grounded in the assumption that we can change how we feel by consciously changing how we think and what we believe. This means that cognitive therapy focuses on language and thought, both of which are located in the left brain. People who have trouble regulating their emotions typically have a left brain that is already more developed than their right brain, and they may well have learned to use rational thinking and words to obscure the deeper emotional experiences and to keep them dissociated. Cognitive therapy may strengthen the very strategies that keep the affect dampening defense of dissociation in place. Even if the left brain becomes more able to control the emotions of the right brain, it can only control emotional arousal that is of low or moderate intensity. As a rule, when emotional arousal reaches a certain level of intensity the left brain goes off-line and the right brain becomes dominant. Changes made in the cognitive strategies of the left brain are unavailable when this happens. At these times, emotionally-focused therapy may enhance the neural connections between the right amygdala and the right orbifrontal cortex which allows the patient to more effectively tolerate and regulate intense emotions. Cognitive therapy which exclusively focuses on the ability of the left brain to control the right cannot directly alter changes within the right-lateralized limbic system. The final problem of cognitive therapy is that it is generally a short-term treatment so it is unable to build a strong enough therapeutic alliance to allow the patient to experience the corrective emotional experience.

Deep change does not happen when a patient is consciously reflecting on an emotion. Rather it happens when the patient actively experiences the emotion and when a resonating emotionally present therapist recognizes and regulates that emotion, thereby modeling new ways of being with another while one is under stress. There is no interpersonal space for this repair of attachment ruptures in current models of cognitive therapy, where left brain insight dominates over right brain interactive regulation.

Coming to the end, Sieff asked Schore what message he would like people to take home from this interview. Schore answered that the earliest stages of life are critical as they form the foundation of everything that follows. Our early attachment relationships, for better or worse, shape our right brain unconscious system and have lifelong consequences. An attuned early attachment relationship enables us to grow an interconnected, well-developed right brain and sets us up to become secure individuals, open to new social and emotional experiences. A traumatic early attachment relationship impairs the development of a healthy right brain and locks us into an emotionally dysregulated, amygdala-driven emotional world. As a result, our only way to defend against intense unregulated emotions is via the over reliance on repression and/or pathological characterological dissociation. Faced with relational stress, we are cut off from the world, from other people, from our emotions, from our bodies and from our sense of self. Our right brains cannot further develop or grow emotionally from our interactions with other right brains. Too many people suffer alone with their desperate pain due to their early relational trauma. For somebody struggling with such emotional dysregulation, the way to emotional security, and to a more vital, alive, and fulfilling life, does not come from making the unconscious conscious – which is essentially a left brain process – rather, it arises through physically restructuring, growing and expanding the emotional unconscious itself. The most effective way to achieve these changes is through relationally-based, emotionally-focused psychotherapy with an empathic and psychobiologically attuned therapist who is willing and able to be an active participant in this process.

2.4   Allan Schore on the science of the art of psychotherapy: excerpts from an interview with David Bullard (2015)

The title of the interview refers to Allan Schore's recent book *The Science of the Art of Psychotherapy* (2012) in which he attempted to more deeply understand the relationship between the two central dimensions of the therapeutic process. On the one hand, a rapidly developing large body of interdisciplinary research is now explicating the science that underlies the clinical domain. A good deal of this new data comes from fields outside the clinical domain, that is, from basic scientific research. Clinicians need to be aware of this recent information and objective knowledge in order to succeed in our particular area of expertise – psychotherapeutic change processes. Yet, at the same time, what we practice is an art – involving intrapsychic and interpersonal forces that are extremely subjective and personal. Thus, there are two types of knowledge that underlie psychotherapy change processes: the explicit knowledge of the broader biological and psychological scientific theories, and the implicit relational knowledge of self and other.

With the current emphasis on relational and emotional factors in all forms of therapy there is now consensus that emotionally, intersubjectively, and empathically being with the patient is more important than rationally and objectively enhancing the patient's understanding of his symptomatic behavior. In the critical moments of any session the patient must sense that that the therapist is empathically resonating with his bodily-based emotional experience. Schore suggested that we have to attempt to "listen beneath the words" in order to "reach the affect" which may be unconscious to the patient. Moreso than left brain reason, right brain intuition and empathy are needed to access functions of the unconscious mind that operate beneath levels of awareness. Schore stresses that psychology has placed too much emphasis on the conscious mind and on verbal behavior. However, utilizing a psychodynamic perspective involves more of a focus on the patient's inner world, as well as access to the unconscious "right mind" of both members of the therapeutic dyad. The communication of emotions within the therapeutic alliance are so rapid that they occur beneath conscious awareness. This alliance is a central mechanism in not only psychodynamic therapy but in all other psychotherapies too.

Indeed, over the last two decades psychodynamic theory has seen a reemergence and transformation of psychoanalysis, the science of unconscious processes. This revitalization has been fostered by neuroscience's interest in rapid implicit (nonconscious) processes. In support of Freud's iceberg model, neuroimaging research has established that most essential adaptive processes are so rapid that they take place beneath conscious awareness. Schore has therefore suggested that the self-system is located in the right brain, the biological substrate of the human unconscious. This new conception of an "unrepressed unconscious" is functionally expressed in rapid primary process cognitive operations (implicitly processing faces, voices, gestures), in sending and receiving primary process communications ("relational unconscious"), and in rapid biological and bioenergetic transformations that mediate changes in bodily states. This differs from Freud's dynamic unconscious which mainly contains repressed material, once conscious but now banished from awareness. Other major changes have been the rediscovery of brain lateralization and the appreciation of different structural organizations of the right and left brain, respectively the unconscious and conscious minds. Each has different critical periods and growth spurts and ultimately different specialized functions. Schore's interest has been in deeper early forming nonverbal bodily-based survival processes.

The conversation then moved to the topic "relational trauma" where Schore suggested that it is not just misattunement that leads to the traumatic predisposition but also the lack of repair, and that repair and interactive regulation requires a very personal, authentic response on the part of the therapist. As the therapy progresses and the attachment bond strengthens, there is enough safety for the suffering individual to disassemble the left brain repressive and right brain dissociative defenses and disinhibit affects that can now reach awareness. As a result, what has been buried and packed down underneath consciousness surges into bodily awareness in the presence of a regulating other, allowing for the possibility of interactive repair.

A number of clinicians are now focusing on the same right brain psychobiological mechanisms in couple's work. The couples' therapist who is working with attachment is able to hold the stressed dysregulated couple, to regulate each member of the marital dyad. She's also facilitating and reading nonverbal emotional communications within the dyad, and bringing to awareness affective moments in which they are engaging and disengaging, and switching between various emotional states. The therapeutic action with couples is to allow each member to become more aware of these rapid automatic processes and how each is communicating or blocking transmissions from the other. As always the clinical principle is to follow the affect, especially authentic affect, whether positive or negative. And again, rupture and repair are important contexts for right brain development and emotional growth in both partners.

Moreover, Bullard asked if Buddhist ideas of the self/non-self are of interest for Schore. In his answer Schore stressed that in the Western cultures and in the US the value of autonomous and independent personalities are emphasized over interdependent personality organizations. As a biological organism that depends on the (physical and social) environment and its resources for survival and well-being, an integrated person needs power and autonomy that enables meeting one's individual needs sufficiently and independently. In addition, human beings have an innate psychobiological need for affiliation and social connection, which is necessary for both emotion regulation and personal growth. Neuroscience now clearly demonstrates that power and autonomy are driven by the left hemisphere, while affiliation and prosocial motivations by the right. So, again, that is the reason why Schore has been more interested in the right hemisphere, which processes not only emotional states and higher cognitive functions, but also spiritual and moral experiences. It is here in the right where the self is transcended, where the self becomes larger and expanded. In these states the grandiosity of the self literally is collapsed down and there is a profound understanding that one is part of a much larger organism, a much larger sense of being alive. This sounds very much like the Buddhist autoregulatory self-state.

Finally, Schore and Bullard addressed Winnicott's idea about being alone in the presence of the other. In his writings, Winnincott talks about the child in the second year achieving a complex developmental advance – the adaptive ability to be alone and the creation of true autonomy. That is, to be separate, to be possessing one's own individuality in the close subjective presence of another. The other is a background and not foreground presence, fostering the child's capacity to autoregulate his emotional state, which may be different than the other, and to preserve self-other boundaries. They are literally both individuating in their presence together.

This joint passive context underscores the importance of solitude and privacy, which in this exhibitionistic day and age are being substantially undervalued. Moments of emotional connection like a state of shared joy or shared pain are important, but so also are moments of shared silence and tranquility. Winnicott differentiated active "excited" love from "quiet" passive love. Schore suggested that attachment theory is essentially about intimacy, and that this suggests that patients can use what they have experienced in therapy to expand their abilities for forming close and personally meaningful bonds with others, as in deep friendships and long-term romantic relationships. This achievement represents the growth of the right hemisphere. Schore pointed out that Freud postulated that successful therapy and indeed life is all about an enhancement of (right brain) love and (left brain) work.

References

Bullard, D. (2015). Allan Schore on the science of the art of psychotherapy. *Psychotherapy.net*. Copyright © 2015 David Bullard.

Carroll, R. (2001). An interview with Allan Schore: "The American Bowlby". *The Psychotherapist*, Autumn 2001. Retrieved from psychotherapy.org.uk.

Halasz, G. (2010). G. Halasz in conversation with Allan Schore. Northridge, CA, Thursday 24th December 2009. *Australasian Psychiatry*, 19 (1), 30–36.

Lane, R. D. (2008). Neural substrates of implicit and explicit emotional processes: A unifying framework for psychosomatic medicine. *Psychosomatic Medicine 2008*, 70, 214–231.

Lanius, R. A., Vermetten, E., & Pain, C. (2010). *The impact of early trauma on health and disease: The hidden epidemic*. New York: Cambridge University Press.

Schore, A. N. (1991). Early superego development: The emergence of shame and narcissistic affect regulation in the practicing period. *Psychoanalysis and Contemporary Thought*, 14, 187–250.

Schore, A. N. (1994). *Affect regulation and the origin of the self: The neurobiology of emotional development*. Mahwah, NJ: Erlbaum.

Schore, A. N. (2001). The effects of relational trauma on right brain development, affect regulation, and infant mental health. *Infant Mental Health Journal*, 22, 201–269.

Schore, A. N. (2002). Dysregulation of the right brain: A fundamental mechanism of traumatic attachment and the psychopathogenesis of posttraumatic stress disorder. *Australian and New Zealand Journal of Psychiatry*, 36, 9–30.

Schore, A. N. (2003a). *Affect regulation and the repair of the self*. New York, London: Norton.

Schore, A. N. (2003b). *Affect dysregulation and the disorder of the self*. New York, London: Norton.

Schore, A. N. (12 April 2008). The paradigm shift: The right brain and the relational unconscious. Presentation on the Division 39 Spring Conference in New York.

Schore, J. R. (1983). *A study of the superego: The relative proneness to shame or guilt as related to psychological masculinity and femininity in women*. Unpublished Dissertation, California Institute for Clinical Social Work, Berkeley.

Sieff, D. F. (2012). On the same wavelength: How our emotional brain is shaped by human relationships. In D. F. Sieff (Ed.) (2015), *Understanding and healing emotional trauma: Conversations with pioneering clinicians and researcher*. London: Routledge, 113–136.

3

ORIGINAL SCHORE PAPERS AND LECTURES

3.1 *Preface* and *Introduction* from *Affect Regulation and the Origin of the Self*

Preface[1]

Over the past two decades, a diverse group of disciplines have suddenly and simultaneously intensified their attention on the scientific study of internal processes. The nature of the covert mechanisms that underlie overt behaviors were, for much of this century, deemed to be outside the domain of prevailing psychological models and existing research methodologies. The remarkable productivity of investigations of various cognitive operations has demonstrated the accessibility of internal processes to both qualitative and quantitative analyses, and has legitimized a shift from the formal study of the exterior and observable to the interior and hidden, yet substantive, aspects of human functioning. Even more recently, a sudden surge of multidisciplinary activity, at quite different levels of analysis, has initiated a deeper exploration into another class of internal processes, that of emotional states.

This acceleration of research into affective phenomena has been paralleled by an explosion in the number of studies of early human structural and functional development. Developmental neuroscience is now delving not only into early cognitive and memorial processes, but also into the ontogeny of hierarchically organized brain systems that evolve to support the psychobiological underpinings of socioemotional functioning. Studies of the infant brain demonstrate that its development occurs in stages over critical periods, and that its maturation is influenced by the environment and is experience-dependent. Concurrent developmental psychological research dramatically emphasizes that the infant's emerging socioaffective functions are fundamentally influenced by the dyadic transactions the child has with the primary caregiver. In these fast acting, "hidden" communications, the mother senses and modulates the nonverbal and affective expressions of her infant's psychobiological states. In other words, the experiences that fine-tune brain circuitries in critical periods of infancy are embedded in socioemotional interchanges between an adult brain and a developing brain. In line with these findings, developmental studies are revitalizing contemporary psychoanalysis. This observational data strongly suggests that the mother's regulatory functions not only modulate the infant's internal state, but also indelibly and permanently shape the emerging self's capacity for self-organization. Studies of incipient relational processes and their effects on developing structure are thus an excellent paradigm for the deeper apprehension of the organization and dynamics of affective and affect regulatory phenomena.

The purpose of this book is to integrate two rapidly converging streams of developmental research: psychological studies of the critical interactive experiences that influence the development of socioemotional functions and neurobiological studies of the ontogeny of postnatally maturing brain structures that come to regulate these same functions. A triad of fundamental assumptions underlies this work on the neurobiology of emotional development – that the compelling questions of human emotion and motivation can only be understood in terms of structure-function relationships, that the primordial conditions in which these evolve occur in the context of the caregiver-infant interaction, and that an understanding of the principles of human developmental psychobiology is a prerequisite and powerful impetus to the elucidation of the dynamic mechanisms of all later socioemotional phenomena.

This volume addresses the fundamental problems of how and why early events permanently affect the development of the self. Drawing upon current findings in infant research and neurobiology, a central hypothesis is proposed – that the infant's affective interactions with the early human social environment directly and indelibly influence the postnatal maturation of brain structures that will regulate all future socioemotional functioning. This principle of the experience-dependent development of self-regulatory structures and functions is supported by multidisciplinary evidence from a spectrum of developmental sciences. Furthermore, the structural characteristics and the dynamic functional properties of such a system are identified to be mediated by the orbitofrontal cortex, the major cerebral system involved in social, emotional, motivational, and self-regulatory processes. This cerebral structure is hidden in the anterior undersurface and interior of the cortex, and is especially developed in the right hemisphere. Due to its unique and extensive interconnections with a number of subcortical systems, it represents the hierarchical apex of the limbic system. A critical period for the maturation of this prefrontal structure exactly overlaps the temporal interval extensively investigated by both attachment and psychoanalytic researchers. An understanding of the caregiver-influenced development of this corticolimbic structure elucidates the unique role of the early maturing right hemisphere in affective processes and in the regulation of internal states.

More than just a review of several literatures, the studies cited in this work are used as a multidisciplinary source pool of experimental data, theoretical concepts, and clinical observations that form the base and scaffolding of an overarching heuristic model of socioemotional development that is grounded in contemporary neuroscience. This psychoneurobiological model is then used to generate a number of heuristic hypotheses regarding the proximal causes of a wide array of affect-related phenomena. The keystone of this model is the principle of the development of self-regulation. An emergent property of hierarchically organized cortical-subcortical systems is the capacity to regulate the transitions between various internal states that support affect, cognition, and behavior. A current common focus on the adaptive regulatory processes of living systems, from the molecular up through the social levels, highlights the unique explanatory power of this central linking concept to organize what on the surface appear to be disparate bodies of knowledge and to reveal many of the "hidden" mechanisms of development. My intention in writing this volume is to demonstrate that a deeper understanding of affect regulation and dysregulation can offer penetrating insights into a number of affect-driven phenomena – from the motive force that underlies human attachment to the proximal causes of psychiatric disturbances and psychosomatic disorders, and indeed to the origin of the self.

Introduction[2]

The understanding of early development is one of the fundamental objectives of science. The beginnings of living systems set the stage for every aspect of an organism's internal and external functioning throughout the life span. It is often not appreciated that an individual's genetic inheritance which encodes the unvarying sequence of development is only partially expressed at birth. Genetic systems that program the evolution of biological and psychological structures continue to be activated at very high rates over the stages of infancy, and this process is significantly influenced by factors in the postnatal environment. Of special importance are the incipient interactions the infant has with the most important object in the early environment – the primary caregiver. Events that occur during infancy, especially transactions with the social environment, are indelibly imprinted into the structures that are maturing in the first years of life. The child's first relationship, the one with the mother, acts as a template, as it permanently molds the individual's capacities to enter into all later emotional relationships. These early experiences shape the development of a unique personality, its adaptive capacities as well as its vulnerabilities to and resistances against particular forms of future pathologies. Indeed, they profoundly influence the emergent organization of an integrated system that is both stable and adaptable, and thereby the formation of the self.

The principle that the early events of development have far-reaching and long-enduring effects is one of the very few elemental and overarching postulates that is shared by all disciplines studying living organisms. We now know that the concept of "early experiences" connotes much more than an immature individual being a passive recipient of environmental stimulation. Rather, these primordial events represent active transactions between the infant and the first external environment. Yet despite their fundamental importance, the scientific study of these phenomena has, perhaps until recently, been far from a unified pursuit. Each separate discipline contains a split-off "developmental" branch, and the transfer of information between these bodies of knowledge, especially those at different levels of analysis, has been quite restricted. The recent explosion of infant research has emphasized the essential importance of a multidisciplinary perspective, but it should be remembered that this field spans the gamut from developmental neurochemistry and neurobiology through developmental psychology to developmental psychoanalysis and infant psychiatry. And yet these seemingly disparate fields share the common assumption that the deeper apprehension of the individual's early development can elucidate the mechanisms of all later function and dysfunction. A powerful impetus towards an integrated multilevel approach has come from recent studies which demonstrate that the early transactions with the social environment are "hidden" within the dyadic relations between mother and child, and that in this dialectic the mother acts as a crucial regulator of the child's development. The characterization of these hidden processes is now a major focus of study, since it has been demonstrated that not only the infant's overt behavior but its covert physiology and thereby its internal state are directly regulated by the mother. The consequences of these revolutionary findings to preexisting theory are turning out to be profound.

Perhaps the best way to give the reader a sense of the state-of-the-art, as it were, of current developmental knowledge is to briefly outline some of the major questions that are being addressed by contemporary multidisciplinary researchers. The nature of the problems that are presently being explored reflects a confidence in the rapidly expanding and exciting field of infant research. Questions that have been up until recently considered as outside of scientific exploration are now being translated into testable hypotheses:

1 How do early experiences induce the growth of structure in the developing human infant?
2 What internal and external factors influence development, and how exactly do these factors interact?
3 What kind of psychobiological mechanisms mediate the regulation of developmental processes by these internal and external factors?
4 How does the variation of these influences shape the organism's inherited genetic contributions? What processes transform genotype into phenotype?
5 Because it is now known that the expression of inherited genetic information is not completed at birth but continues at high rates in infancy, what common fundamental gene-environment processes operate both pre- and postnatally?
6 How does the primary caregiver influence genetically programmed mechanisms that are responsible for the infant's growth?
7 What essentially is the early environment, and what part does the organism's contacts with its mother play in establishing the child's social environment?
8 How do various stresses influence the course of development?
9 Why does development occur in stages?
10 What mechanisms regulate the onsets and offsets of critical periods for the maturation of particular structures and functions?

11 Why are early critical periods of development so important to the functioning of the individual throughout the rest of the life span, and why and how do the events of early childhood imprint permanent effects?

In addition to these questions about the general nature of development, more specific ones arise from the study of human socioemotional development:

1 What part do early social-affective experiences play in the postnatal maturation of the human brain?
2 How does the infant's early social environment influence the growth of structural systems involved in emotional functioning that are maturing in infancy?
3 How does the earliest relationship with a specific human being, the attachment to the primary caregiver, permanently influence the individual's capacities to enter into all later relationships?
4 What psychobiological mechanisms underlie the attachment process?
5 What is the role of emotional communications in the child's continuing dialectic between himself and the social environment?
6 How does the child respond to the changes in the social environment that occur over the stages of infancy, and how do these changes effect the course of socioemotional development?
7 How does the developing child retain continuity and self-regulate as it traverses these changes?
8 What factors facilitate or inhibit the emergence of the adaptive capacity for self-regulation?
9 What is the relationship among failures of development, impairments of adaptive capacities, and psychopathology?
10 How can an elucidation of the events of infancy, especially early socioemotional transactions, lead to a deeper understanding of adult normal and abnormal phenomena?
11 How can developmental knowledge be utilized to formulate heuristic strategies toward the treatment of psychological developmental disorders?
12 What defines a self, and how does it evolve?
13 How do early events influence the development of consciousness?

I believe that the answers to the foregoing questions – which are further addressed in subsequent chapters – will not come from single or even multiple discoveries within any one discipline. Rather, an integration of the findings of many related fields is essential to the ultimate creation of a heuristic model of development that can accommodate interdisciplinary data, and can freely shift back and forth between their different levels of analysis.

A primary purpose of this volume is to bring together and to present in one place the latest observations, data, and concepts from the developmental branches of various disciplines. Such an integrative approach prescribes that the reader is presented with a number of different bodies of current literatures. It is difficult enough to keep up-to-date within one's own area of study, let alone to be aware of the newer concepts in related fields. Nevertheless, this is an absolute necessity in light of the current emphasis on multidisciplinary research. To that end, a major goal of this study of socioemotional development is to supply psychological researchers and clinicians with relevant up-to-date developmental neurobiological insights and findings, and to expose neuroscientists to recent developmental psychological and psychoanalytic studies of infants. Contemporary infant research is now directed towards much more than merely describing the development of overt behaviors. Over the past two decades a paradigmatic shift away from the narrow constraints of a strict behaviorism has occurred in all areas of psychology. This has allowed for a sanctioning of the scientific study of internal states, and has created an environment that supports the generation of new methodologies that more directly access the proximal internal causes of overt behavior. As a result, the developmental sciences have produced a large amount of information about the ontogeny of both cognitive and affective internal processes. This approach is paralleled by the rapidly expanding intense interest in the covert, hidden aspects of the relationship the growing child has with a changing environment.

Another fundamental intention of this work is to focus specifically on social and emotional development, particularly as it occurs in the human infant. Much of the data from developmental neuroanatomy and neurochemistry comes from animal research, yet these studies uniquely reveal the biological and chemical changes that comprise the internal processes underlying the complex affective and cognitive capacities that come to be so highly developed in humans. It is now very clear that well before the advent of language the baby's capacities to interact with the social and physical environments, functions supported by these internal processes, are extremely complex and sophisticated. The fast acting, psychobiological mechanisms that mature in early and late infancy continue to operate throughout life. Indeed they serve as the keystone of all future human intraorganismic, intrapsychic, and interpersonal functioning, as the manifestation of all later-developing capacities is contingent upon their initiatory expression.

Many of the latest findings are quite unexpected in terms of the predictions of older theories, and each field is now radically altering the fundamental assumptions that lie at the core of its conceptions of development. Although their methodologies are quite different, the data emerging from what appear to be distantly related fields are converging on certain common conclusions.

One such finding that appears again and again is the interactive nature of development. Development essentially represents a number of sequential mutually driven infant-caregiver processes that occur in a continuing dialectic between the maturing organism and the changing environment. It now appears that affect is what is actually transacted within the mother-infant dyad, and this highly efficient system of emotional communication is essentially nonverbal. Human development, including its internal neurochemical and neurobiological mechanisms, cannot be understood apart from this affect-transacting relationship.

A second fundamental conclusion is that the study of development must include more than just a documentation of changing functions. The problem of the maturation of structures responsible for the onset of new functional capacities must also be simultaneously addressed. In fact, development can only be understood in terms of a progression of structure-function relationships, since structure, by definition, is continually organizing, disorganizing, and reorganizing in infancy. Changes in the child's behavior (studied by developmental psychology) or in the child's internal world (studied by developmental psychoanalysis) can only be understood in terms of the appearance of a more complex structure that performs emergent functions. At this stage of our scientific knowledge, any discipline that theorizes about structure needs to evaluate its models against what is now known about the veritable characteristics of biological structure as it exists in nature. This brings psychology back to biology, and emphasizes the importance of developmental neuroscience.

A third crucial finding is that we now know that the early environment is fundamentally a social environment, and that the primary social object who mediates the physical environment to the infant is the mother. Through her intermediary action environmental stimulation is modulated, and this transformed input impinges upon the infant in the context of socioaffective stimulation. The mother's modulatory function is essential not only to every aspect of the infant's current functioning, but also to the child's continuing development. Thus, she is the major source of the environmental stimulation that facilitates (or inhibits) the experience-dependent maturation of the child's developing biological (especially neurobiological) structures. Her essential role as the psychobiological regulator of the child's immature psychophysiological systems directly influences the child's biochemical growth processes which support the genesis of new structure.

And fourth, the concept of regulation is one of the few theoretical constructs that is now being utilized by literally every developmental discipline. The current focus on adaptive regulatory phenomena, from the molecular to the social levels, represents a powerful central linking concept that could potentially elucidate the "hidden" processes in development and thereby organize what appear to be disparate bodies of developmental knowledge. With respect to socioemotional ontogeny, it is now established that the infant's affect is initially regulated by the mother, but over the course of development it becomes increasingly self-regulated. The elucidation of the psychobiological mechanisms that underlie the experience-dependent maturation of a structural system that can adaptively autoregulate affect is a very active area of current multidisciplinary research.

3.2   Early superego development: the emergence of shame and narcissistic affect regulation in the practicing period

An understanding of superego processes and particularly the role of the malfunctioning superego in symptom formation is an essential part of the treatment process. Historically, the focus has been on the role of undischarged guilt in the etiology of neurotic disorders, with the role of shame, the "keystone affect" of narcissistic pathologies (Broucek, 1982), given much less attention and less clearly traced. Furthermore, the clinical and theoretical distinctions between shame and guilt are still not precisely characterized. One approach at attempting to elucidate the singular nature of each of these superego affects is to study their differential ontogeny in early development. Advances in clinical technique that focus on shame (Basch, 1988; Miller, 1985; Morrison, 1989; Nathanson, 1987) underscore the critical import of "returning internalized shame to its interpersonal origin" (Kaufman, 1985) in effective psychotherapeutic treatment. The specification and delineation of the genesis and functional role of shame in socioaffective development has direct clinical relevance to the understanding of normal and abnormal early superego development, and to the etiology of early-forming self-pathology (Kohut, 1971).

A central tenet of the developmental approach of this chapter is that critical early object relations involving attuned and misattuned affect transactions, reflected in the internalization of early interactive representations, are required for the maturation of effective superego autoregulatory systems. Furthermore, it is postulated that two separate superego affect systems arise in different early stages. S. Miller (1989) pointed out that the exact ontogenetic course of shame is controversial and still uncharted, and Emde (1988) suggested that the "early moral emotion" of shame that appears in the second year is in need of systematic research. The major purpose of this work is to present a developmental object relations model of the emergence of shame during Mahler's practicing period of separation-individuation and to examine the critical functional role of shame in successive stages of socioemotional developement. The shame-regulatory system that has its onset during the practicing phase will be shown to be instrumental to the effective resolution of the later rapprochement crisis, specifically in terms of the modulation of narcissistic rage and the developmental progression of psychological and gender identification processes. Finally, the relevance of the model to the etiology of the fundamental pathology of narcissistic disorders and to the functional characterization of the ego ideal component of the superego as a mood regulator will be presented.

The methodology of this theoretical research involves the integration of current observations from various fields that are studying the problem of socioemotional development-psychoanalysis, infant research, developmental psychology, and neurobiology. Thus, in the course of this pursuit, a sizeable number of studies will be presented, not as a literature review, but as a multidisciplinary source pool of clinical observations, theoretical concepts, and experimental data from which to generate an overarching conceptual model that attempts to elucidate the common underlying functional mechanism of shame, "the primary social emotion" (Scheff, 1988).

A more general objective is an inquiry into the relationship between the dynamics of early interactional development and the ontogeny of the emergent function of self-regulation, particularly the "process of self-regulation of affect" (Krystal, 1988). "Self-regulatory mechanisms are organized . . . in relation both to endogenous activity and to the surrounding life support system" (Sander, 1977, p. 29). Demos and Kaplan framed the central question as "how organized systems retain continuity while changing in response to developmental and environmental pressures" (1986, p. 156). A guiding principle in this investigation is embodied in the assertion that any comprehensive theory of affects needs to include the physiologic segment as well as the psychoanalytic.

The investigation and characterization of a unique affect, emerging in a specific time and with a particular developmental function, thus utilizes various contributions of clinical and experimental work on the development of emotion from within and without psychoanalysis. Basch (1976) argued that the earliest forms of affective behavior are general physiologic reactions such as response to stimulation (autonomic reactivity) mediated by the autonomic nervous system (ANS). In ensuing developmental stages they provide the substrate for all emotional experience. Krystal (1978) proposed that all later-developing affects evolve out of a neonatal state of contentment and a state of distress that differentiate into two developmental lines, an infantile nonverbal affect system and an adult verbalized, desomatisized system. He asserted, "The development and maturation of affects is seen as the key event in infancy" (Krystal, 1988, p. 211), and wrote of nodal points in affect development that allow for the maturation of particular affects. Spitz (1965) concluded that significant organizational shifts occur regularly in development that are signalled by the emergence of new affective behaviors. Buechler and Izard, in a paper on the emergence and regulation of the expression of emotions in infancy, stated that "the age at which the infant is able to regulate expression may differ for each of the discrete emotions" (1983, p. 301), whereas Pine (1980) emphasized that the earliest expressions of affect are automatic responses described as varying along a singular pleasure-unpleasure continuum, but later this is followed by an "expansion in the affect array." As development proceeds:

> [S]ome affects represent alterations, transformations, specifications of earlier affect states, whereas others are first born at later stages in the developmental process when the psychological conditions for their emergence are met. These psychological conditions involve new learnings, new acquisition of mental life, that have consequences for affective experiences.
>
> *(Pine, 1980, p. 232)*

More specifically to the ontogenesis of the later-appearing superego affects, a review of the clinical literature reveals a common observation that shame has an earlier developmental origin than guilt. This conceptualization was first proposed by Freud (1923/1961b), who distinguished shame associated with early narcissistic conflicts from guilt associated with later moral conflicts. Erikson (1950) asserted the psychosocial stage of "autonomy versus shame and self doubt" takes place in the second year, while "initiative versus guilt" occurs at a later age. H.B. Lewis (1980) argued that shame is a more regressed and primitive mode of superego functioning than guilt, in agreement with Wallace (1963) and Jacobson (1964). Levin (1967) and Anthony (1981) also concluded that shame is preoedipal and originates before guilt. S. Miller (1989) differentiated earlyappearing affects on a developmental line with shame from a later-emerging affect developmental line that culminates in guilt.

Despite continuing controversy in the adult psychoanalytic literature (Garza-Guerrero, 1981), developmental infant research has tended to support these clinical deductions. Indeed, it pinpoints the specific period of the onset of the shame response. Darwin (1872/1965) noted that early infants do not show the physiological hallmark of shame, blushing. Confirming this, Tomkins (1963) found no facial expressions expressive of shame in earliest infancy and characterized "shame-humiliation" as an auxillary affect which appears later, and Field (1982) encountered no "ashamed" responses in four-month-old infants. Selfconsciousness, a behavior reflecting embarassment (a component of shame), was earliest observed at 12 months by Dixon (1957). In the most extensive research on this topic, Amsterdam (1972; Amsterdam & Leavitt, 1980) noted that embarassment and affective self-consciousness first appear at 14 months, coinciding with the acquisition of upright, free locomotion. These responses are completely absent before 12 months. In a more recent series of developmental studies, M. Lewis (1982) first observed the self-conscious emotion of shame in the period of 12 to 18 months. Plutchik, citing the work of Piaget, concluded, "in stage 5 (12–18 months) with the development of the cognitive ability to represent the self and external causation, affects such as shame, defiance, and negativism appear" (1983, p. 243). There is thus consistent evidence for the onset of shame in the junior toddler; that is, Mahler's practicing subphase of the separation-individuation stage of development (10–12 to 16–18 months). It should be kept in mind that the effective vocabulary of the average 12-month-old is three words; at 15 months, it is 19 words (Mussen, Conger, & Kagan, 1969). Kaufman noted shame, "a total experience that forbids communication with words" (1974, p. 565), arises prior to language development and is therefore preverbal. In contrast, Pine argued that guilt "comes into being somewhere from age 3 to 6" (1980, p. 222). Izard (1978) and Sroufe (1979) also found guilt appearing at 36 months. Importantly, notice that the shame system emerges in the preverbal toddler, guilt in the neoverbal child. Their separate origins is one factor indicating that these two superego affect systems are dissociable and independent.

The psychophysiological function of shame

In preparation for the exploration of the ontogeny of shame, it is necessary to present a more detailed description of this unique affect, which perhaps more than any other emotion is so intimately tied to the physiological expression of a stress response. This hyperactive physiological state (Darwin, 1872/1965) is associated with ANS reactions like sweating, greater body awareness, intensification of perceptual functions, uncoordinated motor activity, cognitive impairment, and gaze aversion, thus implying "the more primitive, biologically based nature of shame" (Broucek, 1982, p. 375). The deep physiological substrate of shame is perhaps best reflected in blushing (Wurmser, 1981), which represents the end result of a preceeding intense "affective spell"; that is, the end product of the physiological discharge of shame (Miller, 1965). MacCurdy (1930) proposed that the shock-like onset of blushing reflects a shift of balance from sympathetic to parasympathetic components

of the ANS, the system that determines the physiological expression of all emotions. Supporting this, Knapp (1967) explained that activity of the parasympathetic
branch of the ANS accounts for blushing. Thus the activity of the ANS, which is an
effector channel of the emotion-mediating limbic system, is the basis of the acute
phenomenology of shame. In a heightened state of affect, one is overwhelmed by
intense internal physiological sensations over which there is no conscious control;
notice the similarity of this to a classic acute "stress state" (Seyle, 1956). Indeed, in
social psychological experiments, shame, specifically used as a psychosocial stressor
(Buck, Parke, & Buck, 1970), induced a psychophysiologic stress reaction.

Furthermore, Freud's (1905/1953c) original conceptualization of shame was that
it acted as a superego counterforce or counterreaction formation against exhibitionistic excitement and overstimulation that have potential egodisruptive effects.
This underscores the requisite preexisting state of hyperarousal for shame induction,
and the function of shame as an arousal blocker, a regulator of hyperstimulated
(elated, excited, grandiose, manic, euphoric) states. Tomkins (1963), who identified the function of this "affect auxillary" as a specific inhibitor of the activated,
ongoing affects of interest-excitement and enjoyment-joy, pointed out that shame
reduces self-exposure or self-exploration powered by these positive affects. Shame
signals the self-system to terminate interest in whatever has come to its attention
(Nathanson, 1987). Thus, the "superegomediated flight from positively experienced
exhibitionism to negatively experienced shame" (Miller, 1985) changes the affective valence and diminishes the arousal level of the organism, thereby blocking the
further escalation and intensification of stimulation. The end result is a painfully
stimulated state of shame. Kohut (1971) presented a similar model: at a moment of
exhibitionism of the self, the sudden unexpected impact of shame is to ground the
person who is overstimulated by omnipotent, grandiose affective states.

A model of shame is proposed here in which the neo-individuating self, in a
hyperstimulated, elated, grandiose, narcissistically charged state of heightened arousal,
exhibits itself during a reunion with the caregiver. Despite an excited anticipation
of a shared affect state, the self unexpectedly experiences an affective misattunement,
thereby triggering a sudden stress, shock-induced deflation. It is proposed that this
first occurs in the preverbal practicing subphase of the separation-individuation
period, and that this specific object relation and its internalization is the prototype
of the shame experience.

The ascendancy of narcissism, elation, and heightened arousal during the practicing period

The onset of the practicing period is usually marked by rapid changes in motor
behavior (i.e., of upright posture and locomotion supporting the child's first independent steps), but it is its affective characteristics that are unique and definitional.
Bowlby (1969) pointed out important affective changes occur when locomotion emerges; Bertenthal, Campos, and Barrett (1984) found that mobile infants
show different types of emotional reactions than prelocomotor infants; and Fox

and Davidson noticed "tight linkages exist between the onset of locomotion and the occurrence of important changes in affective behavior" (1984, p. 370). Mahler described the practicing junior toddler as "intoxicated with his own faculties and with the greatness of his world . . . He is exhilarated by his own capacities" (1980, p. 7). Mahler et al. wrote of the stage-specific omnipotent exhilaration and elation of this period (high arousal affects), and noted that at this time more than any other in development, "narcissism is at its peak" (1975, p. 71), while Johnson affirmed, "The practicing period offers a release into manic excitement and involvement in a world far more reinforcing than that of the unreliable nurturance offered earlier" (1987, p. 26).

The one-year-old's frequent mood of elation has also been described by other psychoanalytic (Emde, 1989) and developmental (Sroufe, 1979) researchers. Confirming this, in a neuropsychological study of infant emotional expression, Rothbart, Taylor, and Tucker (1989) found a statistically significant increase in positive emotion and decrease in negative emotion over the developmental period of 10 to $13^1/_2$ months.

In an important paper tracing the development of narcissistic systems and their affects, Parkin referred to the omnipotence, grandiosity, and elation of the emergent "ideal ego," a precursor of the superego ego ideal component and the embodiment of the "narcississtic perfection of childhood." The illusion of omnipotence central to the ideal ego normally arises out of the experience of being merged with the attuned, powerful mother. During the practicing period, the child "has reached the highest point in the development of his primary narcissism and in the overestimation of his powers. His ideal ego is at its full" (1985, p. 146). Parkin (in agreement with the developmental studies reported earlier) noted that it is at this time when shame, self-consciousness, and embarassment first appear and that the toddler first becomes aware of himself/herself as an object for observation and evaluation by another. Broucek, also studying shame and its relationship to early narcissistic development, similarly concluded, "Significant shame experiences may occur in the first one and a half years of life" (1982, p. 372).

In addition to the developmental affective changes at practicing onset, major maturational behavioral (Plooij & van de Plooij, 1989) and cognitive (Zelazo, 1982) reorganizations are known to occur at 12 months. Lester (1983) pointed out that the practicing period represents Piaget's fifth stage of sensorimotor intelligence, a time of the first appearance of tertiary circular reactions that enable the toddler to actively and spontaneously explore for newness in the environment (curiosity onset?). By one year of age, stimulation-seeking exploratory play time may amount to as much as six hours of the child's day. Pine asserted that elated affect (excitement and joy) is "coupled with boundless energy in the constantly moving toddler" (1980, p. 229), and cited White's (1963) discussion of "pleasure in function" associated with the elation of the period. Indeed, it could be speculated that White's concepts of competence and effectance have their roots in the practicing phase. He defined effectance as the infant's sense of what can and cannot be accomplished; it is an emotional mood that characterizes the infant's mastery experiences. Interestingly,

White (1960) asserted that shame is always associated with incompetence. Along the same lines, Broucek (1982) suggested that inefficacy experiences may be the earliest releasers of shame.

Two important points should be made at this juncture. It is proposed that shame modulates high arousal affective states; these states first appear during the practicing period (a developmental period of hyperarousal), and the onset of shame at this time acts as a regulator of hyperstimulated states. Second, hyperaroused narcissistic states developmentally occur at this critical period only if the infant-caregiver dyad has successfully negotiated the preceding stages, allowing the child to tolerate much higher arousal states than earlier. Under optimal conditions, thresholds of stimulation decrease and the ability to tolerate higher levels of stimulation increases during infancy (Field, 1985a). Fogel (1982) referred to a major developmental task of the first year as the evolution of increasing affective tolerance for high arousal. This occurs in attachment transactions in which the psychobiologically attuned (Field, 1985a) caregiver amplifies the infant's highly stimulated state of excitement and joy, one that fuels his/her grandiosity.

On the other hand, Parkin (1985) asserted that certain forms of inadequate mothering in the third quarter of the first year of life inhibit identification of the child with the fantasied omnipotence of the mother and lead to a hypocathected, dormant, and impoverished ideal ego. The ability to experience the practicing high arousal states of elation and interest-excitement depends upon precedent successful experiences of merger with the omnipotent mother. If this does not occur earlier in the symbiotic phase there will be a drastic reduction in primary narcissism. In support of this, the expression of interest, which Piaget (1967) pointed out underlies the process of assimilation and is essential for the development of sensorimotor intelligence, was shown by Bell (1970) to be predicated upon a "harmonious relationship" between mother and infant.

Interestingly, it is known that the practicing characteristic hedonic tone of elation (Lipsitt, 1976), high levels of arousal (Field, 1985b), and elevated activity level (boundless energy, Breese et al., 1973) are all associated with heightened activation of the sympathetic component of the ANS. Furthermore, in various animal models, it has been found that young mammals typically pass through a hyperactive period of mid-infancy in which they display a state of organismic hyperarousal and increased energy metabolism (Reite, Kaufman, Pauley, & Stynes, 1974), especially when apart from the mother, reflecting unmodulated excitatory activity of early maturing, reticular formation brain stem systems responsible for arousal (Campbell & Mabry, 1972; Moorcroft, 1971). In late infancy this activity is decreased due to the later onset of forebrain inhibitory systems. The high level of behavioral arousal that reflects unchecked subcortical reticular excitability is proposed to be identical to the excitement component of Tomkins's "interest-excitement," and to underlie Kohut's (1971) "age-appropriate exhibitionism."

Sympathetic and parasympathetic components are known to have different timetables of development, resulting in unique physiological organizations at different stages of postnatal life. Hofer (1984a) consistently observed high levels of energy-expending sympathetic activity and high resting heart rates in midinfancy, followed by a reduction in late infancy due to the neural maturation of energy-conserving parasympathetic (vagal) restraint.

Parasympathetic inhibitory function, associated with heart rate deceleration, is expressed·by two distinct brain stem systems. A primitive dorsal motor vagal system responsible for metabolic shutdown and immobilization ontogenetically precedes a later maturing more flexible nucleus ambiguus vagal system (Schwaber, Wray, & Higgins, 1979; Geis & Wurster, 1980; Daly, 1991). Over 100 years ago, the British neurologist Hughlings Jackson (1931) postulated that the infant will pass through an excitable stage in ontogenesis that is diminished by the later functional onset of cortical inhibitory centers, reflecting the sequential caudal to rostral development of the brain. Furthermore, it is known that essential subcortical limbic system substrates involved in emotional and cognitive behavior postnatally mature earlier than corresponding systems in the cerebral cortex (Meyersburg & Post, 1979). It could be speculated that the affective, behavioral, and cognitive aspects unique to the practicing period reflect a biologically timed period of sympathetic dominant limbic hyperarousal and behavioral overexcitation, and that the shame system that emerges in this period represents an evolving cortical inhibitory control mechanism of excessive, hyperstimulated states.

Shame stress and the neurophysiology of arousal dysregulation during practicing reunion episodes

An even closer inspection of the practicing terrain reveals the unique and specific nature of "practicing" object relations that engender shame and elucidates the more general process of the socialization of emotion during infancy. Parens (1980) described the typical practicing behavior in which the child brings the things he/she is exploring and attempting to master to the mother's vicinity. Mahler (1979) noted:

> The functions, during the practicing period, attract so much libido that the junior toddler is emotionally relatively independent of the love object and absorbed in his own narcissistic pleasures. Upon the attainment of mastery of some autonomous ego functions, however, he becomes increasingly aware of his separateness and pari passu very much aware of his need for his mother's acceptance and renewed participation.
>
> *(p. 63)*

It is this moment of reunion of the "returning," highly aroused, elated, practicing toddler, in a state of excited expectation, reconnecting with the mother, that is the prototypical object relation in the emergence of shame. The "attachment emotion" of shame (Lewis, 1980) occurs at the point of reattachment. Infant socioemotional research specifically reveals that separation does not activate shame (Izard, Hembree, & Huebner, 1987). Notice the self-exhibiting nature of this practicing transaction, keeping in mind Freud's emphasis on exhibitionistic excitement and overstimulation in shame dynamics. Research utilizing a behavioral microanalysis of reunion episodes has produced rich material concerning stage-specific object relations. This methodology derives from Ainsworth's (Ainsworth, Blehar, Waters, & Wall, 1978) studies of infant attachment patterns after periods of separation, and the work of Mahler, Pine, and Bergman (1975) on "emotional refueling," which is conceptualized as an exchange of energy between the partners in the caregiver-infant dyad. "Reunion between baby and mother serves to regulate either high or low levels of arousal, to a more organized affective and attentional state" (Brent & Resch, 1987, p. 16). It is during these moments of caregiver-infant interaction that the mother acts to maintain the child's arousal within a moderate range that is high enough to foster interactions, yet not so intense as to cause distress and avoidance (Brazelton, Koslowski, & Main, 1974; Stern, 1977).

Reunion microinteractions are therefore critical moments of early object relations involving emotional reconnection after separations, specifically reentering into patterned affective transactions with the object. This moment of initial interface in a dyadic affectively communicating system has been shown to be critical to the infant's modulation of arousal, affect, and attention. Optimal reunion experiences, lasting only 30 seconds to three minutes, have been shown not only to "enable the infant to differentiate internal needs but . . . allow for increasingly active regulation of both separation and individuation of the self" (Brent & Resch, 1987, p. 25). Practicing reunions represent affectively significant "central moments" of the growing child's daily experience that are associated with high intensity object relations (Pine, 1985).

Germinative memories and percepts are organized around these moments of highly narcissistically charged affect transactions common in this developmental period. Stern noted that "important experiences (and their memory and representation) are affect state-dependent . . . the affect state acts as the cardinal organizing element" (1985, p. 245). Importantly, early reunion transactions act as a developmental matrix for the evolution of affects and affect tolerance: "In the further course of development, repeated experiences of separation and reunion are remembered and anticipated, providing the structural basis for progressively more varied and modulated affective responses, whether basically painful or basically pleasurable" (Pao, 1971 p. 788).

But these reunion episodes can also be moments engendering arousal dysregulation and psychosocial stress. Mahler specifically noted that the practicing infant's burgeoning narcissism is "particularly vulnerable to the danger of delation" (Mahler et al., 1975, p. 228). The neo-toddler's first ambulatory, exploratory forays away from the mother and into the world represent critical initial attempts to separate himself/herself from his/her mother (Rheingold & Eckerman, 1970) and define the onset of the separation-individuation period. The ambulatory infant, now able to physically separate himself/herself from the mother for longer periods of time, is able to explore realms of the physical and social environment that are beyond her watchful eye. However, upon return from these forays, the nature of their face-to-face reunions is altered in that they now more than any time previously can engender intense interactive stress. More specifically, the grandiose practicing toddler, highly aroused by what he/she (but not necessarily the caregiver) appraises to be a mastery experience, returns to the mother after a brief separation. The nascent self, in a state of accelerating positive arousal, exhibits itself in a reunion transaction. Despite an excited expectation of a psychobiologically attuned shared positive affect state with the mother and a dyadic amplification of the positive affects of excitement and joy, the infant unexpectedly encounters a facially expressed affective misattunement. The ensuing break in an anticipated visual-affective communication triggers a sudden shock-induced deflation of positive affect, and the infant is thus propelled into a state that he/she cannot yet autoregulate. Shame represents this rapid state transition from a preexisting positive state to a negative state.

Translating this into self-psychology terms, the returning toddler, eagerly looking forward to the maternal smile of recognition and the expected satisfaction of "the need of the budding self for the joyful response of the mirroring selfobject" (mutually attuned elation Kohut, 1977, p. 788) is suddenly and unpreparedly confronted with the "unexpected noncooperation of the mirroring object" (Kohut, 1971, p. 655). This is specifically communicated visually not only in the "absence of the smile of contact" (Basch, 1976, p. 765), but in the presence of the mother's "strange face," a physical expression denoting her negative emotional state. Basch stated, "The shame-humiliation response . . . represents the failure or absence of the smile of contact, a reaction to the loss of feedback from others" (p. 765).

Broucek (1982) noted that:

> shame arises in the infant's contacts with mother at those moments when mother becomes a stranger to her infant. This happens when the infant is disappointed in his excited expectation that certain communicative and interactional behavior will be forthcoming in response to his communicative readiness . . . Shame arises from a disturbance of recognition, producing familiar responses to an unfamiliar person, as long as we understand the "different" mother to be the unfamiliar person. That a mother (even a "good-enough" mother) can be a stranger to her own infant at times is not really surprising since the mother's moods, preoccupations, conflicts and defenses will disturb her physiognomy and at times alter her established communication patterns.
>
> (p. 370)

It is the sudden and rapid processing of this dissonant visuoaffective information that underlies the "unexpected" quality of shame (Lynd, 1958). Research on face scanning indicates that infants are most sensitive to affective expressions in which specifically the eyes vary the most (Haith, Bergman, & Moore, 1979). The instant state of shame distress derives not so much from the perception of the mother's face or smile as much as from the infant's recognition of the mother's break in participation from anticipated communicative visuoaffective eye-to-eye contact. The induction of a stress state at this point is understandable in that "stress is defined as a change or a threat of change demanding adaptation by an organism" (Schneider-man & McCabe, 1985, p. 13). The experience of shame has been associated with unfulfilled expectations (Wurmser, 1981). The shock of shame results from the violation of the infant's expectation of affective attunement based on a memory of the last contact with the mother that was energizing, facilitating, and rewarding for the grandiose self.

McDevitt (1975) argued that the practicing infant maintains an illusion (holds a memory) that the mother is with him/her whenever he/she chooses to move away from her. Sherwood furthered this idea in postulating a "practicing illusion" of maintaining oneness while at a distance from the mother, which reflects the grandiose cognition "that the mother is constantly available in her mirroring func-tion" (1989, p. 15). Shame stress experiences puncture this illusion at reunion as the emerging self encounters a discrepancy between the memory of an ideal symbiotic attunement and the current perceptual input of dyadic affective misattunement. The mother's mirroring function suddenly vanishes, and there is a rapid deenergiz-ing affective experience, a deactivation of the attachment system, a reduction of interest-excitement, and a "sudden decrement in mounting pleasure" (enjoyment-joy; Tomkins, 1963) in the precipitous fall from positively experienced pleasurable exhibitionism to negatively experienced painful shame. The infant switches from an affectively elated externally focused state to an affectively deflated internally focused state, and active expressive affective communication is suddenly displaced by passive receptive emotional surveillance. Interest, curiosity, focused attention, and positive hedonic tone are instantly transformed into diffuse distress, unfocused attention, and negative hedonic tone.

This deflated, "toned-down" state of low arousal, negative emotion, and unfo-cused attention has been described in practicing infants under ongoing separation stress. Mahler noted that, in opposition to periods of elation, when separated from mother for a period of time "they become low-keyed . . . At such times, their gestural and performance motility slowed down; their interest in their surroundings diminished; and they appeared to be preoccupied . . . with inwardly concentrated attention" (1979, p. 127). The low-keyed state, isomorphic to the shame state in which interest and attention to the external environment is suddenly terminated, is a defensive and adaptive phenomenon that comes to the foreground and is most vis-ible under situations of extended separation stress. It has been suggested to represent a narcissistic regressive defense (McDevitt, 1980); as such it reflects a passive rather than an active coping mechanism.

Mahler likened this state to Kaufmann and Rosenblum's (1969) separation state of "conservation-withdrawal," which occurs in "helpless" stressful situations where active coping responses are unavailable, and which "may be adaptive for the 'exhausted' organism in replenishing energy stores and restoring physiological equilibrium" (Field, 1985b, p. 215). This state is driven by dorsal motor vagal activ-ity associated with immobilization and hiding behaviors. Recall Erikson's (1950) assertion that the defensive reaction of shame is expressed as hiding or conceal-ment. Furthermore, it is similar to Bowlby's (1969) "profound detachment" phase of infant separations in which metabolic conservation and inhibition (e.g., a dorsal motor vagal induced heart rate deceleration) is maintained until reunion with the mother becomes possible (during the high arousal, agitated "protest" stage heart rate acceleration occurs). Also note that in the shame transaction the break in the attachment bond is not caused by the highly aroused child's movement away from the mother, or even the mother's movement away from the child, but instead by the active blockade of the child's return to and emotional reconnection with the mother; a separation-induced stress response is triggered in the presence of and by the mother.

The shame-induced failure in the modulation of affect, attention, cognition, and motor activity is produced by the sudden plummeting mood shift and propulsion of the toddler into a disorganized deflation state of sensory underload-induced low arousal. Since this low-keyed state is below the limits of the infant's "optimal activation band" (Field, 1981) or "optimal range of stimulation" (Stern, 1985), it produces a shame state of "narcissistic distress" (Miller, 1988) which he/she cannot at this age actively self-regulate. It is known that moderate levels of arousal are associated with positive affect and focused attention, while extreme levels of arousal (high or low) are related to negative emotion and distracted attention (Malmo, 1959). Brent and Resch (1987) specifically observed this with practicing infants. Activation theorists have shown that extremely low levels of arousal, like high levels, are associated with uncomfortable negative emotional states and behavioral inefficiency (Cofer & Appley, 1964); both understimulation stress and overstimulation stress are known to be aversive (Goldberger, 1982). Phenomenologically, the toddler experiences a hyperactive physiological state, as reflected in suddenly increased dorsal motor vagal parasympathetic ANS activity (i.e., a stress state). Interestingly, the heightened autonomic reactions in shame, blushing, sweating, and so on, have been likened to the infantile preverbal psychosomatic state (Anthony, 1981). Broucek (1982) also equated an infant "distress state" with a primitive shame experience. It is proposed that in the toddler, as well as the adult, the brake of incrementing arousal seen in shame (e.g., reflected in cardiac deceleration, switch in mood, gaze aversion, and blushing) reflects a sudden dynamic switch from sympathetic dominant to parasympathetic dominant ANS activity (drive reduction). The diminution of sympathetic activity in shame underlies the hedonic mood change and the disruption of motor (behavioral) and cognitive activities, and the replacement of parasympathetic passive for sympathetic active coping processes is reflected in the common shame experience of helplessness and passivity accompanying the exquisitely painful sensitivity to critical reactions of others (Morrison, 1985); that is, the loss of a mechanism to actively cope with narcissistic pain. (I suggest that as opposed to the elevated dorsal motor vagal parasympathetic autonomic component that always accompanies shame, humiliation involves an elevated parasympathetic plus a heightened sympathetic reactivity.)

The two components of the centrally, brain-stem-regulated ANS are known to be antagonistic, reciprocally integrated circuits (Hess, 1954) that control arousal, with the catabolic sympathetic branch responsible for energy-mobilizing excitatory activity and heart rate acceleration and the anabolic parasympathetic branch involved in energy-conserving inhibitory activity and heart rate deceleration (Porges, 1976). Broverman, Klaiber, Kobayashi, and Vogel noted that "the sympathetic and parasympathetic autonomic nervous systems are frequently in competition and the final effect then depends upon the relationship between the momentary activity of the two systems" (1968, p. 29).

It has long been acknowledged that "the physiological expression of emotion is dependent, in part, upon both sympathetic and parasympathetic components of the autonomic nervous system" (Truex & Carpenter, 1964, p. 431). It is posited that predominant sympathetic activity underlies high intensity, narcissistically cathected affect states, and dominant dorsal motor vagal parasympathetic function is reflected in low-keyed emotional states. Hofer's work (1983) indicated that attachment and separation responses reflect the activity of not a single but multiple emotional systems. Again, it should be remembered that the practicing period represents a developmental phase of imbalance, of unregulated sympathetic overexcitation.

The idea that the prototypical shame transaction involves a break in attachment, a barrier to a reconnection after a separation, an expectation of seeing the gleam in the mother's eye in a reunion, but suddenly encounters a frustration and experiences instead a bodily-based autonomic stress response may seem unfamiliar. And yet in "The Interpretation of Dreams" (1900/1953b), Freud, in his longest exposition on shame, described:

> If you are wandering about in a foreign land, far from your home and from all that you hold dear, if you have seen and heard many things, have known sorrow and care, and are wretched and forlorn, then without fail you will dream one night that you are coming near to your home; you will see it gleaming and shining in fairest colors, and the sweetest, dearest and most beloved forms will move towards you. Then suddenly you will become aware that you are in rags, naked and dusty. You will be seized with a nameless shame and dread, you will seek to find covering and to hide yourself, and you will awake bathed in sweat. This, so long as men breathe, is the dream of the unhappy wanderer.
>
> *(p. 265)*

Maternal response and the regulation of shame-deflated narcissistic affect

Shame induction triggers an assault on the burgeoning narcissism of the practicing infant, on the ideal ego (primary narcissism), and represents the first experience of narcissistic injury and narcissistic depletion associated with all later shame experiences. It is at the point of this painful type of rupture in the infant-mother bond that the neoevolving, emotionally fragile, differentiating nascent self collapses, triggering physiological upheaval (the infantile psychosomatic state). Schneider (1977) noted that in shame a break occurs in the self's relationship to others and to itself; the self is no longer whole but divided. In Kohutian terminology, shame is related to an empathic break between the mirroring self object and the grandiose self (Josephs, 1989). In an attachment theory conception, H. B. Lewis (1980) noted that the "attachment emotion" of shame is an "implosion" or transient destruction of the self (while the self is intact in guilt). And in Mahlerian terms, Broucek pointed out that early experiences of large toxic doses of shame may impair ongoing development by "undermining separation-individuation processes and promoting regressive efforts to reestablish a symbiotic type of relationship" (1982, p. 37).

As maturation proceeds, this object relations sequence and its associated shame affect is internalized; ultimately shame is associated with the self's vicarious experience of the other's negative evaluation (Lewis, 1979). What once took place within the caregiver-infant unit is subsequently performed intrapsychically. As Parkin noted, the "awareness of the discrepancy or conflict between the self-admiring ideal ego and the reality ego's perception of the absence or contradiction of the admiration in the outside world constitutes the experience of shame" (1985, p. 150). As Basch maintained:

> Later in life this same reaction occurs under similar circumstances, i.e., when we think we have failed to achieve or have broken a desired bond with another. The exquisite painfulness of that reaction in later life harks back to the earliest period when such a condition is not simply uncomfortable but threatens life itself.
>
> *(1976, p. 767)*

In the shame transaction there is thus a state of dysynchrony, a break of attachment, of "misattunement" between the toddler and caregiver, a "mismatch of need and anticipation in the caregiver-infant pairing" (Lichtenberg, 1983). However, the object relation sequence within the dyad is not quite completed – the pair may attempt to resynchronize. In fact, an adaptation by the infant to the psychosocial stress can only be established with the mother's cooperation at reunion. Indeed, stress has been defined as the occurrence of an asynchrony in an interactional sequence. Further, "a period of synchrony, following the period of stress, provides a 'recovery' period" (Chapple, 1970, p. 631).

The frustrative state in shame has been conceptualized as arising from "an inability to effectively arouse the other person's positive reactions to one's communication" (Basch, 1976, p. 767). The overt behavior of the toddler, his/her facial expression of shock, his/her motionless headbang and body posture due to a reduction in tonus of the neck, body, and facial muscles causing a loss of the social smile, his/her averting the eyes, and the hallmark of shame, blushing, act as a signal to the attuned mother of the toddler's internal state of distress. Indeed, the preverbal infant communicates to her the dysregulation of his/her ANS, because "the language of mother and infant consists of signals produced by the autonomic, involuntary nervous system in both parties" (Basch, 1976, p. 766), and the mother is the regulator of the infant's developing ANS (Hofer, 1984b).

The infant's averted gaze, which reflects the alternation of an object-relating interactional mode, has been shown to be a potent elicitor of attention from mothers of securely attached infants, but not from those of insecurely attached infants (Leavitt & Donovan, 1979). Darwin (1872/1965) originally pointed out that the function of emotional facial gestures is to communicate the individual's internal state to another. Sroufe (1979) suggested that infant affects have three functions: the amplification and exaggeration of behavior, the communication of information about internal states, and the elicitation of helpful reactions from the mother. Stern (1985) emphasized that the infant uses facial behaviors to invite higher levels of stimulation from the caregiver when the level of excitation has fallen too low. The child's face thus powerfully signals the caregiver of his/her internal shame-dominated affective state, isolation, and experience that the object relation link has been severed. Basch noted, "The shame–humiliation reaction in infancy of hanging the head and averting the eyes . . . indicates that affective contact with another person has been broken" (1976, p. 765). Yet there is a need to repair the sundered attachment bond: "In shame the individual wishes to resume his or her commerce with the exciting state of affairs, to reconnect with the other, to recapture the relationship that existed before the situation turned problematic" (Tomkins, 1987, p. 144).

The nature of the caregiver's response (or lack of it) at this point is critical to the regulation of the shame affect, that is, shame recovery and the subsequent evolution of an internalized mechanism to regulate shame stress states. An important principle of attachment theory is that parental sensitivity and responsiveness to the child's affective communications is critical to the child's organization and regulation of his/her emotional experiences (Sroufe & Waters, 1977). Sensitive mothers offer stimulation contingent upon the infant's facial orientation: "At the most basic, 'security of attachment' relates to a physiological coding that the universe is benign and need-satisfying, that is, homeostatic disruptions will be set right" (Pipp & Harmon, 1987, p. 650). Demos and Kaplan pointed out that the caregiver's response to the infant's affective states is fundamental to the attachment phenomenon: "[T]he baby will become attached to the caregiver who can help to modulate and to minimize the experience of negative and who maximizes and expands opportunities for positive affect" (1986, p. 169).

Mothers of securely attached infants show a tendency to respond appropriately and promptly to their infants' emotional expressions (Ainsworth et al., 1978). This facilitates the creation of a system of reciprocal regulation, and fosters an expectation that during times of stress the attachment object will remain available and accessible. It also engenders a precursor of self-confidence, a sense in the infant that his/her own activity can control the effect that his/her environment will have on the infant (Ainsworth & Bell, 1974). This sense of "control" could underlie the emergence of "active" (as opposed to passive) coping responses to emotional stress, and the ontogeny of early intrapsychic psychological defenses, which have been characterized as a subset of coping mechanisms (Rutter, 1987). Notice the critical role of early object relations in the ontogeny of stress coping systems, mechanisms to cope with mismatches in the social environment. Indeed, Levine (1983) argued that the development of coping responses is dependent upon early experience.

The work of Tronick (1989) with two- to nine-month-old infants demonstrated that interactive stress is a ubiquitous component of maternal-infant transactions and that it is the caregiver who is responsible for the reparation of dyadic misattunements and the transformation of the infant's negative emotion to this stress into a positive emotion. Tronick argued that mismatches allow for the development of interactive, coping, and self-regulatory skills, and enable the child to maintain engagement with the social environment in the face of stress. He also noted that the capacity for interactive repair will later contribute to the security of attachment. Infants of mothers who were responsive during early dyadic affect transfer interactions show, at 12 months, persistent efforts to overcome an interactive stress. Furthermore, under the aegis of a sensitive and cooperative caregiver, the infant develops an internal representation of himself/herself as effective, of his/her interactions as positive and reparable, and of the caregiver as reliable. Although Tronick's studies include symbiotic and not practicing-phase toddlers, he noted that the process of interactive repair is central to the regulation of later-emerging affects, specifically mentioning shame and guilt.

It is important to distinguish among shame stress, the narcissistic affect shame, and the process which regulates this affect, shame regulation. As outlined earlier, practicing caregiver-induced shame stress produces a state of dyadic mismatch and misattunement, triggering rapid offset of narcissistic, positive hedonic affect and onset of negative affective shame distress, propelling the previously hyperaroused child into an internally focused, passive, hypoaroused shame state. The maternal response to the reengaging toddler at reunion after an attachment break is critical to the reparative process of affect regulation. If she is responsive and approachable, the object relations link is reconnected, the infant's attachment system is reactivated, the arousal deceleration is inhibited, and shame is metabolized. As a result, the child recovers from the injury to narcissism and recovers from shame.

This active recovery mechanism develops in the context of effective early object relations in an "average, expectable environment" (Plutchik, 1983) in order to regulate affective perturbations associated with disruptions in self- and object relationships. The prototype for the evolution of this mechanism lies in the mother's response to the child's shame distress. Kaufman asserted that the shame state that "originates from an interpersonal severing process" may be ameliorated by the process of "restoring the interpersonal bridge" (1985, p. 143).

This practicing onset-shame modulation is identical to the maternal response and regulation of the practicing child's low-keyed states (earlier shown to be isomorphic to shame states) that represent a drop in the child's level of arousal and is reminiscent of a miniature anaclitic depression (Mahler, 1972).

Previously, a description was given of the practicing toddler's venturing away from the mother and becoming exhilarated during exploratory forays into the novel physical environment. At reunion, he/she may return in an excited state and attempt to emotionally share the elation resulting from his/her mastery experiences with the caregiver, or in a depleted low-keyed state, triggered by inefficacy, in which he/she is less inclined to re-engage the physical surroundings. Mahler noted that this toned-down state is visibly terminated at reunion with the briefly absent mother: "The wilting and fatigued infant 'perks up' in the shortest time, following such contact, after which he quickly goes on with his explorations, once again absorbed in pleasures in his own functioning" (1980, p. 6) . In this transaction the under aroused practicing baby is energized by the mother. Consequently, unfocused attention and negative hedonic tone is transformed within ten seconds into focused attention and positive hedonic tone.

In the dyadic shame transaction the infant's low-keyed state was triggered by the caregiver's misattunement, and so, subsequent to her induction of the infant's stressful low arousal state, she now acts to interactively regulate the shame state. In doing so, the shame-modulating caregiver and the infant again cocreate a psychobiological bond of interactive regulation, which switches off the infant's dorsal motor vagal parasympathetic-mediated low arousal that fuels the child's anhedonic depressive state, thereby allowing for a reignition of sympathetic activity which supports higher levels of arousal. The stress regulating caregiver thus facilitates a transition from the primitive dorsal motor vagal to the later maturing and flexible nucleus ambiguus vagal system in the infant's developing brain. Recall, as opposed to the "vegetative" or "reptillian" parasympathetic system in the dorsal motor nucleus that shuts down metabolic activity during immobilization, death feigning, and hiding behaviors, the "smart" or "mammalian" vagal system in the nucleus ambiguus allows for the ability to communicate via facial expressions (mutual gaze), vocalizations, and gestures in contingent social interactions. This interactive regulation produces a shift from passive to active coping, and negative/passive to positive/active mood.

It should be pointed out that these shame regulating transactions are carried out repeatedly throughout the practicing period, and that a characteristic and prototypical pattern of dealing with misattuned states and distressing affects develops between the primary attachment figure and the child; Waters (1978) found stable reunion patterns of affect regulation at 12 and 18 months (practicing and rapprochement).

It is the child's experiencing of an affect and the caregiver's response to this particular affect that is internalized as an affect regulating interactive representation during reunion episodes. The internalization of affective and cognitive components of relationships operationally defines the construction of internal working models (Pipp & Harmon, 1987) that organize the individual's construction of subsequent relationships. These practicing-imprinted models are equated with Stern's (1985) "generalized episodes of interactions that are mentally represented," and with Kernberg's (1984) internalized representations of the self affectively transacting with objects in the social environment. According to Bowlby (1973), these models of attachment relationships contain internalized representations of early parental attributes, particularly conceptions of the caregiver's accessibility and responsiveness. Bretherton (1985) stressed the involvement of internal working models in superego formation.

Kobak and Sceery noted that these internal models that define "styles of affect regulation" provide "rules for regulating distress-related affect . . . in the context of parental responsiveness to the child's signals of distress" (1988, p. 142). This principle also refers to distress that is maternally induced (i.e., shame distress) and the caregiver's responsiveness to the infant's narcissistic stress that she has triggered. Importantly, practicing shame transactions and the maternal regulation of shame stress act as a developmental matrix for the evolution of the capacity to experience, tolerate, and regulate shame, and represent an interpersonal source of the emergence of adaptive coping strategies for dealing with subsequent narcissistic stress. These practicing-internalized models involving the attachment emotion of shame are imprinted into the earliest episodic memory, which stores events that have meaning for the concept of self (Tulving, 1972), and are the source of early, preverbal (and therefore later unconscious), deep transference patterns. Bowlby (1988) posited that the uncovering and reassessment of early internalized working models is the essential task of psychotherapy.

It is in this particular interpersonal context late in the practicing period that the developmental transition of external to internal regulation via increasing levels of internalization occurs (McDevitt, 1980). Hofer (1984b) proposed that internal representations of human relationships serve as "biologic regulators;" the physiological regulatory function of the infant's ANS is initially performed by the mother, and subsequently internalized by the infant. Greenspan (1981) argued that in the ontogeny of homeostatic regulation of the infant's arousal or excitation, the function is first performed by the responsive mother, and then gradually acquired by the infant. Thus, interactive regulation of the infant's external emotional expression that is observable and exogenous in the symbiotic phase (Tronick's interactive repair) is a precursor to self-regulation of internal emotional states that is unobservable, endogenous, and subjective at the end of the practicing phase.

Similarly, Kohut noted that "there may be some internalization of the actual functions carried out by the mother and the 'transmuting' into regulatory mental structures to deal with uncomfortable emotions, in much the same way as the mother provided relief" (1971, p. 13). These maternal "self object" functions are specifically affect regulatory functions, of both arousal reduction and arousal induction. Stolorow, Brandchaft, and Atwood (1987) argued that the caregiver's attuned responsiveness to the child's intense, shifting affective states allows for the evolution of an internalized structure that can modulate and contain strong affect. Such opportunities for internalization determine the structural development of an affect regulator allowing for later emotional self-regulation that provides for constancy of internal affective states, that is, mood autoregulation.

Furthermore, this affect regulator is critical to the maintenance of recurrent positive mood and the establishment of Emde's (1983) "affective core" that regulates the infant's interactive behavior. In securely attached infants, distress does not endure for long periods beyond the conditions that elicit them; rapid recovery to positively toned emotions is typical (Gaensbauer & Mrazek, 1981). In contrast, infants who are insecurely attached show "a greater tendency for negative emotional states to endure beyond the precipitating stimulus events" (Gaensbauer, 1982, p. 169).

Shame and affect regulation through the rapprochement crisis

Within the major developmental transition from practicing to rapprochement, important affective, cognitive, and behavioral changes occur. The emergence of new function and structure during this boundary period rests upon successful passage through preceeding stages. Mahler and colleagues asserted: "Normal autism and normal symbiosis are prerequisite to the onset of the normal separation and individuation process" (1975, p. 47). Similarly, adequate development in the practicing subphase is a prerequisite for rapprochement success. More specifically, it is required for successful passage from one stage into the next; that is, through the portal of the rapprochement crisis.

Mahler and colleagues described that at practicing offset/rapprochment onset "the toddler's elated preoccupation with locomotion and exploration *per se* [is] beginning to wane" (1975, p. 90). Pine referred to the "rapprochement crisis" involving the collapse of the illusion of omnipotence: "Now he is small and alone in a big world, rather than sharing in the (imagined) omnipotence of the mother–child unit" (1980, p. 226). (This omnipotence, supported by the tolerance of high arousal affect, reflects a fairly successful transition through all stages up to and including the practicing phase; a poor symbiotic experience would obviate this.) Parkin (1985) described the transition from the exhilarated practicing state, which represents the highest point in the development of primary narcissism and in the overestimation of the child's powers, into rapprochement. Parkin defined the "narcissistic crisis" (Mahler's rapprochement crisis) as "the necessity of yielding up to reality the child's illusory claims to omnipotence" (1985, p. 146). Freud wrote of the reluctant "departure from primary narcissism" (1914/1957, p. 100), and Fast (1984) pointed out that the child's emergence from this early state of infantile narcissism is marked by considerable resistance, evasion, and a sense of injury.

This critical developmental transition emotionally tests the mother–child dyad and their ability to remain connected during the stage-specific narcissistic distress that unfolds. The crucial import of the continued libidinal availability of the mother to a healthy resolution of the crisis has been stressed (Settlage, 1977). More specifically, although during the crisis the ambitendent toddler moves away from the mother, he/she returns during periods of distress. The mother's "quiet availability" in these reunions for regulation of distressing affects (arousal modulation) is an essential caregiver function. During this period of developmental crisis, separation anxiety is intensified due to fear of loss of the mother as a newly discovered separate object, and narcissistic rages and tantrums are used by the child to regain control. As mentioned earlier, the response of attachment figures to this behavior is critical.

The markers of a successful developmental passage through this stage transition are well known. Kohut (1971) underscored the principle that a true sense of self is a product of the accommodation or neutralization of the individual's grandiosity and idealization. Parkin emphasized that "with this resolution there is a subsidence of the child's rages and of his external struggles with his mother for power" (1985, p. 147), and Settlage (1977) asserted that one of the major developmental tasks of the rapprochement phase is the modulation of infantile rage.

What fundamental internal transformations are being reflected in these changes? Kagan (1979) found the period of 17 to 21 months (the practicing rapprochement border) to be a critical developmental point, noting a shift from spatial-perceptual to a more symbolic-linguistic cognitive mode of problem solving. Lester (1983) noted that rapprochement onset parallels the transition from Piaget's fifth stage to the sixth and final stage of sensorimotor development, "invention of new means through mental combinations." Focusing on the emergent cognitive functions at this time, Lester stated:

> The child can now perform true mental operations with ever-increasing speed, and he can deal with a large segment of reality at once. This level of maturation of the mental apparatus correlates with and possibly explains the phenomenon of the rapprochement crisis.
>
> *(1983, p. 151)*

It should be pointed out, however, that the child at this point in development is still essentially "preverbal." The effective vocabulary (words spoken or understood) of the average 18-month-old is only 22 words (Mussen, Conger, & Kagan, 1969), and emotion-descriptive language does not first emerge until 20 months of age (Bretherton, McNew, & Beeghly, 1981).

Notice the focus solely on the appearance of new cognitive abilities, presumably reflecting the ongoing postnatal maturation of the cerebral cortex (Yakovlev & LeCours, 1967), especially the early maturing right cerebral hemisphere (Geschwind & Galaburda, 1987). This could explain the more efficient ability to process and internally store symbolic representations of the external world, but, to my mind, does not reveal the essential transformation in affect and affect regulation that marks the rapprochement crisis – the deflation of practicing "elation" and "exhilaration" that supports the illusion of omnipotence. Mahler emphasized that during the rapprochement crisis, which is essentially an emotional crisis, the toddler shows "an increasing differentiation of his emotional life" (1980, p. 9). Krystal, also stressing the importance of affect at this developmental phase, noted, "Separation-individuation is a process of growth and development regulated by the intensity of the feelings that can be tolerated during . . . separation. This process provides an opportunity to develop the affect and increase this tolerance" (1988, p. 35).

It is posited here that the shame system, the regulator of hyperstimulated (excited, elated, grandiose, manic) states, critical to the modulation of high arousal narcissistic affects characteristic of the practicing period, is required for deflation of omnipotence and resolution of the rapprochement (narcissistic) crisis. McDevitt (1980) asserted that the formation of superego structure is instrumental to the resolution of the rapprochement crisis. Johnson (1987) pointed out that from the practicing phase onward, the parents must supply repeated but supportive and not humiliating frustration of the child's illusion of grandiosity. In optimal situations this deflation should be gradual and not precipitous and overwhelming; the nascent self is plastic, yet fragile.

These early-frustrative socializing events may serve as stress immunization experiences that allow for tolerance, coping, and recovery from later attachment stresses; Greenspan (1981) pointed out that the ultimate indicator of attachment capacity is resilience in the face of stress. Hunt (1965) suggested that regularly sheltering children from stressors is counterproductive for optimal emotional development. Moreover, Kohut proposed, "Small (subliminal) shame signals play a role in maintaining a homeostatic narcissistic equilibrium" (1971, p. 181). These may represent the mechanism of modulated phase-appropriate empathic failures that allow for transmuting internalizations. Kohut stipulated, "Tolerable disappointments in the pre-existing (and externally sustained) primary narcissistic equilibrium lead to the establishment of internal structures which provide the ability for self-soothing and the acquisition of basic tension tolerance in the narcissistic realm" (1971, p. 64).

Broucek asserted, "In small, unavoidable 'doses,' shame may enhance self and object differentiation and assist the individuation process because it involves acute awareness of one's separateness from the important other" (1982, p. 37). Similarly, Nathanson (1987) pointed out that shame experiences producing lapses in the smooth physiological functioning of the organism act as a major force in shaping the infantile self. Basch (1988), maintained that shame acts to protect the self-system by modifying patterns of expectations in the interest of social maturation. The positive aspect of this unique affect "which in contrast to all other affects . . . is an experience of the self by the self" (Schneider, 1977, p. 25), and which reflects "heightened self-consciousness" (Tomkins, 1963), can be seen in its role in protecting individuation, the growth process of delimiting the boundaries and nature of the self. Spero (1984) argued that the constructive function of shame can be seen in the process of differentiation of the self in the presence of danger of self-other merger; and Severino, McNutt, and Feder (1987), using clinical case material, concluded that the capacity to experience shame is crucial for the achievement of autonomy.

The importance of experienced, regulated (as opposed to bypassed, unregulated) shame to ongoing development (Shane, 1980; Ward, 1972) may lie in its role as a socializing agent. Measured, repeated exposures to limitation may dilute primary infantile narcissism and neutralize primitive aggressive drives, especially during the narcissistic crisis. Mahler (1979) noted that a surplus of unneutralized aggression thwarts favorable development. Parens (1980) described the upsurge in aggressive drive that occurs specifically in the practicing phase, and Kagan (1976) characterized "separation protest" that peaks at 12 months and diminishes between 15 to 24 months (rapprochement). In a study of 13-month-old infants, Izard found that the dominant, typical negative emotional response to brief separation at this age is anger, not sadness, and not "separation anxiety" (Shiller, Izard, & Hembree, 1986). Bowlby (1969) observed a "bitter" separation protest as a response to a broken attachment tie, which H. B. Lewis (1985) specifically equated with "shame-rage" (humiliated fury). Willock (1986) observed the phenomenon of narcissistic vulnerability in hyperaggressive children.

It is proposed that these phenomena commonly reflect "narcissistic rage," the unmodulated, overexcited sympathetic arousal triggered by object loss, which is characteristic of this period. The activation of high levels of sympathetic arousal is known to facilitate aggressive behavior (Zillman & Bryant, 1974). At this age, the infant can not yet autoregulate this state, as it propels him/her into extremely high levels of arousal in excess of his/her optimal activation band, and is therefore beyond his/her active coping capacities. It is known that "negative emotional responses occur in high arousal situations in which active coping methods are not available" (Dienstbier, 1989, p. 93). This unregulated hyperstimulated condition consequently precipitates an explosive (as opposed to shame-induced implosive) self-fragmentation.

Fox and Davidson (1984) asserted that a major developmental milestone occurs in the middle of the second year (practicing offset/rapprochement onset). At this time a system of affect regulation emerges with the capacity for inhibition of distress and other negative affects. Pine (1980) suggested that "control/delay/inhibition processes" (affect regulatory processes) are involved in the expansion of the affect array. This principle may be demonstrated in the transformation of diffuse, explosive rage of the infant into focused and modulated anger. In a classic study of the early expressions of aggression within the first two years of life, Goodenough (1931) reported a developmental transition from frustration-induced anger manifested as tantrums, undirected energy, and outbursts of motor activity into directed motor and language responses. The initiation of the modulation of this negative/active affect during the late-practicing/early-rapprochement period (Settlage, 1977) reflects the onset of functional activity of the shame regulator's control of sympathetic, hyperaroused limbic aggressive states and may underlie "the transformation of narcissistic rage into mature aggression" (Kohut, 1978, p. 649).

Furthermore, the emergence of evocative memory (Fraiberg, 1969) at the practicing rapprochement border can only be maintained if preexisting forms of infantile rage can be regulated (Adler & Buie, 1979). During this developmental period the child's anger:

> interferes with the capability to maintain a sense of the good internal object image during the mother's absence, so that the serene state of mind implied in the capacity to be alone (Winnicott, 1958) is frequently not attainable. This ability to be alone includes the sense of being alone with an ego supportive other, and this image is not available at times of anger or frustration.
>
> *(Wagner & Fine, 1981, p. 11)*

A further fundamental consequence of the importance of shame downregulation of the practicing infant's hyperstimulated, high arousal states is found in its critical effect on ongoing internalization and subsequent identification processes. Wallace (1963) noted that, in adults, there is an association between shame predominance (unregulated shame) and a "deficiency of introjects," A. P. Morrison (1989) high-lighted the relationship of shame to "faulty identity-formation," and Spero (1984) observed that shame-prone personalities manifest "deficits in capacity for internal-ization." Freud postulated that anaclitic identification occurs when the mother, to whom the child has developed an attachment, frustrates the child by withholding rewards she had previously freely dispensed; this motivates the child to "introject" her. Thus, the stress of frustration (as outlined earlier in shame) is requisite to the child's internalization of dyadic object relations sequences and the construction of internalized working models of attachment in episodic memory.

Unmodulated hyperaroused manic affect is known to interfere with learning and memory processes (Johnson & Magaro, 1987), and to specifically disrupt long-term memory processes, particularly retrieval (Henry, Weingartner, & Murphy, 1971). Bandura and Walters's (1963) studies of social learning phenomena indicate that "imitation," which they equate with "identification," is facilitated by moder-ate arousal, but becomes more and more limited and fragmentary as the level of arousal increases. It follows that the extremely high arousal levels of unregulated, self-fragmenting narcissistic rage disrupt identification processes critical to the reso-lution of the rapprochement crisis. This phenomenon is reflected in McDevitt's (1975) demonstration of prolonged states of unmetabolized aggression producing "interferences with identification" in this critical period.

The critical import of shame regulation of hyperaroused, grandiose practicing affect to identification processes also applies to emerging gender identification that is actively occurring at 18 months (Money & Ehrhardt, 1968), rapprochement onset. Nathanson (1987) pointed out that "the earliest manifestations of geni-tality and gender identity are exactly contemporaneous with the period during which shame takes on its deepest significance in terms of the self" (p. 39), and Amsterdam and Leavitt (1980) noted that parental response to the rapprochement onset upsurge in genital sexuality is critical to developing shame affect. Fast (1979) asserted that early gender development in girls involves the transition from an early undifferentiated, grandiose, omnipotent, narcissistic state to a more differentiated state of feminine identification in which earlier illusory claims of omnipotence are yielded up to reality. If this does not occur, an "incompletely differentiated feminine gender" results.

Furthermore, the narcissistic mother either overstimulates or does not modulate her infant's high arousal grandiose affect. Mahler and Kaplan (1977) described the developmental history of a very aggressive narcissistic girl who manifested a pre-dominance of shame and a "poor feminine identification." In an unpublished study (J. Schore, 1983), shame-prone women with inefficient shame-regulatory systems were shown to have weak feminine identifications, presumably reflecting poor early maternal internalizations and attachment. It is posited that this occurred because the narcissistic mother did not downregulate the practicing toddler's hyperarousal, a state detrimental to the learning and memory processes underlying identifica-tion. If the mother does not shameregulate phase-typical hyperarousal, the maternal introjection and gender identification will be "weak." Also, in psychotherapeutic work with adults, Kaufman (1985) noted a strong connection between "failures in identification" due to intense early shame histories and homosexual manifestations.

As pointed out earlier, in addition to the shame experience and its consequent affective misattunement, the caregiver's response of deactivating and subsequently reactivating sympathetic arousal is critical to the organization of a system to regulate the negative effect of shame (i.e., the shame regulator). Thus, at the critical period of the practicing/rapprochement boundary, a favorable resolution of the narcissistic (rapprochement) crisis and the emergence of a system to regulate narcissistic affects depends on the emergence, by the end of the practicing phase, of an internalized, efficient, affect-autoregulatory system that can bidirectionally modulate the high arousal affects intrinsic to the grandiose, narcissistically charged practicing stage, even in the caregiver's absence. This mechanism underlies Freud's (1923/1961b) observation that by both frustrating and satisfying the infant in the correct proportion, the mother facilitates the transformation of the pleasure into the reality principle.

Implications for the etiology of narcissistic disorders

The developmentally impaired narcissistic disorders, which manifest shamesensitivity (DSM-III-R, 1987; Kohut, 1971; Lewis, 1980), defective superego formation, vulnerability to narcissistic injuries, low self-esteem, and unmodulated narcissistic rage do not effectively negotiate the rapprochement crisis. In support of this, Mahler and Kaplan (1977) speculated that the early etiology of the narcissistic disorder of a 13-year-old girl involved the absence of practicing phase refueling and the irresolution of the rapprochement crisis. Masterson correctly pointed out, "The narcissistic personality disorder must be fixated or arrested before the development of the rapprochement crisis, since one of the important tasks of that crisis is not performed, i.e., the deflation of infantile grandiosity and omnipotence" (1981, p. 29). Spitz (1965) described a type of "psychotoxic" maternal care, manifest in an overdose of affective stimulation, that is dispensed by the narcissistic mother who is concerned more with her own emotional needs than her infant's.

When the child is in a grandiose state, mirroring of her narcissism, the primary caregiver is emotionally accessible. However, because the infant's hyperaroused state mirrors the mother's heightened narcissism, the mother may do little to modulate it. On the other hand, when the infant is in a negative hyperaroused state, such as aggressive separation protest, she either fails to modulate it (in herself or in her child) or even hyperstimulates the infant into a state of dyscontrol. She also may be ineffective in regulating the infant up out of hypoaroused states that she herself triggers, such as occurs in maternal shame stress depletion of narcissistic affect. Kohut described this inconsistent attunement of the mother as an important element in the etiology of narcissistic disorders:

> On innumerable occasions she appeared to have been totally absorbed in the
> child – overcaressing him, completely in tune with every nuance of his needs

and wishes – only to withdraw from him suddenly, either by turning her attention totally to other interests or by grossly and grotesquely misunderstanding his needs and wishes.

(1977, p. 52)

Thus, after a shame-induced infant-caregiver misattunement, at reunion, a moment of emotional reconnection, the infant encounters a narcissistically injured, aggressively teasing, and humiliating mother who, rather than decreasing shame distress, hyperstimulates the child into an agitated state of narcissistic rage. The caregiver does not act to modulate shame and allow for the internalization and organization of a shame-regulatory system in the child that can reduce hyperstimulated states and enable recovery from hypostimulated states. Repeated early failures of attunement create "a belief that one's affective needs generally are somehow unacceptable and shameful" (Basch, 1985, p. 35). The inner experience of the affect of shame therefore becomes associated with an expectation of a painful, self-disorganizing internal state that cannot be regulated, and therefore is consciously avoided or "bypassed" (Lewis, H. B., 1971). The developmental arrest of narcissism regulation thus occurs specifically at rapprochement onset, and is due to the failure to evolve a practicing affect regulatory system that can neutralize grandiosity, regulate practicing excitement, or modulate narcissistic distress.

Kohut noted that the specific pathological affective experiences of narcissistic disorders "fall into a spectrum ranging from anxious grandiosity and excitement on the one hand to mild embarassment and self-consciousness or severe shame, hypochondria, and depression on the other" (1971, p. 200). Broucek (1982) described:

With the advent of objective self-awareness, the child becomes more acutely conscious of his comparative smallness, weakness and his relative incompetence in the larger scheme of things. The shame evoked by this self-consciousness is more intense and more threatening for the child with a grandiose self than for the child with a less fantastic, more "normal" ideal self, due to the greater discrepancy between objectively derived self-observation and the defensively exalted grandiose self.

(p. 375)

This phenomenon is due to a failure to downregulate the high arousal affects that fuel the "fantastic" grandiose self. As a result, "the ideal ego may remain sequestered from the developing reality ego as a persisting structure ready for grandiose revival" (Parkin, 1985, p. 146). The hypercathected archaic ideal ego (Kohut's archaic grandiose self), as an unintegrated persisting remnant, moves forward in development, and may be activated and expressed in "the appearance of affects similar to those associated with the earlier system such as grandiosity, omnipotence and euphoria or even elation " (Parkin, 1985, p. 152). Kohut described a personality structure "with a poorly integrated grandiose self concept and intense exhibitionistic-narcissistic tensions who is most prone to experience shame" (1978, p. 441). Shame-prone narcissistic personalities

(Lewis, 1980) defend "against feelings of unworthiness and self-contempt by assuming an attitude of grandiosity and entitlement, which is often accompanied by feelings of elation and contempt for others" (Hartocollis, 1980, p. 137).

Referring to self object (preoedipal) transferences in narcissistic personality disorders, Dorpat pointed out:

> The narcissistic transference object (or self object) serves as a substitute for the patient's missing or defective psychic structures. In analysis and in their everyday life, such patients seek self objects to carry out functions (guiding, controlling, comforting) that persons with more differentiated ego and superego structures are capable of doing for themselves.
>
> *(1981, p. 162)*

In early development, preoedipal caregivers serve as self objects, specifically to perform psychological functions "such as tension management and selfesteem regulation that the infant is unable to perform for himself" (Glassman, 1988, p. 601). This developmental principle underlies the clinical transferential phenomenon of the uneasy dependence of the narcissistic patient on the psychotherapist for self-esteem regulation and the stabilization of narcissistic equilibrium (Bleiberg, 1987), thus promoting the clinician's critical role as an "auxilliary superego" (Strachey, 1934). Self object functions are specifically and exclusively unconscious, nonverbal affect regulatory functions that stabilize selfstructure against the hyperstimulated-explosive fragmenting or hypostimulated-implosive depleting potential of stressful levels of stimulation and affect. An effective structural superego system to autoregulate mood and narcissistic affects, which is required for self-esteem homeostasis and for restoration and recovery of narcissistic equilibrium subsequent to affective stress and narcissistic injury, never ontogenetically evolves. Kernberg (1984) and Tyson and Tyson (1984) emphasized the clinical observation that superego pathology plays a central role in narcissistic disturbances.

The essential psychological lesion in these individuals (as well as in borderline personalities who also manifest a heightened vulnerability to shame and a failure to self-regulate emotional experience; Grotstein, 1990) is that they do not have the capacity to tolerate or recover from narcissistic injuries that expose distressing negative affect, especially hyperaroused affects like narcissistic rage and hypoaroused shame, while maintaining constructive engagement with others. The coping ability to affectively reconnect with an emotionally significant other after a shame stress separation, and indeed to use the other to recover from shame associated narcissistic injury and object loss, has never effectively developed in this personality structure due to its early practicing experiences. Narcissistic disorders are thus disorders of the regulation of narcissistic affect, especially shame, the central affective experience of narcissism (Broucek, 1982; Kinston, 1983; Morrison, 1989), and their pathology is most observable during times of stress of narcissistic affect. Self-regulatory failure has recently been proposed to be responsible for the "affectomotor lability" of narcissistic disorders (Rinsley, 1989).

Despite this inefficient capacity to autoregulate distress, during periods of stress, when it may be more adaptive to communicate one's disorganized affective state to a significant other, such individuals emotionally withdraw from object relations in order to protect against the unconsciously anticipated painful exposure of shame-humiliation. Shame-prone narcissistic personalities are known to suffer from narcissistic injury-triggered, overwhelming, internal selfshaming tendencies (Morrison, 1984) and repetitive oscillations of self-esteem, which necessitate "endless attempts at repair" (Reich, 1960). Bursten noted, "The task of the narcissistic repair mechanism is to be rid of shame" (1973, p. 294), an affect state that "tends to linger for quite a long time until the subject recovers" (Nathanson, 1987, p. 26), and which "spreads out from one specific content . . . to all of inner reality and hence to the entire function of expressing oneself" (Wurmser, 1981, p. 272). When a narcissistically undesirable trait is suddenly exposed (to the self and/or the other), an uncontrolled escalating shame reaction occurs, and there is no adequate affect regulating mechanism for the personality to use to modulate or recover from this painful affective state. Without a system to actively cope with and thereby tolerate this potent affect, the immature, undeveloped, archaic superego avoids risk experiences that are potential points of shameful self-exposure, thereby diminishing the expansion and the province of the ego ideal.

The emergence of ego ideal regulation of narcissistic affect

Under optimal growth conditions a developmental transformation of narcissism occurs: the omnipotence and grandiosity of the psychic system of primary narcissism, the ideal ego, is diminished in the narcissistic crisis, giving way to the dominant emergence of the system of secondary narcissism, the nascent ego ideal. The ego ideal has been conceptualized to have its origins in the early introjection of the idealized loved and loving omnipotent mother (if the child has had such an experience). As a result of this internalization, "internal regulation of self-esteem becomes possible for the first time" (Parkin, 1985, p. 147). The function of the ego ideal, a system by which the self measures itself, is in general similar to other self-regulatory systems that modulate the internal milieu and stabilize the relationship between the organism and the internal environment. However, in particular it acts to autoregulate narcissistic affects that underlie self-esteem, thereby sustaining autonomous emotional control, especially in response to social-environmental induced affective stress.

Blos (1974) characterized the ego ideal as a controlling agency that regulates maintenance of self-esteem and narcissistic balance. "Fulfillment of the ideal results in an increase of self-esteem, while a failure to meet the standards of the ideal [shame] results in a decrease in self-esteem" (Turiell, 1967). Self-esteem has been conceptualized as an "affective picture of the self," with high self-esteem connoting a predominance of positive affects and low self-esteem connoting a predominance of negative ones (Pulver, 1970). Stolorow and Lachmann defined narcissism functionally: "Mental activity is narcissistic to the degree that its function is to maintain the structural cohesion, temporal stability and positive affective coloring of the self representation" (1980, p. 10). The maintainance of narcissistic equilibrium, a functional role of the superego (Tyson & Tyson, 1984), is manifest in the ego ideal regulation of narcissistic affect that underlies self-esteem. Self-esteem regulation has been identified as a function of the superego system (Josephs, 1989; Kernberg, 1984); and Nathanson (1987) described the superego as functionally capable of processing "minute gradations of self-esteem." Pulver (1970) noted that the maintainance of self-esteem is the personality's best protection against narcissistic vulnerability and shame propensity. The functioning of the ego ideal is thus intimately tied into the ego mechanism of episodic memory, which stores events that have meaning for the concept of self and are significant for the maintenance of self-esteem (Tulving, 1972).

The ego ideal, which originates at the end of the practicing period, allows for a successful transition through the rapprochement crisis via its mediation in the efficient regulation of high and low arousal states. Brickman noted, "The evolution of a properly functioning superego system may be seen to be contingent on the successful resolution of developmental . . . issues" (1983, p. 90); and Grotstein (1983) referred to the critical importance of the establishment of a particular internal object to the function of the superego/ego ideal. The work presented here specifically outlines the importance of shame in the genesis of the evolving superego. Notice a psychological function (affect regulation) that is externally regulated in one phase is internalized and autoregulated in the succeeding phase. The ego ideal, a narcissistic component of the superego along with the conscience (Hartmann & Loewenstein, 1962), contains grandiose fantasies and ideals and a "core of narcissistic omnipotence (which) . . . represents the sum of the positive identifications with the parental images" (Piers & Singer, 1953, p. 14). These latter authors also theorized that it contains the goals of striving for mastery, or a "maturation drive," which "would signify a psychic representation of all the growth, maturation, and individuation processes in the human being" (p. 15).

Shame, which is associated with a "narcissistic depletion within the self-structure" (Spero, 1984, p. 264), and is an affective component of low self-esteem (Josephs, 1989), has been commonly conceptualized in the psychoanalytic literature as the affect that arises when a self-monitoring and self-evaluating process concludes that there has been a failure to live up to ego ideal images (Piers & Singer, 1953). From a sociological viewpoint, Scheff (1988) pointed out that this affect, the primary social emotion, though it is usually almost invisible, is generated by the virtually constant monitoring of the self in relation to others. Shame is typically triggered by incompetence (White, 1960) and the concomitant threat of abandonment or rejection by the "significant object" (Levin, 1967), and is thus the affective response to the self's failure to approximate its ideal state of maximized positive and minimized negative narcissistic affect when contrasted to the current level of the actual state.

The ontogenetic origin of shame similarly involves an appraisal process in which a discrepancy exists between the memory of the caregiver in an ideal, attuned, positive affective state and the perception of the reality of a misattuned mother in a negative affective state. Though the developmental origin of the negative evaluation of the self that produces shame arises from the interpersonal failure of expectation (excited anticipation), shame later occurs when certain intrapersonal self-expectations (goals), the predominantly unconscious standards of the ego ideal, are not fulfilled. The central role of the self-monitoring ego ideal to the understanding of shame has been stressed by Morrison (1989).

Due to its intrinsically nonverbal nature, the subjective experience of shame is ineffable. Despite this, various authors have attempted to describe the phenomology of the moment of shame. This ubiquitous primary social emotion in which one is visible and not ready to be visible (Erikson, 1950) operates subtly in even the healthiest of human interactions (Kaufman, 1974). This misattuned relational transaction triggers gaze aversion (Tomkins, 1963), a response of hiding the face "to escape from this being seen or from the one who sees" (Wright, 1991, p. 30), and a state of withdrawal (Lichtenberg, 1989). Under the lens of a "shame microscope" which amplifies and expands this negative affect (Malatesta-Magai, 1991), visible defects, narcissistically charged undesirable aspects of the self, are exposed (Jacobson, 1964). "It is as though something we were hiding from everyone is suddenly under a burning light in public view" (Izard, 1991, p. 332). Shame throws a "flooding light" upon the individual (Lynd, 1958), who then experiences "a sense of displeasure plus the compelling desire to disappear from view" (Frijda, 1988, p. 351), and "an impulse to bury one's face, or to sink, right then and there, into the ground" (Erikson, 1950, p. 223) which impels him to "crawl through a hole" and culminates in feeling as if he "could die" (H. B. Lewis, 1971, p. 198).

The sudden shock-induced deflation of positive affect which supports grandiose omnipotence has been phenomenologically characterized as a whirlpool – a visual representation of a spiral (Potter-Effron, 1989) and as a "flowing off " or "leakage" through a drain hole in the middle of one's being (Sartre, 1957, p. 256). The individual's subjective conscious experience of this affect is thus a sudden, unexpected, and rapid transition from what Freud (1914/1957b) called "primary narcissism"– a sense of being "the center and core of the universe," to what Sartre (1957) described as a shame triggered "crack in my universe."

Furthermore, the unique potency of this bodily-based negative affect has been described by Tomkins (1963):

> Though terror speaks of life and death and distress makes of the world a vale of tears, yet shame strikes deepest into the heart of man. While terror and distress hurt, they are wounds inflicted from outside which penetrate the smooth surface of the ego; but shame is felt as an inner torment, a sickness of the soul. It does not matter whether the humiliated one has been shamed by derisive laughter or whether he mocks himself. In either event he feels himself naked, defeated, alienated, lacking in dignity or worth.
>
> *(p. 118)*

Broucek (1982) argued that shame is the basic affective experience of mental unpleasure and pain associated with disturbances of narcissism, and Amsterdam and

Leavitt (1980) equated it with painful, heightened self-consciousness. Campos, Barrett, Lamb, Goldsmith, and Stenberg (1983) posited that it results from injury to any salient aspect of one's self-concept, Kohut (1977) spoke of "narcissistic injury," and Lynd described this affect as "a peculiarly painful feeling of being in a situation that incurs the scorn or contempt of others" (1958, p. 24). Shame stress, a social "microstressor"of daily living, like physical injury and pain, activates a classical stress response; the physiological expression of physical and mental pain is thus identical. Work on brain opioids and social emotions suggests that visceral pain and the affective response to social isolation share common evolutionary histories and neurochemical substrates (Panksepp, Siviy, & Normansell, 1985). Affect tolerance, which allows for the conscious experience of emotions, was proposed by Krystal (1988) to be analogous to the capacity to bear pain. Parkin (1985) equated the mental pain of disorders of narcissism with shame. Blos (1974) characterized a major function of the ego ideal to be repair of narcissistic injuries produced by comparison with or slights by others, thus underscoring the recovery function of this autoregulatory agency.

Notice that the earliest-evolving component of the internal monitoring superego system is the autoregulatory ego ideal. This dovetails nicely with Brickman's formulation that "the origins of the superego may be traced to the earliest attempts of the child to differentiate himself from his environment" (1983, p. 83). The earlier origin of the ego ideal component before the conscience component of the superego has been posited by others as well (e.g., Anthony, 1981; Parkin, 1985). Further support for this was seen in Kagan's developmental study of preverbal two-year-olds in which he concluded, "The appearance of internal standards is not a late development that occurs after the child learns to fear adult punishment, but is present early in ontogeny. These first standards are concerned with task competence" (1979, p. 1053). Note that these internal standards are preverbal, supporting the concept that the preverbal ego ideal forms before the verbal conscience. Early superego function is first manifested at 18 months (the practicing/rapprochement boundary), when toddlers begin to exhibit "moral" prosocial behavior in the form of approaching persons in distress and initiating positive, other-oriented, affective, and instrumental activities in order to comfort the other (Radke-Yarrow & Zahn-Waxler, 1984).

Although the content of the ego ideal is modified throughout development (aspirations are altered and what triggers shame changes), its homeostatic function of narcissistic affect regulation in infancy, childhood, adolescence, and adulthood is not. Related to this is the problem of the distinction between a system's functional onset as a "primitive ego ideal" and its attainment of a "definitive structure" as a "mature ego ideal" (Blos, 1974). Although ego ideal content (i.e., self-representations and images in episodic memory) may not reflect complex identifications and "definitive organization" until adolescence (Blos, 1974), the basic mechanism underlying its functional onset and therefore its origin traces directly back to the early separation-individuation period. Indeed, Blos dated the origin of the infantile ego ideal at the age of attainment of object constancy, 18 months; this coincides with the rapprochement crisis genesis outlined earlier. Spiegel (1966) pointed out that the function of the primordial ego ideal is the "dampening of extreme affects" and is associated with "the early appearance of shame." The necessity for a psychic structural system to autoregulate affect, shame, and self-esteem is required from toddlerhood through adulthood, and its existence and availability depends on early object relations experiences in the practicing-critical period.

The self-regulatory ego ideal, a stress-sensitive coping system involved in the modulation of affects by "toning down" intense "all good" (positive hedonic tone) or "all bad" (negative hedonic tone) affective dispositions (Garza-Guerrero, 1981), (modulates "splitting defenses") is here proposed to be an affect regulatory system that monitors, adjusts, and corrects emotional responses, thereby providing flexibility and unity in socioemotional function. The superego system here described is equivalent to Fox and Davidson's (1984) negative affect regulating system that first appears in the middle of the second year. The ego ideal shame regulator is composed of two components that control the biphasic process of narcissistic affect regulation. The functional operation of this structural system is relevant to the process by which shame plays a central role in maintaining narcissistic equilibrium (Kohut, 1971). The shame stimulator component acutely reduces hyperaroused and hyperstimulated states; diminishes positive narcissisitic affective coloring of self-representations; contracts the self; lowers expectations; decreases self-esteem, active coping, interest, and curiosity; interferes with cognition; and increases overt consciously experienced shame, parasympathetic supported passive coping, blushing, gaze aversion, and depressive affect-toned mood.

The second component, the shame modulator, reduces consciously experienced shame (narcissistic pain), negative affective self-representations, low-keyed depressive states, and passive coping, and initiates recovery of sympatheticsupported positive hedonic-toned mood and narcissistic affect, facilitation of the cathexis of the self-representation, expansion of the self, increased self-esteem, and active stress coping capacities. This dual-component, dual-process system thus homeostatically reestablishes an optimal sympathetic-parasympathetic limbic balance of autonomic-affective functioning, (autonomic balance underlying an optimal level of emotionality), thereby maintaining self-identity and self-continuity in the face of continuously changing external environmental conditions.

The bulk of contemporary psychoanalytic developmental theory (Emde, 1989; Loewald, 1978; Pine, 1985; Stern, 1985) and research (Lichtenberg, 1983) strongly suggests that the infant's early object relations with the mother are indispensable to the development and organization of psychic structure responsible for self-regulation and adaptation. Studies in developmental neuroscience reveal that the stupendous accelerated growth of brain structure in infancy is critically influenced by "social forces" (Lecours, 1982), and it has been suggested that the neurodevelopmental processes that are responsible for postnatal structural brain growth are influenced by events at the interpersonal and intrapersonal levels (Scheflen, 1981). The critical nature of early socioemotional experiences may lie in their effects of enhancing or inhibiting the maturation of adaptive self-regulating systems, especially limbic and cortical structures that anatomically and physiologically mature during particular periods of infancy, and the subsequent socioemotional functions that these structures will subserve.

Utilizing a neuropsychoanalytic perspective, it is suggested that the psychoanalytic ego ideal can be identified as an affect regulatory structure with the orbital prefrontal cortex. This cortical inhibitory system is expanded in the right hemisphere and has extensive limbic connections; regulates emotion (Jouandet & Gazzaniga, 1979), attachment behavior (Steklis & Kling, 1985), and aggression (DeBruin, Van Oyen, & Vande Poll, 1983); and influences parasympathetic and sympathetic autonomic function (Fuster, 1980). The rapid growth and development of this prefrontal system during the first 18 months of life is critically influenced by early "social contact" (Luria, 1980), and its maturation enables the self-modulation of arousal in late infancy (Bowden, Goldman, Rosvold, & Greenstreet, 1971). During the practicing-critical period, shame experiences associated with the socialization process specifically influence the maturation of this superego affect regulatory system.

Superego function in mood regulation and further theoretical considerations

Pine stated, "The awareness of separateness . . . culminates in the rapprochement stage, in sadness or depressive mood" (1980, p. 227). Noting the transition from the "good mood" of the practicing period to the lingering depressive rapprochement, McDevitt asserted, "Thoughts and feelings persist beyond the situation in which they had their origin. Conflicts with the mother no longer simply flare up and disappear; they appear to continue in the child's mind for longer periods of time" (1975, p. 728). Mahler observed, "A basic mood is established during the separation-individuation process . . . . The characteristic baseline of the child's emotional responsiveness seems to derive from the preponderance and perpetuation of one or the other of the subphases of the separationindividuation process" (1979, p. 63).

The onset of superego (ego ideal) autoregulatory functions at the end of the practicing period that enables the successful resolution of the rapprochement crisis in which there is a transformation of mood states fits well with Jacobson's (1964) conceptualization of the superego as an affect regulatory system, a mood (defined as a general enduring highly persistent state of affect) regulator:

> I have stated that the centralised, regulating power of the superego can modify the course of the self- and object-directed discharge processes in a generalized way. But generalized modifications of all discharge patterns lend our thoughts, actions, and above all our feelings a characteristic color which finds expression in what we call our mood. Thus the superego also becomes a governing force for our moods and keeps them at a comparatively even level. This is why any pathology and deficiency of the superego functions will manifest itself in conspicuous disturbances of the mood level.
>
> *(p. 133)*

Kernberg (1984) postulated that the mature superego exerts functional control by modulating mood swings. The function of the internal monitoring superego system, originally proposed by Freud to regulate drive (hyperstimulated aggression and sexuality), later described by Jacobson (1964) as an autonomous central system for the regulation of libidinal and aggressive cathexes of selfrepresentations, is fundamentally to regulate affect.

The hallmark of a developmentally and functionally evolved superego, which is often too narrowly defined in terms of cognitive and verbal aspects of conscience, is reflected in mood stability and a relatively rapid recovery from disruptive emotional distress states to positively toned emotional states. On the other hand, a developmentally and functionally immature superego, especially under narcissistic stress, would manifest a tendency to slip easily from a positive or neutral state into a negative emotional state. These negative emotional states endure well beyond the precipitating stimulus event as a lingering dysphoric mood.

This conceptualization fits well with Wallace's (1963) clinical observation that shame-prone individuals have undeveloped or partially developed superegos, and Freud's concept, presented in "The Ego and the Id" (1923/1961), that psychiatric disturbances reflect a malfunctioning superego. Structural defects in the undeveloped superego are particularly exposed under high pressure. Superego lacunae (Aldrich, 1987) and the failure of internal controls to regulate internal aggressive impulses will form in response to intense, unmodulated stress states. Superego dysfunction is thus manifest in impaired affect regulation as found, for example, in affective disturbances (Giovacchini, 1979) and mood disorders, as well as in self-esteem pathology as found in narcissistic and borderline patients. Eisnitz noted, "Rapid shifts in self-esteem may be an indicator of superego function dominated by highly aggressivized and libidinized energy" (1988, p. 156).

I suggest that this symptomatology reflects an unevolved, inefficient ego ideal shame regulator that is unable to modulate these hyperenergetic states. Furthermore, I agree with Kernberg's assertion that a lack of superego integration is diagnostic of narcissistic and borderline personality organizations, and with his clinical postulate that as a "criterion for the indication or contraindication of long-term, intensive psychotherapy . . . the quality of object relations and the quality of superego functioning are probably the two most important prognostic criteria" (1984, p. 21). However, the focus should be shifted from the later-forming conscience component and guilt to the developmentally earlier ego ideal and its associated superego affect, shame.

The essential psychological (and biochemical) lesions of disorders of affective functioning are found in structurally unevolved, physiologically altered, inefficient prefrontal regulatory systems that impair active recovery processes. Self-regulatory failure has been proposed to be responsible for the pathological "affectomotor lability" of narcissistic disorders (Rinsley, 1989), and to be the proximal cause of depressive disorders (Morris, 1989; Pyszczynski & Greenberg, 1987). Patients with cyclothymic and dysthymic affective pathology recover more slowly from negative life events than do normals (Goplerud & Depue, 1985). These regulatory impairments are manifest very early in specific vulnerable critical periods. For example, a generalized disturbance in affect regulation, as reflected in long-enduring negative affective states, which is identifiable at 12 months and increases to prominence by 18 months (the span of the practicing period), has been found in infants of manic-depressive parents (Gaensbauer Harmon, Cytryn, & McKnew, 1984).

With the practicing rapprochement transition, a period in which attachment ties with the mother are loosened (Galenson & Roiphe, 1976) yet attachment intensity to the father is significantly increased (Abelin, 1971), the practicing subphase-specific, obligatory, and dominant mood of elation is supplanted by the subphase-specific mood of rapprochement, soberness, and even temporary depression. Notice the typical high arousal affect of the "elated" practicing subphase versus the low arousal, "depressed" affect of the rapprochement phase. At reunion, the practicing caregiver is predominantly regulating an elated junior toddler; the rapprochement caregivers are generally regulating a senior toddler who is in a very different mood state, low energy, and deflated. Again, it should be remembered that emotional distress can take the form of hyperaroused or hypoaroused affects. The "affective climate" of the two subphases is qualitatively very different, both in terms of the predominant affective valence and in terms of the tempo (arousal level) of the predominant emotional state. Practicing elation, characterized as positive/active, is supplanted by rapprochement depression, which is negative/passive.

"Nameless shame" (Kohut, 1977), which originates in the sensorimotor nonverbal practicing period, and the ego ideal component of the superego are both operative at this transitional point in development. However, guilt, which first emerges in the verbal child, and the conscience component, which relies on the internalization of verbal, moral values and parental standards, do not first appear until the end of rapprochement/beginning of the phallic stage (i.e., Mahler's fourth subphase and Piaget's first stage of preoperational representations; Izard, 1978; Pine, 1980; Sroufe, 1979). This dual model of superego onset and function fits well with S. Miller's (1989) division of an early-appearing developmental line associated with shame from a later-emerging affect line associated with guilt, and with Krystal's (1978) differentiation of two lines of emotional development, an infantile nonverbal affect system and a verbal adult system; he specifically cited guilt as an "adult type of affect."

Similarly, in the neuroscience literature, Gazzaniga (1985) postulated the existence of two affect-mediating systems, a basic primitive system and a verbal-conceptual system, that are localized in separate hemispheres. Neuropsychological research with very young children has indicated early autonomous affective as well as cognitive functioning of the two hemispheres. I propose that the earlier development of nonverbal shame and the ego ideal before verbal guilt and conscience reflects the known biologically determined earlier differentiation and functional onset of the nonverbal visuospatial-holistic right hemisphere (Geschwind & Galaburda, 1987; Giannitrapani, 1967; Whitaker, 1978), and the later maturation of the linguistic-rational capacity of the verbal analytic left hemisphere (Miller, 1986; Taylor, 1969). Indeed, a developmental neuropsychological study (Rothbart et al., 1989) of practicing infants has revealed that right, but not left, hemispheric specialization for emotions begins at the end of the first year, with greater right hemispheric cortical inhibition of subcortical emotional processes. In contrast, Thatcher, Walker, and Giudice (1987) showed that the left hemisphere growth spurt does not begin until age two.

In addition, an impressive volume of research on hemispheric lateralization of emotions reveals the existence of dual affective systems, a right hemisphere system dominant for nonverbal mood and affect, and a left hemisphere system involved in verbally mediated affective and mood states (Silberman & Weingartner, 1986). The function of these two systems may be reflected in the processing of unconscious and conscious affective information, respectively. In adults, the right hemisphere is known to be "predominant in the experience, expression and discrimination of emotion and . . . differentially important for the regulation of arousal" (Levy, Heller, Banich, & Burton, 1983, p. 332), preferentially activated under stress conditions (Tucker, Roth, Arneson, & Buckingman, 1977), responsible for maintaining important controls over autonomic activities (Heilman, Schwartz, & Watson, 1977), and to be particularly well connected with subcortical processes (Tucker, 1981). Joseph concluded, "Right hemispheric involvement with emotional functioning is due to greater abundance of reciprocal interconnections with the limbic system" (1982, p. 16).

The emergent ego ideal is here conceptualized to be the right hemispheric, dual-component, narcissistic affect shame regulator that manifests structural organization and functional onset at the end of the practicing period. Ego ideal shame regulation may be pertinent to the dynamic mechanism by which the right hemisphere, which is responsible for primary process functions ascribed to the unconscious (Galin, 1974) and transference phenomena (Watt, 1986), regulates emotional information. The superego components of ego ideal and conscience may thus respectively represent systems of right and left hemispheric affect regulation.

References

Abelin, E. (1971). The role of the father in the separation-individuation process. In J. B. McDevitt & C. F. Settlage (Eds.), *Separation-individuation*, 229–252. New York: International University Press.

Adler, G., & Buie, D. H. J. (1979). Aloneness and borderline psychopathology: The possible relevance of child development issues. *International Journal of Psycho-Analysis*, 60, 83–96.

Ainsworth, M. D. S., & Bell, S. M. (1974). Mother-infant interaction and the development of competence. In K. Connolly & J. Bruner (Eds.), *The growth of confidence*, 97–118. New York: Academic Press.

Ainsworth, M. D. S., Blehar, M. C., Waters, E., & Wall, S. (1978). *Patterns of attachment*. Hillsdale, NJ: Erlbaum.

Aldrich, C. K. (1987). Acting out and acting up: The superego lacuna revisited. *American Journal of Orthopsychiatry*, 57, 402–406.

Amsterdam, B. (1972). Mirror self-image reactions before age two. *Developmental Psychobiology*, 5, 297–305.

Amsterdam, B., & Leavitt, M. (1980). Consciousness of self and painful self-consciousness. *Psychoanalytic Study of the Child*, 35, 67–83.

Anthony, E. J. (1981). Shame, guilt, and the feminine self in psychoanalysis. In S. Tuttman (Ed.), *Object and self: A developmental approach*, 191–234. New York: International Universities Press.

Bandura, A., & Walters, R. H. (1963). *Social learning and personality development*. New York: Holt, Rinehart & Winston.

Basch, M. F. (1976). The concept of affect: A re-examination. *Journal of the American Psychoanalytic Association*, 24, 759–777.

Basch, M. F. (1985). Interpretation: Toward a developmental model. In A. Goldberg (Ed.), *Progress in self psychology*, Vol. 1, 33–42. New York: Guilford Press.

Basch, M. F. (1988). *Understanding psychotherapy*. New York: Basic Books.

Bell, S. M. (1970). The development of the concept of object as related to infant – mother attachment. *Child Development*, 41, 291–311.

Bertenthal, B., Campos, J., & Barrett, K. (1984). Self-produced locomotion: An organizer of emotional, cognitive, and social development in infancy. In R. Emde & R. J. Harmon (Eds.), *Continuities and discontinuities in development*, 175–210. New York: Plenum.

Bleiberg, E. (1987). Stages in the treatment of narcissistic children and adolescents. *Bulletin of the Menninger Clinic*, 51, 296–313.

Blos, P. (1974). The genealogy of the ego ideal. *Psychoanalytic Study of the Child*, 29, 43–88.

Bowden, D. M., Goldman, P. S., Rosvold, H. E., & Greenstreet, R. L. (1971). Free behavior of rhesus monkeys following lesions of the dorsolateral and orbital prefrontal cortex in infancy. *Experimental Brain Research*, 12, 265–274.

Bowlby, J. (1969). *Attachment and loss: Vol. 1. Attachment*. New York: Basic Books.

Bowlby, J. (1973). *Attachment and loss: Vol. 2. Separation, anxiety and anger*. New York: Basic Books.

Bowlby, J. (1988). Attachment, communication, and the therapeutic process. In J. Bowlby (Ed.), *A secure base: Clinical applications of attachment theory*, 137–157. London: Routledge.

Brazelton, T. B., Koslowski, B., & Main, M. (1974). The origins of reciprocity: The early mother-infant interaction. In M. Lewis & L. Rosenblum (Eds.), *The effect of the infant on its caregiver*, 49–77. New York: Wiley.

Breese, G. R., Smith, R. D., Mueller, R. A., Howard, J. L., Prange, A. J., Lipton, M. A., Young, L. D., McKinney, W. T., & Lewis, J. K. (1973). Induction of adrenal catecholamine synthesizing enzymes following mother-infant separation. *Nature New Biology*, 246, 94–96.

Brent, L., & Resch, R. C. (1987). A paradigm of infant-mother reciprocity: A reexamination of "emotional refueling". *Psychoanalytic Psychology*, 4, 15–31.

Bretherton, I. (1985). Attachment theory: Retrospect and prospect. *Monographs of the Society for Research in Child Development*, 50, 3–35.

Bretherton, I., McNew, S., & Beeghly, M. (1981). Early person knowledge in gestural and verbal communication: When do infants acquire a "theory of mind"? In M. Lamb & L. Sherrod (Eds.), *Infant social sognition*, 335–373. Hillsdale, NJ: Erlbaum.

Brickman, A. S. (1983). Pre-oedipal development of the superego. *International Journal of Psycho-Analysis*, 64, 83–92.

Broucek, F. J. (1982). Shame and its relationship to early narcissistic developments. *International Journal of Psycho-Analysis*, 63, 369–378.

Broverman, D. M., Klaiber, E. L., Kobayashi, Y., & Vogel, W. (1968). Roles of activation and inhibition in sex differences in cognitive abilities. *Psychological Review*, 75, 23–50.

Buck, R. W., Parke, R. D., & Buck, M. (1970). Skin conductance, heart rate, and attention to the environment in two stressful situations. *Psychonomic Science*, 18, 95–96.

Buechler, S., & Izard, C. E. (1983). On the emergence, functions, and regulation of some emotion expressions in infancy. In R. Plutchik & H. Kellerman (Eds.), *Emotion: Theory, research, and experience*, Vol. 3, 292–313. New York: Academic Press.

Bursten, B. (1973). Some narcissistic personality types. *International Journal of Psycho-Analysis*, 54, 287–300.

Campbell, B. A., & Mabry, P. D. (1972). Ontogeny of behavioral arousal: A comparative study. *Journal of Comparative and Physiological Psychology*, 81, 371–379.

Campos, J. J., Barrett, K. C., Lamb, M. C, Goldsmith, H. H., & Stenberg, C. (1983). Socio-emotional development. In P. H. Mussen (Ed.), *Handbook of child psychology* (4th ed.), 783–915. New York: Wiley.

Chapple, E. D. (1970). Experimental production of transients in human interaction. *Nature*, 228, 630–633.

Cofer, C. N., & Appley, M. H. (1964). *Motivation: Theory and research*. New York: Wiley.

Daly, M. de Burgh. (1991). Some reflex cardioinhibitory responses in the cat and their modulaton by central inspiratory activity. *Journal of Physiology*, 422, 463–480.

Darwin, C. (1965). *The expression of emotion in man and animals*. Chicago: University of Chicago Press. (Original work published 1872).

DeBruin, J. P. C., Van Oyen, H. G. M., & Vande Poll, N. E. (1983). Behavioral changes following lesions of the orbital prefrontal cortex in male rats. *Behavioral and Brain Research*, 10, 209–232.

Demos, V., & Kaplan, S. (1986). Motivation and affect reconsidered: Affect biographies of two infants. *Psychoanalysis and Contemporary Thought*, 9, 147–221.

Diagnostic and Statistical Manual of Mental Disorders: DSM-III-R. (1987). Washington, D.C.: American Psychiatric Association.

Dienstbier, R. A. (1989). Arousal and physiological toughness: Implications for mental and physical health. *Psychological Review*, 96, 84–100.

Dixon, J. C. (1957). Development of self-recognition. *Journal of Genetic Psychology*, 91, 251–256.

Dorpat, T. L. (1981). Basic concepts and terms in object relations theories. In S. Tuttman, C. Kaye & M. Zimmerman (Eds.), *Object and self: A developmental approach*, 149–178. New York: International Universities Press.

Eisnitz, A. J. (1988). Some superego issues. *Journal of the American Psychoanalytic Association*, 36, 137–163.

Emde, R. (1983). The pre-representational self and its affective core. *Psychoanalytic Study of the Child*, 38, 165–192.

Emde, R. (1988). Development terminable and interminable. I. Innate and motivational factors from infancy. *International Journal of Psycho-Analysis*, 69, 23–42.

Emde, R. (1989). The infant's relationship experience: Developmental and affective aspects. In A. J. Sameroff & R. N. Emde (Eds.), *Relationship disturbances in early childhood*, 33–51. New York: Basic Books.

Erikson, E. (1950). *Childhood and society*. New York: Norton.

Fast, I. (1979). Developments in gender identity: Gender differentiation in girls. *International Journal of Psycho-Analysis*, 60, 443–453.

Fast, I. (1984). *Gender identity: A differentiation model*. Hillsdale, NJ: Analytic Press.

Field, T. (1981). Infant arousal, attention and affect during early interactions. *Advances in Infancy Research*, 1, 58–96.

Field, T. (1982). Affective displays of high-risk infants during early interactions. In T. Field & A. Fogel (Eds.), *Emotion and early interaction*, 101–125. Hillsdale, NJ: Erlbaum.

Field, T. (1985a). Attachment as psychobiological attunement: Being on the same wavelength. In M. Reite & T. Field (Eds.), *The psychobiology of attachment and separation*, 415–454. Orlando: Academic Press.

Field, T. (1985b). Coping with separation stress by infants and young children. In T. Field, P. M. McCabe & N. Schneiderman (Eds.), *Stress and coping*, 197–219. Hillsdale, NJ: Erlbaum.

Fogel, A. (1982). Affect dynamics in early infancy: Affective tolerance. In T. Field & A. Fogel (Eds.), *Emotion and early interaction*. Hillsdale, NJ: Erlbaum, 25–56.

Fox, N. A., & Davidson, R. J. (1984). Hemispheric substrates of affect: A developmental model. In N. A. Fox & R. J. Davidson (Eds.), *The psychobiology of affective development*, 353–381. Hillsdale, NJ: Erlbaum.

Fraiberg, S. (1969). Libidinal object constancy and mental representation. *Psychoanalytic Study of the Child*, 24, 9–47.

Freud, S. (1953b). The interpretation of dreams. In J. Strachey (Ed. & Trans.), *Standard edition of the complete psychological works of Sigmund Freud*, Vols. 4 & 5, 1–627. London: Hogarth Press. (Original work published 1900).

Freud, S. (1953c). Three essays on the theory of sexuality. In J. Strachey (Ed. & Trans.), *Standard edition of the complete psychological works of Sigmund Freud*, Vol. 7, 135–243. London: Hogarth Press. (Original work published 1905).

Freud, S. (1957). On narcissism: An introduction. In J. Strachey (Ed. & Trans.), *Standard edition of the complete psychological works of Sigmund Freud*, Vol. 14, 67–102. London: Hogarth Press. (Original work published 1914).

Freud, S. (1961). The ego and the id. In J. Strachey (Ed. & Trans.), *Standard edition of the complete psychological works of Sigmund Freud*, Vol. 19, 12–63. London: Hogarth Press. (Original work published 1923).

Frijda, N. H. (1988). The laws of emotion. *American Psychologist*, 43, 349–358.

Fuster, J. M. (1980). *The prefrontal cortex: Anatomy, physiology, and neurophysiology of the frontal lobe*. New York: Raven Press.

Gaensbauer, T. J. (1982). Regulation of emotional expression in infants from two contrasting caretaking environments. *Journal of the American Academy of Child Psychiatry*, 21, 163–171.

Gaensbauer, T. J., Harmon, R. J., Cytryn, L., & McKnew, D. H. (1984). Social and affective development in infants with a manic-depressive parent. *American Journal of Psychiatry*, 141, 223–229.

Gaensbauer, T. J., & Mrazek, D. (1981). Differences in the patterning of affective expression in infants. *Journal of the American Academy of Child Psychiatry*, 20, 673–691.

Galenson, E., & Roiphe, H. (1976). Some suggested revisions concerning early female development. *Journal of the American Psychoanalytic Association*, 24(Suppl.), 29–57.

Galin, D. (1974). Implications for psychiatry of left and right cerebral specialization: A neurophysiological context for unconscious processes. *Archives of General Psychiatry*, 31, 572–583.

Garza-Guerrero, A. C. (1981). The superego concept: Part I: Historical review; object relations approach. *Psychoanalytic Review*, 68, 321–342.

Gazzaniga, M. S. (1985). *The social brain: Discovering the networks of the mind*. New York: Basic Books.

Geis, G. S., & Wurster, R. D. (1980). Cardiac responses during stimulation of the dorsal motor nucleus and nucleus ambiguus in the cat. *Circulation Research*, 46, 606–611.

Geschwind, N., & Galaburda, A. M. (1987). *Cerebral lateralization: Biological mechanisms, associations, and pathology*. Boston: MIT Press.

Giannitrapani, D. (1967). Developing concepts of lateralization of cerebral functions. *Cortex*, 3, 353–370.

Giovacchini, P. (1979). *Treatment of primitive mental states*. New York: Jason Aronson.

Glassman, M. (1988). A test of competing psychoanalytic models of narcissism. *Journal of the American Psychoanalytic Association*, 36, 597–625.

Goldberger, L. (1982). Sensory deprivation and overload. In L. Goldberger & S. Breznitz (Eds.), *Handbook of stress: Theoretical and clinical aspects*, 410–418. New York: Free Press.

Goodenough, F. L. (1931). *Anger in young children*. Institute of Child Welfare Monographs. Minneapolis: University of Minnesota Press.

Goplerud, E., & Depue, R. A. (1985). Behavioral response to naturally occurring stress in cyclothymia and dysthymia. *Journal of Abnormal Psychology*, 94, 128–139.

Greenspan, S. I. (1981). *Psychopathology and adaptation in infancy and early childhood*. New York: International Universities Press.

Grotstein, J. S. (1983). Some perspectives on self psychology. In A. Goldberg (Ed.), *The future of psychoanalysis*, 165–203. New York: International Universities Press.

Grotstein, J. S. (1990). Invariants in primitive emotional disorders. In L. B. Boyer & P. L. Giovacchini (Eds.), *Master clinicians on treating the regressed patient*, 139–163. Northvale, NJ: Jason Aronson.

Haith, M. M., Bergman, T., & Moore, M. (1979). Eye contact and face scanning in early infancy. *Science*, 218, 179–181.

Hartmann, H., & Loewenstein, R. M. (1962). Notes on the superego. *Psychoanalytic Study of the Child*, 17, 42–81.

Hartocollis, P. (1980). Affective disturbances in borderline and narcissistic patients. *Bulletin of the Menninger Clinic*, 44, 135–146.

Heilman, K. M., Schwartz, H., & Watson, R. T. (1977). Hypoarousal in patients with the neglect syndrome and emotional indifference. *Neurology*, 38, 229–232.

Henry, G. M., Weingartner, H., & Murphy, D. L. (1971). Idiosyncratic patterns of learning and word association during mania. *American Journal of Psychiatry*, 128, 564–574.

Hess, W. R. (1954). *Diencephalon, autonomic and extrapyramidal functions*. New York: Grune & Stratton.

Hofer, M. A. (1983). On the relationship between attachment and separation processes in infancy. In R. Plutchik & H. Kellerman (Eds.), *Emotion: Theory, research and experience*, Vol. 2, 199–219. New York: Academic Press.

Hofer, M. A. (1984a). Early stages in the organization of cardiovascular control. *Proceedings of the Society of Experimental and Biological Medicine*, 175, 147–157.

Hofer, M. A. (1984b). Relationships as regulators: A psychobiologic perspective on bereavement. *Psychosomatic Medicine*, 46, 183–197.

Hunt, J. M. (1965). Traditional personality theory in light of recent evidence. *American Scientist*, 53, 80–96.

Izard, C. E. (1978). On the ontogenesis of emotions and emotion-cognition relationships in infancy. In M. Lewis & L. Rosenblum (Eds.), *The development of affect*, 389–413. New York: Plenum.

Izard, C. E. (1991). *The psychology of emotions*. New York: Plenum Press.

Izard, C. E., Hembree, E. A., & Huebner, R. R. (1987). Infants' emotion expressions to acute pain: Developmental change and stability of individual differences. *Developmental Psychology*, 23, 105–113.

Jackson, J. H. (1931). *Selected writings of John Hughlings Jackson*, Vols 1 & 2. London: Hodder & Stoughton.

Jacobson, E. (1964). *The self and the object world*. New York: International Universities Press.

Johnson, M. H., & Magaro, P. A. (1987). Effects of mood and severity on memory processes in depression and mania. *Psychological Bulletin*, 101, 28–40.

Johnson, S. M. (1987). *Humanizing the narcissistic style*. New York: Norton.

Joseph, R. (1982). The neuropsychology of development: Hemispheric laterality, limbic language, and the origin of thought. *Journal of Clinical Psychology*, 38, 4–33.

Josephs, L. (1989). Self psychology and the analysis of the superego. *Psychoanalytic Psychology*, 6, 73–86.

Jouandet, M., & Gazzaniga, M. S. (1979). The frontal lobes. In M. S. Gazzaniga (Ed.), *Handbook of behavioral neurobiology*, Vol. 2, 25–59. New York: Plenum Press.

Kagan, J. (1976). Emergent themes in human development. *American Scientist*, 64, 186–196.

Kagan, J. (1979). The form of early development. *Archives of General Psychiatry*, 36, 1047–1054.

Kaufman, G. (1974). The meaning of shame: Toward a self-affirming identity. *Journal of Counseling Psychology*, 21, 568–574.

Kaufman, G. (1985). *Shame: The power of caring.* Boston: Schenkman.

Kaufmann, I. C., & Rosenblum, L. A. (1969). Effects of separation from mother on the emotional behavior of infant monkeys. *Annals of the New York Academy of Science*, 159, 681–695.

Kernberg, O. (1984). *Severe personality disorders: Psychotherapeutic strategies.* New Haven: Yale University Press.

Kinston, W. (1983). A theoretical context for shame. *International Journal of Psycho-Analysis*, 64, 213–226.

Knapp, P. H. (1967). Purging and curbing: An inquiry into disgust, satiety and shame. *Journal of Nervous & Mental Disease*, 144, 514–544.

Kobak, R. R., & Sceery, A. (1988). Attachment in late adolescence: Working models, affect regulation, and representations of self and others. *Child Development*, 59, 135–146.

Kohut, H. (1971). *The analysis of the self.* New York: International Universities Press.

Kohut, H. (1977). *The restoration of the self.* New York: International Universities Press.

Kohut, H. (1978). Forms and transformations of narcissism. In P. Ornstein (Ed.), *The search for the self*, 427–460. New York: International Universities Press.

Krystal, H. (1978). Trauma and affects. *Psychoanalytic Study of the Child*, 33, 81–116.

Krystal, H. (1988). *Integration and self-healing: Affect-trauma-alexithymia.* Hillsdale, NJ: Analytic Press.

Leavitt, L. A., & Donovan, W. L. (1979). Perceived infant temperament, locus of control, and maternal physiological response to infant gaze. *Journal of Research in Personality*, 13, 267–278.

Lecours, A. R. (1982). Correlates of developmental behavior in brain maturation. In T. G. Bever (Ed.), *Regressions in mental development: Basic phenomena and theories*, 267–298. Hillsdale, NJ: Erlbaum.

Lester, E. P. (1983). Separation-individuation and cognition. *Journal of the American Psychoanalytic Association*, 31, 127–156.

Levin, S. (1967). Some metapsychological considerations on the differentiation between shame and guilt. *International Journal of Psycho-Analysis*, 48, 267–276.

Levine, S. (1983). A psychobiological approach to the ontogeny of coping. In N. Garmezy & M. Rutter (Eds.), *Stress, coping, and development in children*, 107–131. New York: McGraw-Hill.

Levy, J., Heller, W., Banich, M. T., & Burton, L. A. (1983). Are variations among right-handed individuals in perceptual asymmetries caused by characteristic arousal differences between hemispheres? *Journal of Experimental Psychology: Human Perception and Performance*, 9, 329–359.

Lewis, H. B. (1971). *Shame and guilt in neurosis.* New York: International Universities Press.

Lewis, H. B. (1979). Shame in depression and hysteria. In C. E. Izard (Ed.), *Emotions in personality and psychopathology*, 399–414. New York: Plenum Press.

Lewis, H. B. (1980). "Narcissistic personality" or "shame-prone superego mode". *Comprehensive Psychotherapy*, 1, 59–80.

Lewis, H. B. (1985). Depression vs. paranoia: Why are there sex differences in mental illness? *Journal of Personality and Social Psychology*, 53, 150–178.

Lewis, M. (1982). Origins of self-knowledge and individual differences in early self-recognition. In J. Suls (Ed.), *Psychological perspectives on the self*, Vol. 1, 55–78. Hillsdale, NJ: Erlbaum.

Lichtenberg, J. D. (1983). *Psychoanalysis and infant research.* Hillsdale, NJ: Analytic Press.

Lichtenberg, J. D. (1989). *Psychoanalysis and motivation.* Hillsdale, NJ: Analytic Press.

Lipsitt, L. P. (1976). Developmental psychology comes of age: A discussion. In L. P. Lipsitt (Ed.), *Developmental psychology: The significance of infancy,* 109–127. Hillsdale, NJ: Erlbaum.

Loewald, H. (1978). Instinct theory, object relations, and psychic structure formation. *Journal of the American Psychoanalytic Association,* 26, 493–506.

Luria, A. R. (1980). *Higher cortical functions in man* (2nd ed.). New York: Basic Books.

Lynd, H. M. (1958). *On shame and the search for identity.* New York: Harcourt, Brace & Company.

MacCurdy, J. T. (1930). The biological significance of blushing and shame. *British Journal of Psychology,* 21, 174–182.

Mahler, M. S. (1972). On the first three subphases of the separation-individuation process. In Dies. (Ed.), *The selected papers of Margaret S. Mahler,* Vol. 2, 119–130. London/New York: Jason Aronson 1979.

Mahler, M. S. (1979). Notes on the development of basic moods: The depressive affect. In M. S. Mahler (Ed.), *The selected papers of Margaret S. Mahler,* 59–75. New York: Jason Aronson.

Mahler, M. S. (1980). Rapprochement subphase of the separation-individuation process. In R. Lax, S. Bach & J. A. Burland (Eds.), *Rapprochement: The critical subphase of separation-individuation,* 3–19. New York: Jason Aronson.

Mahler, M. S., & Kaplan, L. (1977). Developmental aspects in the assessment of narcissistic and so-called borderline personalities. In P. Hartocollos (Ed.), *Borderline personality disorders,* 71–85. New York: International Universities Press.

Mahler, M. S., Pine, F., & Bergman, A. (1975). *The psychological birth of the human infant.* New York: Basic Books.

Malatesta-Magai, C. (1991). Emotional socialization: Its role in personality and developmental psychopathology. In D. Cicchetti & S. L. Toth (Eds.), *Internalizing and externalizing expressions of dysfunction: Rochester symposium on developmental psychopatholgy,* Vol. 2, 203–224. Hillsdale, NJ: Erlbaum.

Malmo, R. B. (1959). Activation: A neurophysiological dimension. *Psychological Review,* 66, 367–386.

Masterson, J. F. (1981). *The narcissistic and borderline personality disorders.* New York: Brunner/Mazel.

McDevitt, J. (1975). Separation-individuation and object constancy. *Journal of the American Psychoanalytic Association,* 23, 713–742.

McDevitt, J. (1980). The role of internalization in the development of object relations during the separation-individuation phase. In R. F. Lax, S. Bach & J. A. Burland (Eds.), *Rapprochement: The critical subphase of separation-individuation,* 135–149. New York: Jason Aronson.

Meyersburg, H. A., & Post, R. M. (1979). An holistic developmental view of neural and psychological processes: A neurobiologic-psychoanalytic integration. *British Journal of Psychiatry,* 135, 139–155.

Miller, J. P. (1965). The psychology of blushing. *International Journal of Psycho-Analysis,* 146, 188–199.

Miller, L. (1986). Some comments on cerebral hemispheric models of consciousness. *Psychoanalytic Review,* 73, 129–144.

Miller, S. (1985). *The shame experience.* Hillsdale, NJ: Analytic Press.

Miller, S. (1988). Humiliation and shame: Comparing two affect states as indicators of narcissistic stress. *Bulletin of the Menninger Clinic,* 52, 40–51.

Miller, S. (1989). Shame as an impetus to the creation of conscience. *International Journal of Psycho-Analysis,* 70, 231–243.

Money, J., & Ehrhardt, A. (1968). *Man, woman, boy, and girl.* Baltimore: Johns Hopkins University Press.

Moorcroft, W. H. (1971). Ontogeny of forebrain inhibition of behavioral arousal in the rat. *Brain Research*, 35, 513–522.

Morris, W. N. (1989). *Mood: The frame of mind*. New York: Springer.

Morrison, A. P. (1984). Working with shame in psychoanalytic treatment. *Journal of the American Psychoanalytic Association*, 32, 479–505.

Morrison, A. P. (1989). *Shame, the underside of narcissism*. Hillsdale, NJ: Erlbaum.

Morrison, N. K. (1985). Shame in the treatment of schizophrenia: Theoretical considerations with clinical illustrations. *Yale Journal of Biological Medicine*, 58, 289–297.

Mussen, P. H., Conger, J. J., & Kagan, J. (1969). *Child development and personality*. New York: Harper & Row.

Nathanson, D. L. (1987). A timetable for shame. In D. L. Nathanson (Ed.), *The many faces of shame*, 1–63. New York: Guilford Press.

Panksepp, J., Siviy, S. M., & Normansell, L. A. (1985). Brain opioids and social emotions. In M. Reite & T. Field (Eds.), *The psychobiology of attachment and separation*, 3–49. Orlando, FL: Academic Press.

Pao, P. (1971). Elation, hypomania, and mania. *Journal of the American Psychoanalytic Association*, 19, 787–798.

Parens, H. (1980). An exploration of the relations of instinctual drives and the symbiosis/separation-individuation process. *Journal of the American Psychoanalytic Association*, 28, 89–114.

Parkin, A. (1985). Narcissism: Its structures, systems and affects. *International Journal of Psycho-Analysis*, 66, 143–156.

Piaget, J. (1967). *Six psychological studies*. New York: Random House.

Piers, G., & Singer, M. B. (1953). *Shame and guilt*. Springfield, IL: Charles C. Thomas.

Pine, F. (1980). On the expansion of the affect array: A developmental description. In R. Lax, S. Bach & J. A. Burland (Eds.), *Rapprochement: The critical subphase of separation-individuation*, 217–233. New York: Jason Aronson.

Pine, F. (1985). *Developmental theory and clinical process*. New Haven, CT: Yale University Press.

Pipp, S., & Harmon, R. J. (1987). Attachment as regulation: A commentary. *Child Development*, 58, 648–652.

Plooij, F. X., & van de Plooij, H. (1989). Vulnerable periods during infancy: Hierarchically reorganized systems. Control, stress, and disease. *Ethology and Sociobiology*, 10, 279–286.

Plutchik, R. (1983). Emotion in early development: A psychoevolutionary approach. In R. Plutchik & H. Kellerman (Eds.), *Emotion: Theory, research, and experience*, 221–257. New York: Academic Press.

Porges, S. W. (1976). Peripheral and neurochemical parallels of psychopathology: A psychophysiological model relating autonomic imbalance to hyperactivity, psychopathy, and autism. *Advances in Child Development and Behavior*, 11, 35–65.

Potter-Effron, R. T. (1989). *Shame, guilt, and alcoholism: Treatment issues in clinical practice*. New York: The Haworth Press.

Pulver, S. E. (1970). Narcissism: The term and the concept. *Journal of the American Psychoanalytic Association*, 18, 319–341.

Pyszczynski, T., & Greenberg, J. (1987). Self-regulatory perseveration and the depressive self-focusing style: A self-awareness theory of reactive depression. *Psychological Bulletin*, 102, 122–138.

Radke-Yarrow, M., & Zahn-Waxler, C. (1984). Roots, motives and patterns in children's prosocial behavior. In E. Staub, D. Bar-Tal, J. Karylowski & J. Reykowski (Eds.), *Development and maintenance of prosocial behavior*, 81–99. New York: Plenum Press.

Reich, A. (1960). Pathologic forms of self-esteem regulation. *Psychoanalytic Study of the Child*, 15, 215–234.

Reite, M., Kaufman, I. C., Pauley, J. D., & Stynes, A. J. (1974). Depression in infant monkeys: Physiological correlates. *Psychosomatic Medicine*, 36, 363–367.

Rheingold, H. L., & Eckerman, C. O. (1970). The infant separates himself from his mother. *Science*, 168, 78–83.

Rinsley, D. B. (1989). *Developmental pathogenesis and treatment of borderline and narcissistic Personalities*. Northvale, NJ: Jason Aronson.

Rothbart, M. K., Taylor, S. B., & Tucker, D. M. (1989). Right-sided facial asymmetry in infant emotional expression. *Neuropsychologia*, 27, 675–687.

Rutter, M. (1987). Temperament, personality and personality disorder. *British Journal of Psychiatry*, 150, 443–458.

Sander, L. (1977). Regulation of exchange in the infant caretaker system: A viewpoint on the ontogeny of structures. In N. Freedman & S. Grand (Eds.), *Communicative structures and psychic structures*, 13–34. New York: Plenum Press.

Sartre, J.-P. (1957). *Being and nothingness*. London: Methuen. (Original work published 1943).

Scheff, T. J. (1988). Shame and conformity: The deference-emotion system. *American Sociological Review*, 53, 395–406.

Scheflen, A. E. (1981). *Levels of schizophrenia*. New York: Brunner/Mazel.

Schneider, C. D. (1977). *Shame, exposure and privacy*. Boston: Beacon Press.

Schneiderman, N., & McCabe, P. M. (1985). Biobehavioral responses to stress. In T. M. Field, P. M. McCabe & N. Schneiderman (Eds.), *Stress and coping*, 13–61. Hillsdale, NJ: Erlbaum.

Schore, J. R. (1983). *A study of the superego: The relative proneness to shame or guilt as related to psychological masculinity and femininity in women*. Unpublished Dissertation, California Institute for Clinical Social Work, Berkeley.

Schwaber, J. S., Wray, S., & Higgins, G. A. (1979). Vagal cardiac innervation: Contributions of the dorsal motor nucleus and the nucleus ambiguus determined by liquid scintillation counting. *Society of Neuroscience Abstracts*, 4, 809.

Settlage, C. (1977). The psychoanalytic understanding of narcissistic and borderline personality disorders: Advances in developmental theory. *Journal of the American Psychoanalytic Association*, 25, 805–833.

Severino, S., McNutt, E., & Feder, S. (1987). Shame and the development of autonomy. *Journal of the American Academy of Psychoanalysis*, 15, 93–106.

Seyle, H. (1956). *The stress of life*. New York: McGraw-Hill.

Shane, P. (1980). Shame and learning. *American Journal of Orthopsychiatry*, 50, 348–355.

Sherwood, V. R. (1989). Object constancy: The illusion of being seen. *Psychoanalytic Psychology*, 6, 15–30.

Shiller, V. M., Izard, C. E., & Hembree, E. A. (1986). Patterns of emotion expression during separation in the strange-situation procedure. *Developmental Psychology*, 22, 378–382.

Silberman, E. K., & Weingartner, H. (1986). Hemispheric lateralization of functions related to emotion. *Brain and Cognition*, 5, 322–353.

Spero, M. H. (1984). Shame: An object-relational formulation. *Psychoanalytic Study of the Child*, 39, 259–282.

Spiegel, L. A. (1966). Affects in relation to self and object: A model for the derivation of desire, longing, pain, anxiety, humiliation, and shame. *Psychoanalytic Study of the Child*, 21, 69–92.

Spitz, R. A. (1965). *The first year of life: A psychoanalytic study of normal and deviant development of object relations*. New York: International Universities Press.

Sroufe, L. A. (1979). Socioemotional development. In J. D. Osofsky (Ed.), *Handbook of infant development*, 462–516. New York: Wiley.

Sroufe, L. A., & Waters, E. (1977). Attachment as an organizational construct. *Child Development*, 48, 1184–1189.

Steklis, H. D., & Kling, A. (1985). Neurobiology of affiliative behavior in nonhuman primates. In M. Reite & T. Field (Eds.), *The psychobiology of attachment and separation*, 93–134. Orlando, FL: Academic Press.

Stern, D. N. (1977). *The first relationship*. Cambridge, MA: Harvard University Press.

Stern, D. N. (1985). *The interpersonal world of the infant*. New York: Basic Books.

Stolorow, R. D., Brandchaft, B., & Atwood, G. (1987). *Psychoanalytic treatment: An intersubjective approach*. Hillsdale, NJ: Analytic Press.

Stolorow, R. D., & Lachmann, F. M. (1980). *Psychoanalysis of developmental arrests*. New York: International Universities Press.

Strachey, J. (1934). The nature of the therapeutic action of psychoanalysis. *International Journal of Psycho-Analysis*, 15, 117–126.

Thatcher, R. W., Walker, R. A., & Giudice, S. (1987). Human cerebral hemispheres develop at different rates and ages. *Science*, 236, 1110–1113.

Tomkins, S. (1963). *Affect/imagery/consciousness: Vol. 2. The negative affects*. New York: Springer.

Tomkins, S. (1987). Shame. In D. L. Nathanson (Ed.), *The many faces of shame*, 133–161. New York: Guilford Press.

Tronick, E. Z. (1989). Emotions and emotional communication in infants. *American Psychologist*, 44, 112–119.

Truex, R., & Carpenter, B. A. (1964). *Strong and Elwyn's human neuroanatomy* (5th ed.). Baltimore: Williams & Ilkins.

Tucker, D. M. (1981). Lateral brain function, emotion, and conceptualization. *Psychological Bulletin*, 89, 19–46.

Tucker, D. M., Roth, R. S., Arneson, B. A., & Buckingman, V. (1977). Right hemisphere activation during stress. *Neuropsychologia*, 15, 697–700.

Tulving, E. (1972). Episodic and semantic memory. In E. Tulving & W. Donaldson (Eds.), *Organization of memory*, 381–403. New York: Academic Press.

Turiell, E. (1967). An historical analysis of the Freudian conception of the superego. *Psychoanalytic Review*, 54, 118–140.

Tyson, P., & Tyson, R. L. (1984). Narcissism and superego development. *Journal of the American Psychoanalytic Association*, 32, 75–98.

Wagner, H., & Fine, H. (1981). A developmental overview of object relations and ego psychology. In L. Saretsky, G. D. Goldman & D. S. Milman (Eds.), *Integrating ego psychology and object relations theory*. Dubuque, LA: Kendall/Hunt, 3–20.

Wallace, L. (1963). The mechanism of shame. *American Journal of Psychoanalysis*, 32, 62–73.

Ward, H. P. (1972). Shame – a necessity for growth in therapy. *American Journal of Psychotherapy*, 26, 232–243.

Waters, E. (1978). The reliability and stability of individual differences in infant – mother attachment. *Child Development*, 49, 483–494.

Watt, D. F. (1986). Transference: A right hemispheric event? An inquiry into the boundary between psychoanalytic metapsychology and neuropsychology. *Psychoanalysis and Contemporary Thought*, 9, 43–77.

Whitaker, H. A. (1978). Is the right left over? Commentary on Corballis and Morgan, "on the biological basis of laterality". *Behavioral and Brain Sciences*, 1, 1–4.

White, R. (1960). Competence and the psychosexual stages of development. In M. Jones (Ed.), *Nebraska symposium on motivation*, 97–143. Lincoln: University of Nebraska Press.

White, R. (1963). *Ego and reality in psychoanalytic theory: Psychological issues* [Monograph 11]. New York: International Universities Press.

Willock, B. (1986). Narcissistic vulnerability in the hyperaggressive child: The disregarded (unloved-uncared for) self. *Psychoanalytic Psychology*, 3, 59–80.

Winnicott, D. (1958). The capacity to be alone. *International Journal of Psycho-Analysis*, 39, 416–420.

Wright, K. (1991). *Vision and separation: Between mother and baby*. Northvale, NJ: Jason Aronson.

Wurmser, L. (1981). *The mask of shame*. Baltimore: Johns Hopkins University Press.

Yakovlev, P. I., & Lecours, A. R. (1967). The myelogenetic cycles of regional maturation of the brain. In A. Minkow (Ed.), *Regional development of the brain in early life*, 3–70. Oxford, UK: Blackwell.

Zelazo, P. R. (1982). The year-old infant: A period of major cognitive change. In T. G. Beyer (Ed.), *Regressions in mental development: Basic phenomena and theories*, 47–79. Hillsdale, NJ: Erlbaum.

Zillman, D., & Bryant, J. (1974). Effects of residual excitation on the emotional response to provocation and delayed aggressive behavior. *Journal of Personality and Social Psychology*, 30, 782–791.

3.3   Attachment and the regulation of the right brain

In 1969, 29 years after his initial publication of an article on how the early environment could influence the development of character (1944), John Bowlby integrated his career-spanning observations and theoretical conceptualizations into the first of three influential volumes on *Attachment and Loss* (1969, 1973, 1981). This foundational volume, *Attachment* (1969), was groundbreaking for a number of reasons. It focused upon one of the major questions of science, specifically, how and why do certain early ontogenetic events have such an inordinate effect on everything that follows? Bowlby presented these essential problems in such a way that both a heuristic theoretical perspective and a testable experimental methodology could be created to observe, measure, and evaluate certain very specific mechanisms by which the early social environment interacts with the maturing organism in order to shape developmental processes (Schore, 2000a).

But perhaps of even more profound significance was his carefully argued proposition that an interdisciplinary perspective should be applied to the study of developmental phenomena, as they exist in nature. In such an approach, the collaborative knowledge bases of a spectrum of sciences would yield the most powerful models of both the nature of the fundamental ontogenetic processes that mediate the infant's first attachment to another human being, and the essential psychobiological mechanisms by which these processes indelibly influence the development of the organism at later points of the life cycle.

In response to this classic volume, Ainsworth observed, "In effect what Bowlby has attempted is to update psychoanalytic theory in the light of recent advances in biology" (1969, p. 998). Bowlby's deep insights into the potential synergistic effects of combining the literatures of what appeared on the surface to be distantly related realms may now seem like a brilliant flash of intuition. In actuality it represented a natural convergence of his two most important intellectual influences, Darwin and Freud. In order to create a perspective that could describe critical events in both the external and internal world, concepts from both ethology (behavioral biology) and psychoanalysis are presented and interwoven throughout the volume. In essence, a central goal of Bowlby's first book is to demonstrate that a mutually enriching dialogue can be organized between the biological and the psychological realms, something Darwin (1872/1965) had attempted in the first scientific treatise on the biology and psychology of emotion, *The Expression of Emotions in Man and Animals*, and Freud (1895/1966) had attempted in his endeavor to integrate neurobiology and psychology in order to create a "natural science," *Project for a Scientific Psychology* (Schore, 1997b).

Although both Darwin and Freud emphasized the centrality of early development as an important part of their overall work, each primarily focused his observational and theoretical lens on the adaptive and maladaptive functioning of fully matured adult organisms. In *Attachment,* Bowlby (1969) argued that clinical observers and experimental scientists should intensively focus on developing organisms that are in the process of maturing. More specifically, he called for deeper explorations of the fundamental ontogenetic mechanisms by which an immature organism is critically shaped by its primordial relationship with a mature adult member of its species, that is, more extensive studies of how an attachment bond forms between the infant and mother. In this conception, Bowlby asserted that these developmental processes are the product of the interaction of a unique genetic endowment with a particular environment, and that the infant's emerging social, psychological, and biological capacities cannot be understood apart from its relationship with the mother.

Bowlby's original chartings of the attachment landscape

Much has transpired since the original publication of Bowlby's *Attachment*, and the ensuing explosion of attachment research since 1969 is a testament to the power of the concepts it contains. And yet a (re)reading of this classic still continues to reveal more and more subtle insights into the nature of developmental processes, and to shine light upon yet to be fully explored areas of developmental research. In fact, in this seminal work of developmental science, the pioneering Bowlby (1969) presented a survey of what he saw to be the essential topographic landmarks of the uncharted territory of mother-infant relationally-driven psychobiological processes. The essential guideposts of this dynamic domain – the central phenomena that must be considered in any overarching model of how the attachment relationship generates both immediate and long-enduring effects on the developing individual – were presented by Bowlby in not only the subject matter but also the structural organization of the book. The reader will notice that the book is divided into four parts, "The Task," "Instinctive Behaviour," "Attachment Behaviour," and "Ontogeny of Human Attachment," and that Bowlby devoted ten chapters to the first two parts, and seven to the last two parts.

It is now more than 30 years since Bowlby called for "a far-reaching program of research into the social responses of man, from the preverbal period of infancy onwards" (1969, p. 174). In the following, I want to offer a psychoneurobiological perspective of not only the original contents of Bowlby's guidebook, but also some thoughts about the current and future directions of the experimental and clinical explorations of attachment theory as they pass from one century into the next. In doing so, I will specifically attend to not so much the quality of attachment research, which has served as a standard in psychology, psychiatry, and psychoanalysis as a whole, nor to the breadth of the research, which spans developmental psychology, developmental psychobiology, developmental neurochemistry, infant psychiatry, and psychoanalysis, but rather to the foci of current investigations, as measured against the original prescriptions that were offered by Bowlby. And I will suggest that certain uninvestigated areas of this attachment domain, sketched out in Bowlby's cartographic descriptions in his book, are now ready to be explored by interdisciplinary research programs. For a broad overview of the field at the end of the century I refer the reader to two excellent edited volumes, *Attachment Theory: Social, Developmental, and Clinical Perspectives* (Goldberg, Muir, & Kerr, 1995) and *Handbook of Attachment: Theory, Research, and Clinical Applications* (Cassidy & Shaver, 1999).

In Bowlby's book, most current readers are very familiar (or even perhaps only familiar) with the latter two sections on attachment, and most researchers continue to focus their investigation upon the concepts outlined in these later chapters. It is here, as well as in the introductory sections, that Bowlby presented his essential contributions on the infant's sequential responses to separation from the primary attachment figure – protest, despair, and detachment. In the context of emphasizing the importance of studying the infant's behavior specifically during the temporal interval when the mother returns, Bowlby introduced the methodology of Ainsworth, which would soon become the major experimental paradigm for attachment research, the incrementally stress-increasing "strange situation."

But in addition to theorizing on the nature of separation responses, stressful ruptures of the mother-infant bond, Bowlby also described what he saw as the fundamental dynamics of the attachment relationship. In stating that the infant is active in seeking interaction, that the mother's maternal behavior is "reciprocal" to the infant's attachment behavior, and that the development of attachment is related both to the sensitivity of the mother in responding to her baby's cues and to the amount and nature of their interaction, he laid a groundwork that presents attachment dynamics as a "reciprocal interchange" (1969, p. 346), a conceptualization that is perfectly compatible with recent advances in dynamic systems theory (Schore, 1997a; Lewis, 1995, 1999, 2000).

At the very beginning of the section on "Attachment Behavior" Bowlby (1969) offered his earliest model of the essential characteristics of attachment: it is instinctive social behavior with a biological function, "readily activated especially by the mother's departure or by anything frightening, and the stimuli that most efficiently terminate the systems are sound, sight, or touch of the mother," and is "a product of the activity of a number of behavioural systems that have proximity to mother as a predictable outcome" (p. 179). Although the first three postulates remained unaltered in his later writings, in his second volume Bowlby (1973) attempted to more precisely define the set-goal of the attachment system as seeking not just proximity but also access to an attachment figure who is emotionally available and responsive.

A further evolution of this concept is now found in transactional theories that emphasize the central role of the primary caregiver in coregulating the child's facially expressed emotional states (Schore, 1994, 1998a, 2002) and that define attachment as the dyadic regulation of emotion (Sroufe, 1996) and the regulation of biological synchronicity between organisms (Wang, 1997). The development of synchronized interactions is fundamental to the healthy affective development of the infant (Penman, Meares, & Milgrom-Friedman, 1983). Reite and Capitanio (1985) conceptualized affect as "a manifestation of underlying modulating or motivational systems subserving or facilitating social attachments" (p. 248), and suggest that an essential attachment function is "to promote the synchrony or regulation of biological and behavioral systems on an organismic level" (p. 235). In these rapid, regulated face-to-face transactions the psychobiologically attuned (Field, 1985a) caregiver not only minimizes the infant's negative but also maximizes his positive affective states (Schore, 1994, 1996, 1998b). This proximate interpersonal context of "affect synchrony" (Feldman, Greenbaum, & Yirmiya, 1999) and interpersonal resonance (Schore, 1997a) represents the external realm of attachment dynamics.

But due to his interests in the inner world, Bowlby presented a model of events occurring within the internal realm of attachment processes. And so he offered his initial speculations about how the developing child constructs internal working models "of how the physical world may be expected to behave, how his mother and other significant persons may be expected to behave, how he himself may be expected to behave, and how each interacts with the other" (1969, p. 354). This initial concept has evolved into "process-oriented" conceptions of internal working models as representations that regulate an individual's relationship adaptation through interpretive/attributional processes (Bretherton & Munholland, 1999), and encode strategies of affect regulation (Kobak & Sceery, 1988; Schore, 1994). Psychobiological models refer to representations of the infant's affective dialogue with the mother which can be accessed to regulate its affective state (Polan & Hofer, 1999).

Interestingly, Bowlby (1969) also described internal working models in the first part of the volume, the eight chapters devoted to "instinctive behavior". I repeat my assertion that a deeper explication of the fundamental themes of this section of the book represents the frontier of attachment theory and research. In these opening chapters, the aggregate of which represents the foundation on which the later chapters on attachment are built, Bowlby posited that internal models function as "cognitive maps" in the brain, and are accessed "to transmit, store, and manipulate information that helps making predictions as to how . . . set-goals [of attachment] can be achieved" (p. 80). Furthermore, he states that "the two working models each individual must have are referred to respectively as his environmental model and his organismic model" (p. 82). This is because "sensory data regarding events reaching an organism via its sense organs are immediately assessed, regulated, and interpreted . . . The same is true of sensory data derived from the internal state of the organism" (p. 109). Here Bowlby pointed to the need for a developmental theoretical conception of attachment that can tie together psychology and biology, mind and body.

And so at the very onset of his essay, he began "The Task" by describing a theoretical landscape that includes both the biological and social aspects of attachment, a terrain that must be described both in terms of its structural organization as well as its functional properties. Following the general perspective of all biological investigators he attempted to elucidate the structure-function relationships of a living system, but with the added perspective of developmental biology he was specifically focusing on the early critical stages within which the system first self-organizes. Thus the form of the book is to first outline the general characteristics of the internal structural system, and then to describe this system's central functional role in attachment processes.

Bowlby (1969) began the third chapter by quoting Freud's (1926/1959) dictum that "[t]here is no more urgent need in psychology than for a securely founded theory of the instincts." The attempt to do so in this book, an offering of an "alternative model of instinctive behavior," in essence represents Bowlby's conviction that what Freud was calling for was the creation of a model that could explicate the biology of unconscious processes. Toward that end, in the first of eight chapters on the topic, he proposed that attachment is instinctive behavior associated with self preservation, and that it is a product of the interaction between genetic endowment and the early environment.

But immediately after a brief five-page introduction, Bowlby (1969) launched into a detailed description of a biological control system that is centrally involved in instinctive behavior. This control system is structured as a hierarchical mode of organization that acts as "an overall goal-corrected behavioral structure." Bowlby also gave some hints as to the neurobiological operations of this control system – its functions must be associated with the organism's "state of arousal" that results from the critical operations of the reticular formation, and with "the appraisal of organismic states and situations of the midbrain nuclei and limbic system" (p. 110). He even offered a speculation about its anatomical location – the prefrontal lobes (p. 156).

This control system, Bowlby wrote, is "open in some degree to influence by the environment in which development occurs" (p. 45). More specifically, it evolves in the infant's interaction with an "environment of adaptiveness, and especially of his interaction with the principal figure in that environment, namely his mother" (p. 180). Furthermore, Bowlby speculated that the "up-grading of control during individual development from simple to more sophisticated is no doubt in large part a result of the growth of the central nervous system" (p. 156). In fact he even went so far as to suggest the temporal interval that is critical to the maturation of this control system – nine to 18 months (p. 180).

In a subsequent chapter, "Appraising and Selecting: Feeling and Emotion," Bowlby quoted Darwin's (1872/1965) observation that the movements of expression in the face and body serve as the first means of communication between the mother and infant. Furthering this theme on the communicative role of feeling and emotion, Bowlby emphasized the salience of "facial expression, posture, tone of voice, physiological changes, tempo of movement, and incipient action" (p. 120).

The appraisal of this input is experienced "in terms of value, as pleasant or unpleasant" (pp. 111–112) and "may be actively at work even when we are not aware of them" (p. 110), and in this manner feeling provides a monitoring of both the behavioral and physiological state (p. 121). Emotional processes thus, he wrote, lie at the foundation of a model of instinctive behavior.

In following chapters, Bowlby concluded that the mother-infant attachment relation is "accompanied by the strongest of feelings and emotions, happy or the reverse" (p. 242), that the infant's "capacity to cope with stress" is correlated with certain maternal behaviors (p. 344), and that the instinctive behavior that emerges from the coconstructed environment of evolutionary adaptiveness has consequences that are "vital to the survival of the species" (p. 137). He also suggested that the attachment system is readily activated until the end of the third year, when the child's capacity to cope with maternal separation "abruptly" improves, due to the fact that "some maturational threshold is passed" (p. 205).

Contributions from neuroscience to attachment theory

So the next question is, 30 years after the appearance of this volume, at the end of the "decade of the brain," how do Bowlby's original chartings of the attachment domain hold up? In a word, they were prescient. In fact his overall bird's-eye perspective of the internal attachment landscape was so comprehensive that we now need to zoom in for close-up views of not just the essential brain structures that mediate attachment processes but also visualizations of how these structures dynamically self-organize within the developing brain. This includes neurobiological studies of Bowlby's control system, which I suggest may now be identified with the orbitofrontal cortex, an area that is the "senior executive of the emotional brain" (Joseph, 1996) and been shown to mediate "the highest level of control of behavior, especially in relation to emotion" (Price, Carmichael, & Drevets, 1996, p. 523). Keeping in mind Bowlby's previously presented theoretical descriptions, the following is an extremely brief overview of a growing body of studies on the neurobiology of attachment. (For more extensive expositions of these concepts and references see Schore, 1994, 1996, 1997a, 1998a, 1999, 2000b, 2001a, 2001b, 2002).

According to Ainsworth (1967, p. 429), attachment is more than overt behavior, it is internal, "being built into the nervous system, in the course and as a result of the infant's experience of his transactions with the mother." Following Bowlby's lead, the limbic system has been suggested to be the site of developmental changes associated with the rise of attachment behaviors (Anders & Zeanah, 1984). Indeed, the specific period from seven to 15 months has been shown to be critical for the myelination and therefore the maturation of particular rapidly developing limbic and cortical association areas (Kinney, Brody, Kloman, & Gilles, 1988), and limbic areas of the human cerebral cortex show anatomical maturation at 15 months (Rabinowicz, 1979). In a number of works I offered evidence to show that attachment experiences, face-to-face transactions of affect synchrony between caregiver and infant, directly influence the imprinting, the circuit wiring of the orbital prefrontal cortex, a corticolimbic area that is known to begin a major maturational change at 10 to 12 months and to complete a critical period of growth in the middle to end of the second year (Schore, 1994, 1996, 1997a, 1998a). This time frame is identical to Bowlby's maturation of an attachment control system that is open to influence of the developmental environment.

The co-created environment of evolutionary adaptiveness is thus isomorphic to a growth-facilitating environment for the experience-dependent maturation of a regulatory system in the orbitofrontal cortex. Indeed, this prefrontal system appraises visual-facial (Scalaidhe, Wilson, & Goldman-Rakic, 1997) and auditory (Romanski et al., 1999) information, and processes responses to pleasant touch, taste, smell (Francis, Diorio, Liu, & Meaney, 1999) and music (Blood, Zatorre, Bermudez, & Evans, 1999) as well as to unpleasant images of angry and sad faces (Blair, Morris, Frith, Perrett, & Dolan, 1999). But this system is also involved in the regulation of the body state and reflects changes taking place in that state (Luria, 1980).

This frontolimbic system provides a high-level coding that flexibly coordinates exteroceptive and interoceptive domains and functions to correct responses as conditions change (Derryberry & Tucker, 1992), processes feedback information (Elliott, Frith, & Dolan, 1997), and thereby monitors, adjusts, and corrects emotional responses (Rolls, 1986) and modulates the motivational control of goal-directed behavior (Tremblay & Schultz, 1999). So after a rapid evaluation of an environmental stimulus, the orbitofrontal system monitors feedback about the current internal state in order to make assessments of coping resources, and it updates appropriate response outputs in order to make adaptive adjustments to particular environmental perturbations (Schore, 1998a). In this manner, "the integrity of the orbitofrontal cortex is necessary for acquiring very specific forms of knowledge for regulating interpersonal and social behavior" (Dolan, 1999, p. 928).

These functions reflect the unique anatomical properties of this area of the brain. Due to its location at the ventral and medial hemispheric surfaces, it acts as a convergence zone where cortex and subcortex meet. It is thus situated at the apogee of the "rostral limbic system," a hierarchical sequence of interconnected limbic areas in orbitofrontal cortex, insular cortex, anterior cingulate, and amygdala (Schore, 1997a, 2000b). The limbic system is now thought to be centrally involved in the capacity "to adapt to a rapidly changing environment" and in "the organization of new learning" (Mesulam, 1998, p. 1028). Emotionally-focused limbic learning underlies the unique and fast acting processes of imprinting, the learning mechanism associated with attachment, as this dynamic evolves over the first and second year. Hinde pointed out that "the development of social behavior can be understood only in terms of a continuing dialectic between an active and changing organism and an active and changing environment" (1990, p. 162).

But the orbitofrontal system is also deeply connected into the ANS and the arousal-generating reticular formation, and due to the fact that it is the only cortical structure with such direct connections, it can regulate autonomic responses to social stimuli (Zald & Kim, 1996) and modulate "instinctual behavior" (Starkstein & Robinson, 1997). The activity of this frontolimbic system is therefore critical to the modulation of social and emotional behaviors and the homeostatic regulation of body and motivational states, affect regulating functions that are centrally involved in attachment processes. The essential aspect of this function is highlighted by Westen who asserts that "[t]he attempt to regulate affect – to minimize unpleasant feelings and to maximize pleasant ones – is the driving force in human motivation" (1997, p. 542).

The orbital prefrontal region is especially expanded in the right hemisphere, which is specialized for inhibitory control, and it comes to act as an executive control function for the entire right brain. This hemisphere, which is dominant for unconscious processes, computes, on a moment-to-moment basis, the affective salience of external stimuli. Keeping in mind Bowlby's earlier descriptions, this lateralized system performs a "valence tagging" function (Schore, 1998a, 1999a), in which perceptions receive a positive or negative affective charge, in accord with a calibration of degrees of pleasure-unpleasure. It also contains a "nonverbal affect lexicon," a vocabulary for nonverbal affective signals such as facial expressions, gestures, and vocal tone, or prosody (Bowers, Bauer, & Heilman, 1993). The right hemisphere is thus faster than the left in performing valence-dependent, automatic, preattentive appraisals of emotional facial expressions (Pizzagalli, Regard, & Lehmann, 1999).

Because the right cortical hemisphere, more so than the left, contains extensive reciprocal connections with limbic and subcortical regions (Joseph, 1996; Tucker, 1992), it is dominant for the processing of "self-related material" (Keenan et al., 1999) and emotional information, and for regulating psychobiological states (Schore, 1994, 1998a, 1999; Spence, Shapiro, & Zaidel, 1996).

Thus the right hemisphere is centrally involved in what Bowlby described as the social and biological functions of the attachment system (Henry, 1993; Schore, 1994; Shapiro, Jamner, & Spence, 1997; Siegel, 1999; Wang, 1997).

Confirming this model, Ryan, Kuhl, and Deci, using EEG and neuroimaging data, concluded that "[t]he positive emotional exchange resulting from autonomy-supportive parenting involves participation of right hemispheric cortical and subcortical systems that participate in global, tonic emotional modulation" (1997, p. 719). And in line with Bowlby's assertion that attachment behavior is vital to the survival of the species, it is held that the right hemisphere is central to the control of vital functions supporting survival and enabling the organism to cope with stresses and challenges (Wittling & Schweiger, 1993).

There is a growing body of studies that shows that the infant's early maturing (Geschwind & Galaburda, 1987) right hemisphere is specifically impacted by early social experiences (Schore, 1994, 1998b). This developmental principle is now supported in a recent single photon emission computed tomographic (SPECT) study by Chiron and colleagues (1997), which demonstrated that the right brain hemisphere is dominant in preverbal human infants, and indeed for the first three years of life. I suggest that this ontogenetic shift of dominance from the right to left hemisphere after this time may explicate Bowlby's description of a diminution of the attachment system at the end of the third year that is due to an "abrupt" passage of a "maturational threshold."

Neuropsychological studies indicate that "the emotional experience(s) of the infant . . . are disproportionately stored or processed in the right hemisphere during the formative stages of brain ontogeny" (Semrud-Clikeman & Hynd, 1990, p. 198), that "the infant relies primarily on its procedural memory systems" during "the first 2–3 years of life" (Kandel, 1999, p. 513), and that the right brain contains the "cerebral representation of one's own past" and the substrate of affectively-laden autobiographical memory (Fink et al., 1996, p. 4275). These findings suggest that early forming internal working models of the attachment relationship are processed and stored in implicit-procedural memory systems in the right hemisphere.

In the securely attached individual, these models encode an expectation that "homeostatic disruptions will be set right" (Pipp & Harmon, 1987, p. 650). In discussing these internal models Rutter noted, "children derive a set of expectations about their own relationship capacities and about other people's resources to their social overtures and interactions, these expectations being created on the basis of their early parent-child attachments" (1987, p. 449). Such representations are processed by the orbitofrontal system, which is known be activated during "breaches of expectation" (Nobre, Coull, Frith, & Mesulam, 1999) and to generate affect regulating strategies for coping with expected negative and positive emotional states that are inherent in intimate social contexts.

The efficient operations of this regulatory system allow for cortically processed information concerning the external environment (such as visual and auditory stimuli emanating from the emotional face of the attachment object) to be integrated with subcortically processed information regarding the internal visceral environment (such as concurrent changes in the child's emotional or bodily self-state). The relaying of sensory information into the limbic system allows incoming information about the social environment to trigger adjustments in emotional and motivational states, and in this manner the orbitofrontal system integrates what Bowlby termed environmental and organismic models. Findings that the orbitofrontal cortex generates nonconscious biases that guide behavior before conscious knowledge does (Bechara, Damasio, Tranel, & Damasio, 1997), codes the likely significance of future behavioral options (Dolan, 1999), and represents an important site of contact between emotional information and mechanisms of action selection (Rolls, 1986), are consonant with Bowlby's (1981) assertion that unconscious internal working models are used as guides for future action.

These mental representations, according to Main, Kaplan, and Cassidy (1985), contain cognitive as well as affective components and act to guide appraisals of experience. The orbitofrontal cortex is known to function as an appraisal mechanism (Pribram, 1987; Schore, 1998a) and to be centrally involved in the generation of "cognitive-emotional interactions" (Barbas, 1995). It acts to "integrate and assign emotional-motivational significance to cognitive impressions; the association of emotion with ideas and thoughts" (Joseph, 1996, p. 427) and in "the processing of affect-related meanings" (Teasdale et al., 1999). Orbitofrontal activity is associated with a lower threshold for awareness of sensations of both external and internal origin (Goldenberg et al., 1989), thereby enabling it to act as an "internal reflecting and organizing agency" (Kaplan-Solms & Solms, 1996). This orbitofrontal role in "self-reflective awareness" (Stuss, Gow, & Hetherington, 1992) allows the individual's to reflect on one's own internal emotional states, as well as others (Povinelli & Preuss, 1995). According to Fonagy and Target (1997) the reflective function is a mental operation that enables the perception of another's state. The right hemisphere mediates empathic cognition and the perception of the emotional states of other human beings (Voeller, 1986), and orbitofrontal function is essential to the capacity of inferring the states of others (Baron-Cohen, 1995). This adaptive capacity may thus be the outcome of a secure attachment to a psychobiologically attuned, affect regulating caregiver. A recent neuropsychological study indicates that the orbitofrontal cortex is "particularly involved in theory of mind tasks with an affective component" (Stone, Baron-Cohen, & Knight, 1998, p. 651).

Furthermore, the functioning of the orbitofrontal control system in the regulation of emotion (Baker, Frith, & Dolan, 1997) and in "acquiring very specific forms of knowledge for regulating interpersonal and social behavior" (Dolan, 1999, p. 928) is central to self-regulation, the ability to flexibly regulate emotional states through interactions with other humans – interactive regulation in interconnected contexts, and without other humans – autoregulation in autonomous contexts. The adaptive capacity to shift between these dual regulatory modes, depending upon the social context, emerges out of a history of secure attachment interactions of a maturing biological organism and an early attuned social environment.

Attachment theory is fundamentally a regulatory theory

Attachment behavior is thought to be the output of "a neurobiologically based biobehavioral system that regulates biological synchronicity between organisms" (Wang, 1997, p. 168). I suggest that the characterization of the orbitofrontal system as a frontolimbic structure that regulates interpersonal and social behavior (Dolan, 1999), determines the regulatory significance of stimuli that reach the organism, and regulates body state (Luria, 1980), bears a striking resemblance to the behavioral control system characterized by Bowlby in the late 1960s. The *Oxford English Dictionary* defines control as "the act or power of directing or regulating."

Attachment theory, as first propounded in Bowlby's (1969) definitional volume, is fundamentally a regulatory theory. Attachment can thus be conceptualized as the interactive regulation of synchrony between psychobiologically attuned organisms. This attachment dynamic, which operates at levels beneath awareness, underlies the dyadic regulation of emotion. Emotions are the highest order direct expression of bioregulation in complex organisms (Damasio, 1998). Imprinting, the learning process associated with attachment, is described by Petrovich and Gewirtz (1985) as synchrony between sequential infant-maternal stimuli and behavior (see Schore, 1994; Nelson & Panksepp, 1998 for models of the neurochemistry of attachment).

According to Feldman, Greenbaum, and Yirmiya, "face-to-face synchrony affords infants their first opportunity to practice interpersonal coordination of biological rhythms" (1999, p. 223), and acts as an interpersonal context in which "interactants integrate into the flow of behavior the ongoing responses of their partner and the changing inputs of the environment" (p. 224). The visual, prosodic–auditory, and gestural stimuli embedded in these emotional communications are rapidly transmitted back and forth between the infant's and mother's face, and in these transactions the caregiver acts as a regulator of the child's arousal levels.

Because arousal levels are known to be associated with changes in metabolic energy, the caregiver is thus modulating changes in the child's energetic state (Schore, 1994, 1997a). These regulated increases in energy metabolism are available for biosynthetic processes in the baby's brain, which is in the brain growth spurt (Dobbing & Sands, 1973). In this manner, "the intrinsic regulators of human brain growth in a child are specifically adapted to be coupled, by emotional communication, to the regulators of adult brains" (Trevarthen, 1990, p. 357).

In addition, the mother also regulates moments of asynchrony, that is, stressful negative affect. Social stressors can be characterized as the occurrence of an asynchrony in an interactional sequence (Chapple, 1970). Stress describes both the subjective experience induced by a distressing, potentially threatening, or novel situation, and the organism's reactions to a homeostatic challenge. It is now thought that social stressors are "far more detrimental" than nonsocial aversive stimuli (Sgoifo et al., 1999).

Separation stress, in essence, is a loss of maternal regulators of the infant's immature behavioral and physiological systems that results in the attachment patterns of protest, despair, and detachment. The principle that "a period of synchrony, following the period of stress, provides a 'recovery' period" (Chapple, 1970, p. 631) underlies the mechanism of interactive repair (Schore, 1994; Tronick, 1989). The primary caregiver's interactive regulation is therefore critical to the infant's maintaining positively charged as well as coping with stressful negatively charged affects. These affect regulating events are particularly impacting the organization of the early developing right hemisphere.

Bowlby's control system is located in the right hemisphere that is not only dominant for "inhibitory control" (Garavan, Ross, & Stein, 1999), but also for the processing of facial information in infants (Deruelle & de Schonen, 1998) and adults (Kim et al., 1999), and for the regulation of arousal (Heilman & Van Den Abell, 1979). Because the major coping systems, the HPA axis and the sympathetic–adrenomedullary axis, are both under the main control of the right cerebral cortex, this hemisphere contains "a unique response system preparing the organism to deal efficiently with external challenges," and so its adaptive functions mediate the human stress response (Wittling, 1997, p. 55). Basic research in stress physiology shows that the behavioral and physiological response of an individual to a specific stressor is consistent over time (Koolhaas et al., 1999).

These attachment transactions are imprinted into implicit-procedural memory as enduring internal working models, which encode coping strategies of affect regulation (Schore, 1994) that maintain basic regulation and positive affect even in the face of environmental challenge (Sroufe, 1989). Attachment patterns are now conceptualized as "patterns of mental processing of information based on cognition and affect to create models of reality" (Crittenden, 1995, p. 401). The "anterior limbic prefrontal network," which interconnects the orbital and medial prefrontal cortex with the temporal pole, cingulate, and amygdala, "is involved in affective responses to events and in the mnemonic processing and storage of these responses" (Carmichael & Price, 1995, p. 639), and "constitutes a mental control system that is essential for adjusting thinking and behavior to ongoing reality" (Schnider & Ptak, 1999, p. 680). An ultimate indicator of secure attachment is resilience in the face of stress (Greenspan, 1981), which is expressed in the capacity to flexibly regulate emotional states via autoregulation and interactive regulation. However, early social environments that engender insecure attachments inhibit the growth of this control system (Schore, 1997a) and therefore preclude its adaptive coping function in "operations linked to behavioral flexibility" (Nobre et al., 1999, p. 12).

In support of Bowlby's assertion that the child's capacity to cope with stress is correlated with certain maternal behaviors, developmental biological studies are exploring "maternal effects," the influence of the mother's experiences on her progeny's development and ability to adapt to its environment (Bernardo, 1996). This body of research indicates that "variations in maternal care can serve as the basis for a nongenomic behavioral transmission of individual differences in stress reactivity across generations" (Francis et al., 1999, p. 1155), and that "maternal care during infancy serves to 'program' behavioral responses to stress in the offspring" (Caldji et al., 1998, p. 5335).

Developmental neurobiological findings support the idea that "infants' early experiences with their mothers (or absence of these experiences) may come to influence how they respond to their own infants when they grow up" (Fleming, O'Day, & Kraemer, 1999, p. 673). I suggest that the intergenerational transmission of stress coping deficits occurs within the context of relational environments that are growth-inhibiting to the development of regulatory corticolimbic circuits sculpted by early experiences. These attachment-related psychopathologies are thus expressed in dysregulation of social, behavioral, and biological functions that are associated with an immature frontolimbic control system and an inefficient right hemisphere (Schore, 1994, 1996, 1997a). This conceptualization bears directly upon Bowlby's (1978) assertion that attachment theory can be used to frame the early etiologies of a diverse group of psychiatric disorders and the neurophysiological changes that accompany them.

Future directions of attachment research on regulatory processes

Returning to *Attachment*, Bowlby asserted, "The merits of a scientific theory are to be judged in terms of the range of phenomena it embraces, the internal consistency of its structure, the precision of the predictions it can make and the practibility of testing them" (1969, p. 173). The republication of this classic volume is occurring at a point in time, coincident with the beginning of the new millennium, when we are able to explore the neurobiological substrata on which attachment theory is based. In earlier writings I have suggested that "the primordial environment of the infant, or more properly of the commutual psychobiological environment shared by the infant and mother, represents a primal terra incognita of science" (Schore, 1994, p. 64). The next generation of studies of Bowlby's theoretical landscape will chart in detail how different early social environments and attachment experiences influence the unique microtopography of a developing brain.

Such studies will project an experimental searchlight upon events occurring at the common dynamic interface of brain systems that represent the psychological and biological realms. The right brain–right brain psychobiological transactions that underlie attachment processes are bodily-based, and critical to the adaptive capacities and growth of the infant. This calls for studies that concurrently measure brain, behavioral, and bodily changes in both members of the dyad. Autonomic measures of synchronous changes in the infant's and mother's bodily states need to be included in studies of attachment functions, and the development of coordinated interactions between the maturing central nervous system (CNS) and ANS should be investigated in research on attachment structures.

It is accepted that internal working models that encode strategies of affect regulation act at levels beneath conscious awareness. In the *American Psychologist*, Bargh and Chartrand asserted that:

> [M]ost of moment-to-moment psychological life must occur through non-conscious means if it is to occur at all . . . various nonconscious mental systems perform the lion's share of the self-regulatory burden, beneficently keeping the individual grounded in his or her current environment.
>
> *(1999, p. 462)*

This characterization describes internal working models, and since their affective-cognitive components regulate the involuntary ANS, these functions may very well be inaccessible to self-report measures that mainly tap into conscious thoughts and images.

The psychobiological mechanisms that trigger organismic responses are fast acting and dynamic. Studying very rapid affective phenomena in real time involves attention to a different time dimension than usual, a focus on interpersonal attachment and separations on a microtemporal scale. The emphasis is less on enduring traits and more on transient dynamic states, and research methodologies will have to be created that can visualize the dyadic regulatory events occurring at the brain-mind-body interface of two subjectivities that are engaged in attachment transactions. Digital videotape recordings, analyzing split-second events in both members of an affect-transacting dyad, may be particularly suited for this purpose.

Because the human face is a central focus of these transactions, studies of right brain appraisals of visual and prosodic facial stimuli, even presented at tachistoscopic levels, may more accurately tap into the fundamental mechanisms that are involved in the processing of social-emotional information. And in light of the principle that dyadic regulatory affective communications maximize positive as well as minimize negative affect, both procedures that measure coping with negative affect (strange situations), and those that measure coping with positive affect (play situations), need to be used to evaluate attachment capacities.

It is established that face-to-face contexts of affect synchrony not only generate positive arousal but also expose infants to high levels of social and cognitive information (Feldman et al., 1999). In such interpersonal contexts, including attachment-related "joint attention" transactions (Schore, 1994), the developing child is exercising early attentional capacities. There is evidence to show that "intrinsic alertness," the most basic intensity aspect of attention, is mediated by a network in the right hemisphere (Sturm et al., 1999). In light of the known impaired functioning of right frontal circuits in attention deficit/hyperactivity disorders (Casey et al., 1997), developmental attachment studies may elucidate the early etiology of these disorders, as well as of right hemisphere learning disabilities (Gross-Tsur, Shalev, Manor, & Amir, 1995; Semrud-Clikeman & Hynd, 1990).

Furthermore, although most attachment studies refer to infants and toddlers, it is well known that the brain maturation rates of baby girls are significantly more advanced than boys. Gender differences in infant emotional regulation (Weinberg, Tronick, Cohn, & Olsen, 1999) and in the orbitofrontal system that mediates this function (Overman, Bachevalier, Schuhmann, & Ryan, 1996) have been demonstrated. Studies of how different social experiences interact with different female-male regional brain growth rates could elucidate the origins of gender differences within the limbic system that are later expressed in variations of social-emotional information processing between the sexes. This research should include measures of "psychological gender" (see Schore, 1994). And in addition to maternal effects on early brain maturation, the effects of fathers, especially in the second and third years, on the female and male toddler's psychoneurobiological development can tell us more about paternal contributions to the child's expanding stress coping capacities.

We must also more fully understand the very early pre- and postnatally maturing limbic circuits that organize what Bowlby calls the "building blocks" of attachment experiences (see Schore, 2000b, 2001a). Bowlby (1969) referred to a succession of increasingly sophisticated systems of limbic structures that are involved in attachment. Since attachment is the outcome of the child's genetically encoded biological (temperamental) predisposition and the particular caregiver environment, we need to know more about the mechanisms of gene-environment interactions. This work could elucidate the nature of the expression of particular genes in specific brain regions that regulate stress reactivity, as well as a deeper knowledge of the dynamic components of "nonshared" environmental factors (Plomin, Rende, & Rutter, 1991). It should be remembered that DNA levels in the cortex significantly increase over the first year, the period of attachment (Winick, Rosso, & Waterlow, 1970).

A very recent report of an association between perinatal complications (deviations of normal pregnancy, labor-delivery, and early neonatal development) and later signs of specifically orbitofrontal dysfunction (Kinney, Steingard, Renshaw, & Yurgelun-Todd, 2000) may elucidate the mechanism by which an interaction of a vulnerable genetically encoded psychobiological predisposition interacts with a misattuned relational environment to produce a high-risk scenario for future disorders. Orbitofrontal dysfunction in infancy has also been implicated in a later-appearing impairment of not only social but moral behavior (Anderson, Bechara, Damasio, Tranel, & Damasio, 1999).

Furthermore, developmental neuroscientific studies of the effects of attuned and misattuned parental environments will reveal the subtle but important differences in brain organization among securely and insecurely attached individuals, as well as the psychobiological mechanisms that mediate resilience to or risk for later-forming psychopathologies. Neurobiological studies now indicate that although the right prefrontal system is necessary to mount a normal stress response, extreme alterations of such activity are maladaptive (Sullivan & Gratton, 1999). In line with the association of attachment experiences and the development of brain systems for coping with relational stress, future studies need to explore the relationship between different adaptive and maladaptive coping styles of various attachment categories and correlated deficits in brain systems involved in stress regulation. Subjects, classified on the Adult Attachment Inventory (Hesse, 1999), could be exposed to a real-life, personally meaningful stressor, and brain imaging and autonomic measures could then evaluate the individual's adaptive or maladaptive regulatory mechanisms. Such studies can also elucidate the mechanisms of the intergenerational transmission of the regulatory deficits of different classes of psychiatric disorders (see Schore, 1994, 1996, 1997a).

In light of the fact that the right hemisphere subsequently reenters into growth spurts (Thatcher, 1994) and ultimately forms an interactive system with the later maturing left (Schore, 1994, 2002; Siegel, 1999), neurobiological reorganizations of the attachment system and their functional correlates in ensuing stages of childhood and adulthood need to be explored. Psychoneurobiological research of the continuing experience-dependent maturation of the right hemisphere could elucidate the underlying mechanisms by which certain attachment patterns can change from "insecurity" to "earned security" (Phelps, Belsky, & Crnic, 1998).

The documented findings that the orbitofrontal system is involved in "emotion-related learning" (Rolls, Hornak, Wade, & McGrath, 1994) and that it retains plasticity throughout later periods of life (Barbas, 1995) may also help us understand how developmentally based, affectively focused psychotherapy can alter early attachment patterns. A functional magnetic resonance imaging study by Hariri, Bookheimer and Mazziotta provided evidence that higher regions of specifically the right prefrontal cortex attenuate emotional responses at the most basic levels in the brain, that such modulating processes are "fundamental to most modern psychotherapeutic methods" (2000, p. 43), that this lateralized neocortical network is active in "modulating emotional experience through interpreting and labeling emotional expressions" (p. 47), and that "this form of modulation may be impaired in various emotional disorders and may provide the basis for therapies of these same disorders" (p. 48). This process is a central component of therapeutic narrative organization, of turning "raw feelings into symbols" (Holmes, 1993, p. 150). This "neocortical network," which "modulates the limbic system" is identical to the right-lateralized orbitofrontal system that regulates attachment dynamics. Attachment models of mother-infant psychobiological attunement may thus be used to explore the origins of empathic processes in both development and psychotherapy, and reveal the deeper mechanisms of the growth-facilitating factors operating within the therapeutic alliance (see Schore, 1994, 1997c, 2002).

In a sense these deeper explorations into the roots of the human experience have been waiting for not just theoretical advances in developmental neurobiology and technical improvements in methodologies that can noninvasively image developing brain-mind-body processes in real time, but also for a perspective of brain-mind-body development that can bridge psychology and biology. Such interdisciplinary models can shift back and forth between different levels of organization in order to accommodate heuristic conceptions of how the primordial experiences with the external social world alters the ontogeny of internal structural systems. Ultimately, these psychoneurobiological attachment models can be used as a scientific basis for creating even more effective early prevention programs.

In her concluding comments of a recent overview of the field, Mary Main, a central figure in the continuing development of attachment theory, writes;

> We are currently at one of the most exciting junctures in the history of our field. We are now, or will soon be, in a position to begin mapping the relations between individual differences in early attachment experiences and changes in neurochemistry and brain organization. In addition, investigation of physiological 'regulators' associated with infant-caregiver interactions could have far-reaching implications for both clinical assessment and intervention.
>
> *(1999, pp. 881–882)*

But I leave the final word to Bowlby himself, who in the last paragraph of his seminal book (1969), sums up the meaning of his work: "The truth is that the least-studied phase of human development remains the phase during which a child is acquiring all that makes him most distinctively human. Here is still a continent to conquer" (p. 358).

References

Ainsworth, M. D. S. (1967). *Infancy in Uganda: Infant care and the growth of love*. Baltimore: Johns Hopkins University Press.

Ainsworth, M. D. S. (1969). Object relations, dependency and attachment: A theoretical review of the infant-mother relationship. *Child Development*, 40, 969–1025.

Anders, T. F., & Zeanah, C. H. (1984). Early infant development from a biological point of view. In J. D. Call, E. Galenson & R. L. Tyson (Eds.), *Frontiers of infant psychiatry*, Vol. 2, 55–69. New York: Basic Books.

Anderson, S. W., Bechara, A., Damasio, H., Tranel, D., & Damasio, A. R. (1999). Impairment of social and moral behavior related to early damage in human prefrontal cortex. *Nature Neuroscience*, 2, 1032–1037.

Baker, S. C., Frith, C. D., & Dolan, R. J. (1997). The interaction between mood and cognitive function studied with PET. *Psychological Medicine*, 27, 565–578.

Barbas, H. (1995). Anatomie basis of cognitive-emotional interactions in the primate prefrontal cortex. *Neuroscience and Biobehavioral Reviews*, 19, 499–510.

Bargh, J. A., & Chartrand, T. L. (1999). The unbearable automaticity of being. *American Psychologist*, 54, 462–479.

Baron-Cohen, S. (1995). *Mindblindness: An essay on autism and theory of mind*. Cambridge, MA: MIT Press.

Bechara, A., Damasio, H., Tranel, D., & Damasio, A. R. (1997). Deciding advantageously before knowing the advantageous strategy. *Science*, 275, 1293–1295.

Bernardo, J. (1996). Maternal effects in animal ecology. *American Zoologist*, 36, 83–105.

Blair, R. J. R., Morris, J. S., Frith, C. D., Perrett, D. I., & Dolan, R. J. (1999). Dissociable neural responses to facial expressions of sadness and anger. *Brain*, 122, 883–893.

Blood, A. J., Zatorre, R. J., Bermudez, P., & Evans, A. C. (1999). Emotional responses to pleasant and unpleasant music correlate with activity in paralimbic brain regions. *Nature Neuroscience*, 2, 382–387.

Bowers, D., Bauer, R. M., & Heilman, K. M. (1993). The nonverbal affect lexicon: Theoretical perspectives from neuropsychological studies of affect perception. *Neuropsychology*, 7, 433–444.

Bowlby, J. (1944). Forty-four juvenile thieves: Their characters and home life. *International Journal of Psychoanalysis*, 25, 1–57, 207–228.

Bowlby, J. (1969). *Attachment and loss: Vol. 1. Attachment*. New York: Basic Books.

Bowlby, J. (1973). *Attachment and loss: Vol. 2. Separation, anxiety and anger*. New York: Basic Books.

Bowlby, J. (1978). Attachment theory and its therapeutic implications. In S. C. Feinstein & P. L. Giovacchini (Eds.), *Adolescent psychiatry: Developmental and clinical studies*, 5–33. Chicago: University of Chicago Press.

Bowlby, J. (1981). *Attachment and loss: Vol. 3. Loss, sadness, and depression*. New York: Basic Books.

Bretherton, I., & Munholland, K. A. (1999). Internal working models in attachment relationships: A construct revisited. In J. Cassidy & P. R. Shaver (Eds.), *Handbook of attachment: Theory, research, and clinical applications*, 89–111. New York: Guilford.

Caldji, C., Tannenbaum, B., Sharma, S., Francis, D., Plotsky, P. M., & Meaney, M. J. (1998). Maternal care during infancy regulates the development of neural systems mediating the expression of fearfulness in the rat. *Proceedings of the National Academy of Sciences of the United States of America*, 95, 5335–5340.

Carmichael, S. T., & Price, J. L. (1995). Limbic connections of the orbital and medial prefrontal cortex in macaque monkeys. *Journal of Comparative Neurology*, 363, 615–641.

Casey, B. J., Trainor, R., Giedd, J., Vauss, Y., Vaituzis, C. K., Hamburger, S., Kozuch, P., & Rapoport, J. L. (1997). The role of the anterior cingulate in the automatic and controlled processes: A developmental neuroanatomical study. *Developmental Psychobiology*, 30, 61–69.

Cassidy, J., & Shaver, P. R. (Eds.). (1999). *Handbook of attachment: Theory, research, and clinical applications*. New York: Guilford Press.

Chapple, E. D. (1970). Experimental production of transients in human interaction. *Nature*, 228, 630–633.

Chiron, C., Jambaque, I., Nabbout, R., Lounes, R., Syrota, A., & Dulac, O. (1997). The right brain hemisphere is dominant in human infants. *Brain*, 120, 1057–1065.

Crittenden, P. M. (1995). Attachment and psychopathology. In S. Goldberg, R. Muir & J. Kerr (Eds.), *Attachment theory: Social, developmental, and clinical perspectives*, 367–406. Mahwah, NJ: Analytic Press.

Damasio, A. R. (1998). Emotion in the perspective of an integrated nervous system. *Brain Research Reviews*, 26, 83–86.

Darwin, C. (1965). *The expression of emotion in man and animals.* Chicago: University of Chicago Press. (Original work published 1872).

Derryberry, D., & Tucker, D. M. (1992). Neural mechanisms of emotion. *Journal of Clinical and Consulting Psychology*, 60, 329–338.

Deruelle, C., & De Schonen, S. (1998). Do the right and left hemispheres attend to the same visuospatial information within a face in infancy? *Developmental Neuropsychology*, 14, 535–554.

Dobbing, J., & Sands, J. (1973). Quantitative growth and development of human brain. *Archives of Disease in Childhood*, 48, 757–767.

Dolan, R. J. (1999). On the neurology of morals. *Nature Neuroscience*, 2, 927–929.

Elliott, R., Frith, C. D., & Dolan, R. J. (1997). Differential neural response to positive and negative feedback in planning and guessing tasks. *Neuropsychologia*, 35, 1395–1404.

Feldman, R., Greenbaum, C. W., & Yirmiya, N. (1999). Mother-infant affect synchrony as an antecedent of the emergence of self-control. *Developmental Psychology*, 35, 223–231.

Field, T. (1985a). Attachment as psychobiological attunement: Being on the same wavelength. In M. Reite & T. Field (Eds.), *The psychobiology of attachment and separation*, 415–454. Orlando: Academic Press.

Field, T. (1985b). Coping with separation stress by infants and young children. In T. Field, P. M. McCabe & N. Schneiderman (Eds.), *Stress and coping*, 197–219. Hillsdale, NJ: Erlbaum.

Fink, G. R., Markowitsch, H. J., Reinkemeier, M., Bruckbauer, T., Kessler, J., & Heiss, W.-D. (1996). Cerebral representation of one's own past: Neural networks involved in autobiographical memory. *Journal of Neuroscience*, 16, 4275–4282.

Fleming, A. S., O'Day, D. H., & Kraemer, G. W. (1999). Neurobiology of mother-infant interactions: Experience and central nervous system plasticity across development and generations. *Neuroscience and Biobehavioral Reviews*, 23, 673–685.

Fonagy, P., & Target, M. (1997). Attachment and reflective function: Their role in self-organization. *Development and Psychopathology*, 9, 679–700.

Francis, D. D., Diorio, J., Liu, D., & Meaney, M. J. (1999). Nongenomic transmission across generations of maternal behavior and stress responses in the rat. *Science*, 286, 1155–1158.

Francis, D. D., & Meaney, M. J. (1999). Maternal care and the development of stress responses. *Current Opinion in Neurobiology*, 9, 128–134.

Freud, S. (1959). Inhibition, symptoms, and anxiety. In J. Strachey (Ed. & Trans.), *The standard edition of the complete psychological works of Sigmund Freud*, Vol. 20, 77–175. London: Hogarth Press. (Original work published 1926).

Freud, S. (1966). Project for a scientific psychology. In J. Strachey (Ed. & Trans.), *Standard edition of the complete psychological works of Sigmund Freud*, Vol. 1, 295–397. London: Hogarth Press. (Original work published 1895).

Garavan, H., Ross, T. J., & Stein, E. A. (1999). Right hemisphere dominance of inhibitory control: An event-related functional MRI study. *Proceedings of the National Academy of Sciences of the United States of America*, 96, 8301–8306.

Geschwind, N., & Galaburda, A. M. (1987). *Cerebral lateralization: Biological mechanisms, associations, and pathology.* Boston: MIT Press.

Goldberg, S., Muir, R., & Kerr, J. (1995). *Attachment theory: Social, developmental, and clinical perspectives.* Mahwah, NJ: Analytic Press.

Goldenberg, G., Podreka, I., Uhl, F., Steiner, M., Willmes, K., & Deecke, L. (1989). Cerebral correlates of imagining colours, faces and a map – I. SPECT of regional cerebral blood flow. *Neuropsychologia*, 27, 1315–1328.

Greenspan, S. I. (1981). *Psychopathology and adaptation in infancy and early childhood.* New York: International Universities Press.

Gross-Tsur, V., Shalev, R. S., Manor, O., & Amir, N. (1995). Developmental right-hemisphere syndrome: Clinical spectrum of the nonverbal learning disability. *Journal of Learning Disabilities*, 28, 80–86.

Hariri, A. R., Bookheimer, S. Y., & Mazziotta, J. C. (2000). Modulating emotional responses: Effects of a neocortical network on the limbic system. *NeuroReport*, 11, 43–48.

Heilman, K. M., & van den Abell, T. (1979). Right hemispheric dominance for mediating cerebral activation. *Neuropsychologia*, 17, 315–321.

Henry, J. P. (1993). Psychological and physiological responses to stress: The right hemisphere and the hypothalamo-pituitary-adrenal axis, an inquiry into problems of human bonding. *Integrative Physiological and Behavioral Science*, 28, 369–387.

Hesse, E. (1999). The adult attachment interview: Historical and current perspectives. In J. Cassidy & P. R. Shaver (Eds.), *Handbook of attachment: Theory, research, and clinical applications*, 395–433. New York: Guilford.

Hinde, R. (1990). Causes of social development from the perspective of an integrated developmental science. In G. Butterworth & P. Bryant (Eds.), *Causes of development*, 161–185. Hillsdale, NJ: Erlbaum.

Holmes, J. (1993). *John Bowlby and attachment theory*. London: Routledge.

Joseph, R. (1996). *Neuropsychiatry, neuropsychology, and clinical neuroscience* (2nd ed.). Baltimore: Williams & Wilkins.

Kandel, E. R. (1999). Biology and the future of psychoanalysis: A new intellectual framework for psychiatry revisited. *American Journal of Psychiatry*, 156, 505–524.

Kaplan-Solms, K., & Solms, M. (1996). Psychoanalytic observations on a case of frontal-limbic disease. *Journal of Clinical Psychoanalysis*, 5, 405–438.

Keenan, J. P., McCutcheon, B., Freund, S., Gallup, G. C., Jr., Sanders, G., & Pascual-Leone, A. (1999). Left hand advantage in a self-face recognition task. *Neuropsychologia*, 37, 1421–1425.

Kim, J. J., Andreasen, N. C., O'Leary, D. S., Wiser, A. K., Boles Ponto, L. L., Watkins, G. L., & Hichwa, R. D. (1999). Direct comparison of the neural substrates of recognition memory for words and faces. *Brain*, 122, 1069–1083.

Kinney, D. K., Steingard, R. J., Renshaw, P. F., & Yurgelun-Todd, D. A. (2000). Perinatal complications and abnormal proton metabolite concentrations in frontal cortex of adolescents seen on magnetic resonance spectroscopy. *Neuropsychiatry, Neuropsychology, and Behavioral Neurology*, 13, 8–12.

Kinney, H. C., Brody, B. A., Kloman, A. S., & Gilles, F. H. (1988). Sequence of central nervous system myelination in human infancy. II: Patterns of myelination in autopsied infants. *Journal of Neuropathology and Experimental Neurology*, 47, 217–234.

Kobak, R. R., & Sceery, A. (1988). Attachment in late adolescence: Working models, affect regulation, and representations of self and others. *Child Development*, 59, 135–146.

Koolhaas, J. M., Korte, S. M., De Boer, S. F., Van der Vegt, B. J., Van Reenen, C. G., Hopster, H., De Jong, I. C., Ruis, M. A. W., & Blokhuis, H. J. (1999). Coping styles in animals: Current status in behavior and stress-physiology. *Neuroscience and Biobehavioral Reviews*, 23, 925–935.

Lewis, M. D. (1995). Cognition-emotion feedback and the self-organization of developmental paths. *Human Development*, 38, 71–102.

Lewis, M. D. (1999). A new dynamic systems method for the analysis of early socio-emotional development. *Developmental Science*, 2, 457–475.

Lewis, M. D. (2000). The promise of dynamic systems approaches for an integrated account of human development. *Child Development*, 71, 1–23.

Luria, A. R. (1980). *Higher cortical functions in man* (2nd ed.). New York: Basic Books.

Main, M. (1999). Epilogue: Attachment theory: Eighteen points with suggestions for future studies. In J. Cassidy & P. R. Shaver (Eds.), *Handbook of attachment: Theory, research, and clinical applications*, 845–887. New York: Guilford.

Main, M., Kaplan, N., & Cassidy, J. (1985). Security in infancy, childhood and adulthood: A move to the level of representation. *Monographs of the Society for Research in Child Development*, 50, 66–104.

Mesulam, M.-M. (1998). From sensation to cognition. *Brain*, 121, 1013–1052.

Nelson, E. E., & Panksepp, J. (1998). Brain substrates of infant-mother attachment: Contributions of opioids, oxytocin, and norepinephrine. *Neuroscience & Biobehavioral Reviews*, 22, 437–542.

Nobre, A. C., Coull, J. T., Frith, C. D., & Mesulam, M. M. (1999). Orbitofrontal cortex is activated during breaches of expectation in tasks of visual attention. *Nature Neuroscience*, 2, 11–12.

Overman, W. H., Bachevalier, J., Schuhmann, E., & Ryan, P. (1996). Cognitive gender differences in very young children parallel biologically based cognitive gender differences in monkeys. *Behavioral Neuroscience*, 110, 673–684.

Penman, R., Meares, R., & Milgrom-Friedman, J. (1983). Synchrony in mother-infant interaction: A possible neurophysiological base. *British Journal of Medical Psychology*, 56, 1–7.

Petrovich, S. B., & Gewirtz, J. L. (1985). The attachment learning process and its relation to cultural and biological evolution: Proximate and ultimate considerations. In M. Reite & T. Field (Eds.), *The psychobiology of attachment and separation*. Orlando: Academic Press, 259–291.

Phelps, E. A., O'Connor, K. J., Gatenby, J. C., Gore, J. C., Grillon, C., & Davis, M. (2001). Activation of the left amygdala to a cognitive representation of fear. *Nature Neuroscience* 4, 437–441.

Phelps, J. L., Belsky, J., & Crnic, K. (1998). Earned security, daily stress, and parenting: A comparison of five alternative models. *Development and Psychopathology*, 10, 21–38.

Pipp, S., & Harmon, R. J. (1987). Attachment as regulation: A commentary. *Child Development*, 58, 648–652.

Pizzagalli, D., Regard, M., & Lehmann, D. (1999). Rapid emotional face processing in the human right and left brain hemispheres: An ERP study. *NeuroReport*, 10, 2691–2698.

Plomin, R., Rende, R., & Rutter, M. (1991). Quantitative genetics and developmental psychopathology. In D. Cicchetti & S. L. Toth (Eds.), *Internalizing and externalizing expressions of dysfunction: Rochester symposium on developmental psychopathology*, Vol. 2, 155–292. Mahwah, NJ: Erlbaum.

Polan, H. J., & Hofer, M. A. (1999). Psychobiological origins of infant attachment and separation responses. In J. Cassidy & P. R. Shaver (Eds.), *Handbook of attachment: Theory, research, and clinical applications*, 162–180. New York: Guilford Press.

Povinelli, D., & Preuss, T. M. (1995). Theory of mind: Evolutionary history of a cognitive specialization. *Trends in Neuroscience*, 18, 418–424.

Pribram, K. H. (1987). The subdivisions of the frontal cortex revisited. In E. Perecman (Ed.), *The frontal lobes revisited*, 11–39. Hillsdale, NJ: Erlbaum.

Price, J. L., Carmichael, S. T., & Drevets, W. C. (1996). Networks related to the orbital and medial prefrontal cortex: A substrate for emotional behavior? *Progress in Brain Research*, 107, 523–536.

Rabinowicz, T. (1979). The differentiate maturation of the human cerebral cortex. In F. Falkner & J. M. Tanner (Eds.), *Human growth: Vol. 3. Neurobiology and nutrition*, 97–123. New York: Plenum.

Reite, M., & Capitanio, J. P. (1985). On the nature of social separation and attachment. In M. Reite & T. Field (Eds.), *The psychobiology of attachment and separation*, 223–255. Orlando, FL: Academic Press.

Rolls, E. T. (1986). Neural systems involved in emotion in primates. In R. Plutchik & H. Kellerman (Eds.), *Emotion: Theory, research, and practice*, Vol. 3, 125–143. Orlando, FL: Academic Press.

Rolls, E. T., Hornak, J., Wade, D., & McGrath, J. (1994). Emotion-related learning in patients with social and emotional changes associated with frontal lobe damage. *Journal of Neurology, Neurosurgery, and Psychiatry*, 57, 1518–1524.

Romanski, L. M., Tian, B., Fritz, J., Mishkin, M., Goldman-Rakic, P. S., & Rauschecker, J. P. (1999). Dual streams of auditory afferents target multiple domains in the primate prefrontal cortex. *Nature Neuroscience*, 2, 1131–1136.

Rutter, M. (1987). Temperament, personality and personality disorder. *British Journal of Psychiatry*, 150, 443–458.

Ryan, R. M., Kuhl, J., & Deci, E. L. (1997). Nature and autonomy: An organizational view of social and neurobiological aspects of self-regulation in behavior and development. *Development and Psychopathology*, 9, 701–728.

Scalaidhe, S. P., Wilson, F. A. W., & Goldman-Rakic, P. S. (1997). Areal segregation of face-processing neurons in prefrontal cortex. *Science*, 278, 1135–1138.

Schnider, A., & Ptak, R. (1999). Spontaneous confabulators fail to suppress currently irrelevant memory traces. *Nature Neuroscience*, 2, 677–681.

Schore, A. N. (1994). *Affect regulation and the origin of the self: The neurobiology of emotional development*. Mahwah, NJ: Erlbaum.

Schore, A. N. (1996). The experience-dependent maturation of a regulatory system in the orbital prefrontal cortex and the origin of developmental psychopathology. *Development and Psychopathology*, 8, 59–87.

Schore, A. N. (1997a). A Century after Freud's Project – is a rapprochement between psychoanalysis and neurobiology at hand? *Journal of the American Psychoanalytic Association*, 45, 1–34.

Schore, A. N. (1997b). Early organization of the nonlinear right brain and development of a predisposition to psychiatric disorders. *Development and Psychopathology*, 9, 595–631.

Schore, A. N. (1997c). Interdisciplinary developmental research as a source of clinical models. In M. Moskowitz, C. Monk, C. Kaye, & S. Ellman (Eds.), *The neurobiological and developmental basis for psychotherapeutic intervention*, 1–71. Northvale, NJ: Aronson.

Schore, A. N. (1998a). Early shame experiences and infant brain development. In P. Gilbert & B. Andrews (Eds.), *Shame: Interpersonal behavior, psychopathology, and culture*, 57–77. New York: Oxford University Press.

Schore, A. N. (1998b). The experience-dependent maturation of an evaluative system in the cortex. In K. H. Pribram (Ed.), *Fifth appalachian conference on behavioral neurodynamics, "brain and values"*, 337–358. Mahwah, NJ: Erlbaum.

Schore, A. N. (1999). Commentary on emotions: Neuropsychoanalytic views. *Neuro-Psychoanalysis*, 1, 49–55.

Schore, A. N. (2000a). Attachment and the regulation of the right brain. *Attachment & Human Development*, 2, 23–47.

Schore, A. N. (2000b). Attachment, the right brain, and empathic processes within the therapeutic alliance. *Psychologist Psychoanalyst*, 20(4), 8–11.

Schore, A. N. (2001a). Contributions from the decade of the brain to infant mental health: An overview. *Infant Mental Health Journal*, 22, 1–6.

Schore, A. N. (2001b). The effects of a secure attachment relationship on right brain development, affect regulation, and infant mental health. *Infant Mental Health Journal*, 22, 7–66.

Schore, A. N. (2002). Clinical implications of a psychoneurobiological model of projective identification. In S. Alhanati (Ed.), *Primitive mental states: Vol. 3. Pre-and peri-natal influences on personality development*. London: Karnac, 1–65.

Semrud-Clikeman, M., & Hynd, G. W. (1990). Right hemisphere dysfunction in nonverbal learning disabilities: Social, academic, and adaptive functioning in adults and children. *Psychological Bulletin*, 107, 196–209.

Sgoifo, A., Koolhaas, J., De Boer, S., Musso, E., Stilli, D., Buwalda, B., & Meerlo, P. (1999). Social stress, autonomic neural activation, and cardiac activity in rats. *Neuroscience and Biobehavioral Reviews*, 23, 915–923.

Shapiro, D., Jamner, L. D., & Spence, S. (1997). Cerebral laterality, repressive coping, autonomic arousal, and human bonding. *Acta Physiologica Scandinavica*, 640 (Suppl.), 60–64.

Siegel, D. J. (1999). *The developing mind: Toward a neurobiology of interpersonal experience*. New York: Guilford Press.

Spence, S., Shapiro, D., & Zaidel, E. (1996). The role of the right hemisphere in the physiological and cognitive components of emotional processing. *Psychophysiology*, 33, 112–122.

Sroufe, L. A. (1989). Relationships, self, and individual adaptation. In A. J. Sameroff & R. N. Emde (Eds.), *Relationship disturbances in early childhood*, 70–94. New York: Basic.

Sroufe, L. A. (1996). *Emotional development: The organization of emotional life in the early years*. New York: Cambridge University Press.

Starkstein, S. E., & Robinson, R. G. (1997). Mechanism of disinhibition after brain lesions. *Journal of Nervous and Mental Disease*, 185, 108–114.

Stone, V. E., Baron-Cohen, S., & Knight, R. T. (1998). Frontal lobe contributions to theory of mind. *Journal of Cognitive Neuroscience*, 10, 640–656.

Sturm, W., de Simone, A., Krause, B. J., Specht, K., Hesselmann, V., Radermacher, I., Herzog, H., Tellann, L., Müller-Gärtner, H.-W., & Willmes, K. (1999). Functional anatomy of intrinsic alertness: Evidence for a fronto-parietal-thalamic-brainstem network in the right hemisphere. *Neuropsychologia*, 37, 797–805.

Stuss, D. T., Gow, C. A., & Hetherington, C. R. (1992). "No longer Gage": Frontal lobe dysfunction and emotional changes. *Journal of Consulting and Clinical Psychology*, 60, 349–359.

Sullivan, R. M., & Gratton, A. (1999). Prefrontal cortical regulation of hypothalamic-pituitary-adrenal function of the rat and implications for psychopathology: Side matters. *Psychoneuroendocrinology*, 27, 99–114.

Teasdale, J. D., Howard, R. J., Cox, S. G., Ha, Y., Brammer, M. J., Williams, S. C. R., & Checkley, S. A. (1999). Functional MRI study of the cognitive generation of affect. *American Journal of Psychiatry*, 156, 209–215.

Thatcher, R. W. (1994). Cyclical cortical reorganization: Origins of human cognitive development. In G. Dawson & K. W. Fischer (Eds.), *Human behavior and the developing brain*, 232–266. New York: Guilford.

Tremblay, L., & Schultz, W. (1999). Relative reward preference in primate orbitofrontal cortex. *Nature*, 398, 704–708.

Trevarthen, C. (1990). Growth and education of the hemispheres. In C. Trevarthen (Ed.), *Brain circuits and functions of the mind*, 334–363. Cambridge, UK: Cambridge University Press.

Tronick, E. Z. (1989). Emotions and emotional communication in infants. *American Psychologist*, 44, 112–119.

Tucker, D. M. (1992). Developing emotions and cortical networks. In M. R. Gunnar & C. A. Nelson (Eds.), *Minnesota symposium on child psychology: Vol. 24. Developmental behavioral neuroscience*, 75–128. Mahwah, NJ: Erlbaum.

Voeller, K. K. S. (1986). Right hemisphere deficit syndrome in children. *American Journal of Psychiatry*, 143, 1004–1009.

Wang, S. (1997). Traumatic stress and attachment. *Acta Physiologica Scandinavica*, 640(Suppl.), 164–169.

Weinberg, M. K., Tronick, E. Z., Cohn, J. F., & Olsen, K. L. (1999). Gender differences in emotional expressivity and self-regulation during infancy. *Developmental Psychology*, 35, 175–188.

Westen, D. (1997). Towards a clinically and empirically sound theory of motivation. *International Journal of Psycho-Analysis*, 78, 521–548.

Winick, M., Rosso, P., & Waterlow, J. (1970). Cellular growth of the cerebrum cerebellum and brain stem in normal and marasmic children. *Experimental Neurology*, 26, 393–400.

Wittling, W. (1997). The right hemisphere and the human stress response. *Acta Physiologica Scandinavica*, 640(Suppl.), 55–59.

Wittling, W., & Schweiger, E. (1993). Neuroendocrine brain asymmetry and physical complaints. *Neuropsychologia*, 31, 591–608.

Zald, D. H., & Kim, S. W. (1996). Anatomy and function of the orbital frontal cortex, II: Function and relevance to obsessive-compulsive disorder. *Journal of Neuropsychiatry*, 8, 249–261.

3.4 Dysregulation of the right brain: a fundamental mechanism of traumatic attachment and the psychopathogenesis of posttraumatic stress disorders

A large nationally representative study reported that 60% of men and 50% of women experience a traumatic event at some point in their lives (Kessler, Sonnega, Bromet, Hughes, & Nelson, 1995). And yet this same study found that estimates of lifetime PTSD are 5% for men and 10% for women. Other research indicated that roughly one half of those who have an episode of PTSD develop chronic symptoms of the disorder (Zlotnick et al., 1999). These data underscore a central problem: although trauma is a common element of many if not most lives, why do only a certain minor proportion of individuals exposed to the various forms of trauma develop chronic pathological reactions of mind and body to catastrophic life events?

A major change in our approach to this problem is reflected in the shift from *DSM-III-R*, where the severity of the trauma was considered to be the key factor in precipitating PTSD, to the *DSM-IV*, where characteristics of the victim, including the reaction to the trauma, is emphasized. In other words, the etiology of PTSD is best understood in terms of what an individual brings to a traumatic event as well as what he or she experiences afterward, and not just the nature of the traumatic event itself (Schnurr & Friedman, 1997). This implies that certain personality patterns are specifically associated with the unique ways individuals cope or fail to cope with stress.

Psychobiological research on PTSD (Morgan et al., 2001) echoed this principle:

> Although many people are exposed to trauma, only some individuals develop PTSD; most do not. It is possible that humans differ in the degree to which stress induces neurobiological perturbations of their threat response systems, which may result in a differential capacity to cope with aversive experiences.
>
> *(p. 412)*

> These individual differences exist before trauma exposure and may be used to test constructs of stress hardiness and stress vulnerability in humans.
>
> *(p. 420)*

There is agreement that the developmental stage at the time of exposure (Pynoos, 1993) and the specific type of trauma exposure (Davidson & Foa, 1993) are essential factors in PTSD, and yet they have been deemphasized in the recent literature (McFarlane & Yehuda, 2000). Highlighting these factors, however, brings into the foreground a number of fundamental issues: what are the effects of trauma in the earliest developmental stages? Why does this developmental exposure impact the differential capacity to cope with stress, and how is this related to the genesis of premorbid personality organizations vulnerable to PTSD? These questions, which lie at the core of trauma theory, direct clinical psychiatry into the realms of child and especially infant psychiatry.

Attachment and the development of right brain stress coping mechanisms

The exploration of the early development of adaptive coping mechanisms and of the personality is at the core of attachment theory, "the dominant approach to understanding early socioemotional and personality development during the past quarter-century of research" (Thompson, 2000, p. 145). In his groundbreaking volume, *Attachment*, Bowlby (1969) hypothesized that the infant's "capacity to cope with stress" is correlated with certain maternal behaviors, that the developing emotion processing limbic system is impacted by attachment transactions, and that attachment outcome has consequences that are "vital to the survival of the species." Bowlby's speculation that, within the attachment relationship, the mother shapes the development of the infant's coping responses is now supported by a large body of basic experimental studies that characterize maternal care and the development of stress responses (Anisman, Zaharia, Meaney, & Merali, 1998; Essex, Klein, Cho, & Kalin, 2002; Francis & Meaney, 1999; Kuhn & Schanberg, 1998), and the influence of maternal factors on the ontogeny of the limbic-hypothalamic-pituitary-adrenal axis (Hennessy, 1997; Levine, 1994; Suchecki, Nelson, Van Oers, & Levine, 1995).

Recent developmental psychobiological models indicate that:

> An individual's response to stressful stimuli may be maladaptive producing physiological and behavioral responses that may have detrimental consequences, or may be adaptive, enabling the individual to better cope with stress. Events experienced early in life may be particularly important in shaping the individual's pattern of responsiveness in later stages of life.
>
> *(Kehoe et al., 1996, p. 1435)*

These "events" are attachment experiences, shaped by the interaction of the infant's innate psychophysiological predispositions and the social environment of maternal care (Helmeke, Ovtscharoff, Poeggel, & Braun, 2001; Henry & Wang, 1998; Nachmias, Gunnar, Mangelsdorf, Parritz, & Buss, 1996; Ovtsharoff & Braun, 2001; Schore, 1994, 1998b, 1999b, 2000a, 2000d, 2001a; Siegel, 1999; Streeck-Fischer & van der Kolk, 2000; Suomi, 1995; Valent, 1998).

Furthermore, basic stress research suggests that deprivation of maternal care represents a source of "stressful environmental information" for the developmental, maturational pattern of the neural circuitry of the infant's stress system (Korte, 2001). This complements studies indicating that pre- or postnatal stressors negatively impact later mental health, especially when maternal care is absent (Korfman, 2002; Schore,

2001c). Such work is derivative of attachment theory's deep interest in the etiology of not only normal but abnormal development. In applying the theory to links between stress coping features and psychopathology Bowlby (1978) proposed:

> In the fields of etiology and psychopathology [attachment theory] can be used to frame specific hypotheses which relate different family experiences to different forms of psychiatric disorder and also, possibly, to the neurophysiological changes that accompany them.
>
> *(pp. 5–33)*

With respect to the etiology of PTSD, a large body of studies implicates childhood abuse, and suggests that early life trauma produces specific patterns of developmental neurobiological alterations, especially in the limbic system (Kaufman, Plotsky, Nemeroff, & Charney, 2000; Teicher, Glod, Surrey, & Swett, 1993; Vermetten & Bremner, 2002).

In this chapter I will apply the central principle of attachment theory as outlined earlier to the etiology of PTSD. Although etiological models of PTSD have centered primarily on childhood sexual abuse, I will suggest that an increased focus on the neurobiological consequences of relational abuse and dysregulated infant attachment can offer a deeper understanding of the psychoneurobiological stress coping deficits of both mind and body that define the symptomatic presentation of the disorder, especially chronic forms of PTSD.

Stress and the right hemisphere

A growing body of evidence shows that the neural circuitry of the stress system is located in the early developing right brain, the hemisphere that is dominant for the control of vital functions that support survival and the human stress response (Wittling, 1997). Because stress coping strategies are deeply connected into essential organismic functions, they begin their maturation pre- and postnatally, a time of right brain dominance (Chiron et al., 1997). An MRI study of infants reported that the volume of the brain increases rapidly during the first two years, that normal adult appearance is seen at two years and all major fiber tracts can be identified by age three, and that infants under two years show higher right than left hemispheric volumes (Matsuzawa et al., 2001). Attachment experiences of the first two years thus directly influence the experiencedependent maturation of the right brain (Henry, 1993; Schore, 1994, 1996, 1997c, 2000c; Siegel, 1999; Wang, 1997). These include experiences with a traumatizing caregiver, which are well known to negatively impact the child's attachment security, stress coping strategies, and sense of self (Crittenden & Ainsworth, 1989; Erickson, Egeland, & Pianta, 1989).

Recent research is describing pediatric and maltreatment-related PTSD in children (Carrion et al., 2001, 2002; Beers & De Bellis, 2002). These studies in developmental traumatology concluded that "the overwhelming stress of maltreatment in childhood is associated with adverse influences on brain development" (De Bellis et al., 1999, p. 1281). This "maltreatment" specifically refers to the severe affect dysregulation of the two dominant forms of infant trauma – abuse and neglect. It is established that social stressors are far more detrimental than nonsocial aversive stimuli (Sgoifo et al., 1999), and therefore attachment or "relational trauma" from the social environment has more negative impact upon the infant brain than assaults from the nonhuman or inanimate, physical environment.

And so it is now being emphasized that specifically a dysfunctional and traumatized early *relationship* is the stressor that leads to PTSD, that severe trauma of interpersonal origin may override any genetic, constitutional, social, or psychological resilience factor, and that the ensuing adverse effects on brain development and alterations of the biological stress systems may be regarded as "an environmentally induced complex developmental disorder" (De Bellis, 2001). Furthermore, these relational perspectives on PTSD in early childhood emphasize the importance of understanding young children's traumatic responses in the context of their primary caregiving relationships. These efforts call for a deeper exploration of "the mechanism of how parental functioning impinges on child adaptation" (Scheeringa & Zeanah, 2001, p. 812).

The fact that early relational trauma is "ambient" clearly suggests that the infant is frequently experiencing not single-episode or acute stress, but cumulative and chronic unpredictable traumatic stress in his very first interactions with another human. The stress literature, which is investigating "determinants of individual differences in stress reactivity in early development" clearly shows that acute stress produces short-term and reversible deficits, while repeated, prolonged, chronic stress is associated with long-term patterns of autonomic reactivity, expressed in "neuronal structural changes, involving atrophy that might lead to permanent damage, including neuronal loss" (McEwen, 2000, p. 183). Consonant with this principle, in earlier writings I have suggested that early relational trauma has a significant negative impact on the experience-dependent maturation of the right brain, which is in a critical period of growth during the same temporal intervals as dyadic attachment experiences (Schore, 1994, 1997a, 1998e, 1998f, 1999d, 1999e, 2001c).

Because the early developing right hemisphere is, more so than the later maturing left, deeply interconnected into the autonomic, limbic, and arousal systems, it is dominant for the processing of social-emotional and bodily information (Devinsky, 2000; Schore, 1994, 2000b, 2001b). A large number of studies indicated that this hemisphere is dominant not only for the reception (Adolphs, Damasio, Tranel, & Damasios, 1996; Adolphs, 2002; Borod et al., 1998; George & Solomon, 1996; Keil et al., 2002; Nakamura et al., 1999; Pizzagalli et al., 2002), expression (Borod, Haywood, & Koff, 1997), and communication (Blonder, Bowers, & Heilman, 1991) of emotion, but also for the control of spontaneously evoked emotional reactions (Dimberg & Petterson, 2000), the modulation of "primary emotions" (Ross, Homan, & Buck, 1994), and the adaptive capacity for the regulation of affect (Schore, 1994, 1998a, 2001a).

It has been said that the most significant consequence of the stressor of early relational trauma is the lack of capacity for emotional self-regulation (Toth & Cicchetti,

1998), expressed in the loss of the ability to regulate the intensity and duration of affects (van der Kolk & Fisler, 1994). Basic developmental neuropsychobiological studies indicated that perinatal distress leads to a blunting of the stress regulating response of the right (and not left) prefrontal cortex that is manifest in adulthood (Brake, Sullivan, & Gratton, 2000; Sullivan & Gratton, 2002). In light of the essential role of the right hemisphere in the human stress response, this psychoneurobiological conception of trauma-induced right brain pathogenesis bears upon recent data which suggest that early adverse experiences result in an increased sensitivity to the effects of stress later in life and render an individual vulnerable to stress-related psychiatric disorders (Graham, Heim, Goodman, Miller, & Nemeroff, 1999). Affect dysregulation is now seen to be a fundamental mechanism of all psychiatric disorders (Taylor, Bagby, & Parker, 1997).

A developmental neuropsychopathological perspective dictates that to "understand neuropsychological development is to confront the fact that the brain is mutable, such that its structural organization reflects the history of the organism" (Luu & Tucker, 1996, p. 297). A history of early relational traumatic stress is specifically imprinted into the right brain, which is dominant for "autobiographical" (Fink et al., 1996) or "personal" (Nakamura et al., 2000) memory. Terr (1988) wrote that literal mirroring of traumatic events by behavioral memory can be established at any age, including infancy. In fact it is now thought that preverbal children, even in the first year of life, can establish and retain an internal representation of a traumatic event over significant periods of time (Gaensbauer, 2002), and that young children and adults are able to re-enact traumatic experiences that occurred in their infancy. This developmental model suggests that traumatic attachments, occurring in a critical period of organization of the right brain, will create an enduring vulnerability to dysfunction during stress and a predisposition to PTSDs.

Right brain dysregulation, dissociation, and PTSD pathogenesis: introduction

Indeed, in 1996 van der Kolk proposed that the symptoms of PTSD fundamentally reflect an impairment of the right brain, known to be dominant for inhibitory control (Garavan, Ross, & Stein, 1999). This hypothesis subsequently received experimental support in a number of studies (e.g., Rauch et al., 1996; Schuff et al., 1997; Shin et al., 1999; Spivak, Segal, Mester, & Weizman, 1998). In this same period, dysfunction of the frontal lobes, specifically the orbitofrontal system that is expanded in the right hemisphere (Falk et al., 1990) and controls instinctive emotional responses through cognitive processes, was also implicated in PTSD (Bremner et al., 1997; Charney, Deutch, Southwick, & Krystal, 1995; Deutch & Young, 1995; Semple et al., 1992). This line of research has continued in studies that show right hemispheric and orbitofrontal dysfunction in PTSD (e.g., Berthier, Posada, & Puentes, 2001; Galletly, Clark, McFarlane, & Weber, 2001; Koenen et al., 2001; Shin et al., 1999; Vasterling, Brailey, & Sutker, 2000).

The emotional disturbances of PTSD have been suggested to have their origins in the inability of the right prefrontal cortex to modulate amygdala functions (Hariri, Bookheimer, & Mazziotta, 2000; Schore, 1999f, 2001a, 2001c), especially activity of the right amygdala (Adamec, 1997), known to process frightening faces (Adolphs, Tranel, & Damasio, 2001; Whalen et al., 1998) and "unseen fear" (Morris, Ohman, & Dolan, 1999). Morgan and LeDoux (1995) conclude that, without orbital prefrontal feedback regarding the level of threat, the organism remains in an amygdala-driven defensive response state longer than necessary, that in humans, conditioned fear acquisition and extinction are associated with right hemisphere dominant amygdala function (La Bar, Gatenby, Gore, Le Doux, & Phelps, 1998), and that a defective orbitofrontal system operates in PTSD (Morgan, Romanski, & LeDoux, 1993).

We are also seeing a parallel interest in developmental research on the etiology of the primitive defense that is used to cope with overwhelming affective states – dissociation. In part this has been driven by PTSD models that suggest that individuals with a history of early childhood abuse may develop more dissociative responses to subsequent traumas (Bremner, 1999). From the perspective of developmental psychopathology, an outgrowth of attachment theory that conceptualizes normal and aberrant development in terms of common underlying mechanisms, dissociation is described as offering "potentially very rich models for understanding the ontogeny of environmentally produced psychiatric conditions" (Putnam, 1995, p. 582). Disorganized-disoriented insecure attachment, a primary risk factor for the development of psychiatric disorders (Main, 1996), has been specifically implicated in the etiology of the dissociative disorders (Barach, 1991; Liotti, 1992). Intriguingly, clinical psychiatric research suggests that specifically maternal dysfunction contributes to the etiology of adult dissociative psychopathology (Draijer & Langeland, 1999).

Neuroscience is beginning to delve into the neurobiology of dissociation, especially in infancy (Schore, 2001b, 2001e). It is now thought that dissociation at the time of exposure to extreme stress signals the invocation of neural mechanisms that result in long-term alterations in brain functioning (Chambers et al., 1999). This principle applies to long-term alterations in the developing brain, especially the early maturing right brain, the locus of dissociation (Lanius et al., 2002; Schore, 2001c; Weinberg, 2000), activation during acquisition of conditioned fear (Fisher et al., 2002), withdrawal and avoidance (Davidson & Hugdahl, 1995), and a spectrum of psychiatric disorders (Cutting, 1992; Schore, 1996, 1997a).

Traumatic attachment, dyregulation, and the pathogenesis of PTSD

Bowlby (1969) postulated that the major negative impact of early traumatic attachments is an alteration of the organism's normal developmental trajectory:

> [S]ince much of the development and organization of [attachment] behavioral systems takes place whilst the individual is immature, there are plenty of

occasions when an atypical environment can divert them from developing on an adaptive course.

(p. 130)

And sixty years earlier, Janet (1911) proposed:

> All [traumatized] patients seem to have the evolution of their lives checked; they are attached to an unsurmountable object. Unable to integrate traumatic memories, they seem to have lost their capacity to assimilate new experiences as well. It is . . . as if their personality development has stopped at a certain point, and cannot enlarge any more by the addition of new elements.
>
> *(p. 532)*

Janet further postulated that the psychological consequence of trauma is the breakdown of the adaptive mental processes leading to the maintenance of an integrated sense of self. Again, recent studies indicate that the right hemisphere is central to self-recognition (Keenan, Nelson, O'Connor, & Pascual-Leone, 2001) and the ability to maintain a coherent, continuous, and unified sense of self (Devinsky, 2000), but it also is the locus of various self-regulation pathologies (Schore, 1994, 1996, 1997c).

The concept of regulation – shared by the attachment, PTSD, neuroscience, and psychiatric literatures – may be a bridging concept for expanding a biopsychosocial model of psychiatry. According to Taylor et al. (1997):

> The concept of disorders of affect regulation is consistent with a growing realization in medicine and psychiatry that most illnesses and diseases are the result of dysregulations within the vast network of communicating systems that comprise the human organism.
>
> *(p. 270)*

A model of the interactive genesis of psychobiological dysregulation also supports and provides a deeper understanding of the diathesis-stress concept – that psychiatric disorders are caused by a combination of a genetic-constitutional predisposition and environmental or psychosocial stressors that activate the inborn neurophysiological vulnerability. The unique contributions of the intrinsic psychobiological perspective of trauma studies to both clinical psychiatry and neuroscience is articulated by McFarlane (2000):

> [T]he origins of psychiatry in medicine tie the discipline strongly to its biological roots. The field of traumatic stress has the potential to bridge this divide.
>
> *(p. 900)*

> Traumatic stress as a field, has the capacity to show the future direction of functional neurobiology.
>
> *(p. 901)*

In an editorial in the *American Journal of Psychiatry*, Rapoport (2000) called for deeper studies of the association between pre/perinatal adverse events or stressors and adult psychiatric outcomes. Toward that end, in the following I will suggest that recent theoretical models linking developmental affective neuroscience and attachment theory, updated basic research in biological psychiatry on stress mechanisms, and current advances in psychophysiology on the survival functions of the ANS may offer us a deeper understanding of the underlying mechanisms by which early childhood trauma massively dysregulates and thereby alters the developmental trajectory of the right hemisphere. This results in an immature personality organization with vulnerable coping capacities, one predisposed to the pathological hyperarousal and dissociation that characterizes PTSD at later points of stress. These psychoneurobiological models, which link infant, child, and adolescent psychiatry, are offered as heuristic proposals that can be evaluated by experimental and clinical research.

Overview of the neurobiology of a secure attachment

The essential task of the first year of human life is the creation of a secure attachment bond of emotional communication between the infant and the primary caregiver. In order to enter into this communication, the mother must be psychobiologically attuned to the dynamic crescendos and decescendos of the infant's bodily-based internal states of autonomic arousal. During the sequential signalling of play episodes, mother and infant show sympathetic cardiac acceleration and then parasympathetic deceleration in response to the smile of the other, and thus the language of mother and infant consist of signals produced by the autonomic, involuntary nervous system in both parties (Basch, 1976). The attachment relationship mediates the dyadic regulation of emotion (Sroufe, 1996), wherein the mother coregulates the infant's postnatally developing ANS. Also known as the "vegetative" nervous system (from the Latin *vegetare*, to animate or bring to life), it is responsible for the generation of what Stern (1985) called "vitality affects."

In heightened affective moments each partner learns the rhythmic structure of the other and modifies his or her behavior to fit that structure, thereby cocreating a specifically fitted interaction. In play episodes of affect synchrony, the pair are in affective resonance, and in such, an amplification of vitality affects and a positive state occurs especially when the mother's psychobiologically attuned external sensory stimulation frequency coincides with the infant's genetically encoded endogenous rhythms. And in moments of interactive repair the "good-enough" caregiver who induces a stress response in her infant through a misattunement, reinvokes in a timely fashion a reattunement, a regulation of the infant's negative state. Maternal sensitivity thus acts as an external organizer of the infant's biobehavioral regulation (Spangler, Schieche, Ilg, Maier, & Ackerman, 1994).

If attachment is the regulation of interactive synchrony, stress is defined as an asynchrony in an interactional sequence, and, following this, a period of reestablished synchrony allows for stress recovery and coping. The regulatory processes of affect synchrony that creates states of positive arousal and interactive repair that modulates states of negative arousal are the fundamental building blocks of attachment and its associated emotions, and resilience in the face of stress is an ultimate indicator of attachment security. Attachment, the outcome of the child's genetically encoded biological (temperamental) predisposition and the particular caregiver environment, thus represents the regulation of biological synchronicity between organisms, and imprinting, the learning process that mediates attachment, is defined as synchrony between sequential infant-maternal stimuli and behavior.

It is now thought that "attachment relationships are formative because they facilitate the development of the brain's major self-regulatory mechanisms" (Fonagy & Target, 2002, p. 328). The optimally regulated communications embedded in secure attachment experiences directly influence the maturation of both the post-natally maturing CNS limbic system that processes and regulates social-emotional stimuli and the ANS that generates the somatic aspects of emotion (Braun & Poeggel, 2001; Helmeke, Poeggel, & Braun, 2001; Ovtsharoff & Braun, 2001; Poeggel & Braun, 1996; Schore, 1994). The limbic system derives subjective information in terms of emotional feelings that guide behavior (MacLean, 1985), and functions to allow the brain to adapt to a rapidly changing environment and organize new learning (Mesulam, 1998). As mentioned, the higher regulatory systems of the right hemisphere form extensive reciprocal connections with the limbic system and ANS (Spence, Shapiro, & Zaidel, 1996; Tucker, 1992). Both the ANS and the CNS continue to develop postnatally, and the assembly of these limbic-autonomic circuits (Rinaman, Levitt, & Card, 2000) is directly influenced by the interactive regulatory transactions embedded in the attachment relationship (Schore, 1994, 2001a). In this manner, the internalized regulatory capacities of the infant develop in relation to the mother, and thus, as Bowlby suggested, the mother shapes the infant's stress coping systems.

Attachment and right cortical regulation of the autonomic nervous system

In his original formulation Bowlby (1969) described a neurophysiological control system that is centrally involved in regulating instinctive attachment behavior (Schore, 2000c, 2001d). In a number of writings, I indicated that this system is located in the right orbitofrontal area and its cortical and subcortical connections (Schore, 1994, 1996, 1998a, 2000a, 2000b, 2000c, 2001a). Due to its position at the interface of the cortex and subcortex, this ventromedial cortex sits at the hierarchical apex of the limbic system. This frontolimbic system directly connects into the subcortical reticular formation, thus regulating arousal, a central component of all emotional states. Its lateral and medial divisions process positive and negative emotions (Northoff et al., 2000). Indeed, this prefrontal system acts as the highest level of control of behavior, especially in relation to emotion (Price et al., 1996). Referred to as "the thinking part of the emotional brain," it is situated at the hierarchical apex of what is now refered to as the "rostral limbic system" (Devinsky, Morrell, & Vogt,

1995), or "anterior limbic prefrontal network" (Carmichael & Price, 1995), which also includes the anterior cingulate (medial frontal cortex) and the amygdala (see Schore, 2000b, 2001a). This "senior executive" of the social-emotional brain comes to act in the capacity of an executive control function for the entire right brain, the locus of what Devinsky (2000) called the "emotional self," and LeDoux (2002) termed the "implicit self."

But, in addition, the orbitofrontal cortex also represents the apex of the hierarchy of control of autonomic functions (Pribram, 1981). Due to its direct connections into the hypothalamus, the head ganglion of the ANS, it functions as a cortical control center of involuntary bodily functions that represent the somatic components of all emotional states, and acts to control autonomic responses associated with emotional events (Cavada, Company, Tejedor, Cruz-Rizzolo, & Reinoso-Suarez, 2000). Recent studies demonstrated that the right orbitofrontal cortex represents the highest level of organization for processing the interoceptive state, and thus is responsible for the subjective evaluation of the physiological condition of the entire body (Craig, 2002). Indeed, the right hemisphere is dominant for the regulation of selfrelated information and the corporeal self (Devinsky, 2000; Keenan et al., 2001; Ryan, Kuhl, & Deci, 1997; Schore, 1994).

In optimal early environments that promote secure attachments, a right-lateralized regulatory system organizes with a capacity to modulate, under stress, a flexible coping pattern of shifting out of autonomic balance into a coupled reciprocal autonomic mode of control in which homeostatic increases in the activity in one ANS division are associated with decreases in the other (Berntson, Cacioppo, & Quigley, 1991). The two components of the centrally regulated ANS are known to be distinct modular circuits that control arousal expressions, with the catabolic sympathetic branch responsible for energy-mobilizing excitatory activity and the anabolic parasympathetic branch involved in energy conserving inhibitory activity. These dissociable autonomic functions reflect the sympathetic catecholaminergic stimulation of glycogenolysis and parasympathetic vagal and cortisol stimulation of glycogenesis (Hilz, Tarnowski, & Arend, 1963; Shimazu, 1971; Shimazu & Amakawa, 1968).

In light of the fact that primordial representations of body states are the building blocks and scaffolding of development (Damasio, 1994), the current intense interest in emotional development is leading researchers to focus attention upon changes in bodily state, mediated by the ANS, that are crucial to ongoing emotional experience. The right hemisphere, dominant for somatosensory processing (Adolphs et al., 2001; Coghill, Gilron, & Iadorola, 2001), predominantly controls both sympathetic and parasympathetic activity (Erciyas, Topaktas, Akyuz, & Dener, 1999; Wittling, Block, Schweiger, & Genzel, 1998; Yoon, Morillo, Cechetto, & Hachinski, 1997). The ANS, by regulating the strength of the heartbeat and controlling vascular caliber, performs a critical role in ensuring that blood flow is adequate to supply oxygen and nutrients to the bodily organs and the brain, according to their relative needs.

A quick review of the ANS indicates that the sympathetic branch is activated by any stimulus above an orgasmic threshold, and that it functions to increase arousal, trigger an immediate anticipatory state, and rapidly mobilize resources in response to appraised stressors. Physiological activation is expressed in the conversion of glycogen to glucose and elevation of blood sugar for increased energy, quicker and stronger heart beat, increased blood supply to the muscles, dilation of bronchii and increases in breathing rate, dilation of the pupils, increased sweating, and speeding up of mental activity. The opposing parasympathetic branch has a higher threshold of activation and thus initiates its operations after the sympathetic, and its adaptive functions are expressed in slowing the heart rate, relaxing the muscles, lowering blood pressure, and pupillary constriction. Its operations allow for breathing to return to normal rates, increases in digestion, onset of bowel and bladder activities, and reestablishment of immune functions.

An autonomic mode of reciprocal sympathetic-parasympathetic control is behaviorally expressed in an organism that responds alertly and adaptively to a personally meaningful (especially social) stressor, yet as soon as the context is appraised as safe, immediately returns to the relaxed state of autonomic balance. The ANS is not only sensitive to environmental demands and perceived stresses and threats, but will, in a predictable order, also rapidly reorganize to different neural-mediated states (Porges, 2001). These ANS changes are regulated by "higher" limbic structures in the CNS. Indeed, the orbitofrontal cortex acts as a major center of CNS control over the sympathetic and parasympathetic branches of the ANS (Neafsey, 1990), and thereby regulates autonomic responses to social stimuli (Zald & Kim, 1996), the intuitive "gut feelings" that an individual has to other humans. These right-lateralized connections also mediate the adaptive capacity of empathically perceiving the emotional states of other human beings (Adolphs, Damasio, Tranel, Cooper, & Damasio, 2000; Schore, 1994, 1996, 2001a, 2001d).

The early forming right hemisphere stores an internal working model of the attachment relationship (Schore, 1994; Siegel, 1999) that determines the individual's characteristic strategies of affect regulation for coping and survival (Schore, 1994; Valent, 1998). This working model is encoded in implicit memory, which is primarily regulatory, automatized, and unconscious (Bargh & Chartrand, 1999) and right-lateralized (Hugdahl, 1995). This right frontal system thus plays a unique role in the regulation of motivational states and the adjustment or correction of emotional responses. It acts as a recovery mechanism that monitors and regulates the duration, frequency, and intensity of not only positive but negative affect states.

In the securely attached individual the representation of the attachment relationship with the primary caregiver encodes an implicit expectation that homeostatic disruptions will be set right, allowing the child to self-regulate functions which previously required the caregiver's external regulation. In this manner, emotion is initially regulated by others, but over the course of early development it becomes increasingly self-regulated as a result of neurophysiological development (Thompson, 1990). These adaptive capacities are central to self-regulation, the ability to flexibly regulate emotional states through interactions with other humans – interactive regulation in interconnected contexts, and without other humans – that is, auto-regulation in autonomous contexts.

The orbitofrontal system, shaped in its critical period by interpersonal attachment transactions, is fundamentally involved in the regulation of interpersonal behavior (Eslinger, 1999). This control system is specialized to play a critical role in strategic memory by supporting the early mobilization of effective behavioral strategies in novel or ambiguous situations (Savage et al., 2001). Operating at levels beneath awareness, it is activated when there is insufficient information available to determine the appropriate course of action, and is specialized to act in contexts of "uncertainty or unpredictability" (Elliott, Dolan, & Frith, 2000), an operational definition of stress. Efficient orbitofrontal operations organize the expression of a regulated emotional response and an appropriate motivational state for a particular social-environmental context, and in this fashion it contributes to "judicious, adapted behavior" (Cavada et al., 2000). Anatomical, electrophysiological, and imaging studies indicate that the orbitofrontal functions are central to "the integration of past, present, and future experiences, enabling adequate performance in behavioral tasks, social situations, or situations involving survival" (Lipton, Alvarez, & Eichenbaum, 1999, p. 356). As mentioned earlier, neuroscience research indicates that these same adaptive stress–survival capacities are severely impaired in infant, child, and adult with PTSDs.

The neurobiology of infant trauma

It is important to stress that the developmental attainment of an efficient internal system that can adaptively regulate various forms of arousal and psychobiological states, and thereby affect, cognition, and behavior, only evolves in a growth-facilitating emotional environment. The good-enough mother of the securely attached infant permits access to the child after a separation and shows a tendency to respond appropriately and promptly to his/her emotional expressions. She also allows for the interactive generation of high levels of positive affect in shared play states. These regulated events allow for an expansion of the child's coping capacities, and account for the principle that security of the attachment bond is the primary defense against trauma-induced psychopathology.

In contrast to this scenario is a relational growth-inhibiting early environment, in which the abusive caregiver not only shows less play with her infant, but also induces traumatic states of enduring negative affect in the child. Because her attachment is weak, she provides little protection against other potential abusers of the infant, such as the father. This caregiver is inaccessible and reacts to her infant's expressions of emotions and stress inappropriately and/or rejectingly, and therefore shows minimal or unpredictable participation in the various types of arousal regulating processes. Instead of modulating, she induces extreme levels of stimulation and arousal, very high in abuse and/or very low in neglect. And because she provides no interactive repair, the infant's intense negative states last for long periods of time.

The enduring detrimental effects of parent-inflicted trauma on the attachment bond is now well-established:

> The continued survival of the child is felt to be at risk, because the actuality of the abuse jeopardizes (the) primary object bond and challenges the child's capacity to trust and, therefore, to securely depend.
>
> *(Davies & Frawley, 1994, p. 62).*

Freyd (1996), describing the effects of childhood abuse and attachment, referred to "betrayal trauma theory." In contexts of relational trauma, the caregiver(s), in addition to dysregulating the infant, withdraws any repair functions, leaving the infant for long periods in an intensely disruptive psychobiological state that is beyond her immature coping strategies. In studies of a neglect paradigm, Tronick and Weinberg (1997) described:

> When infants are not in homeostatic balance or are emotionally dysregulated (e.g., they are distressed), they are at the mercy of these states. Until these states are brought under control, infants must devote all their regulatory resources to reorganizing them. While infants are doing that, they can do nothing else.
>
> *(p. 56)*

The "nothing else" these authors refer to is a failure to continue to develop. These infants forfeit potential opportunities for socioemotional learning during critical periods of right brain development (Schore, 2001c).

Indeed, we now know that trauma causes biochemical alterations within the developing brain (Bremner et al., 1999; Schore, 1997a). The infant's psychobiological response to trauma comprises two separate response patterns, hyperarousal and dissociation (Perry, Pollard, Blakely, Baker, & Vigilante, 1995; Schore, 2001c), the same two responses of adult PTSD (Bremner, 1999). In the initial stage of threat, a startle or an alarm reaction is initiated, in which the sympathetic component of the ANS is suddenly and significantly activated, resulting in increased heart rate, blood pressure, and respiration. Distress is expressed in crying and then screaming. In very recent work, this dyadic transaction is described by Beebe (2000) as "mutually escalating over arousal" of a disorganized attachment pair:

> Each one escalates the ante, as the infant builds to a frantic distress, may scream, and, in this example, finally throws up. In an escalating over arousal pattern, even after extreme distress signals from the infant, such as ninety-degree head aversion, arching away . . . or screaming, the mother keeps going.
>
> *(p. 436)*

The infant's state of "frantic distress," or what Perry and colleagues (1995) termed fear-terror is mediated by sympathetic hyperarousal, expressed in increased levels of the brain's major stress hormone, corticotropin-releasing factor, which in turn regulates sympathetic catecholamine activity (Brown et al., 1982), and so brain adrenaline, noradrenaline, and dopamine levels are significantly elevated. Noradrenaline is also released from the locus coeruleus (AstonJones, Valentino, Van Bockstaele, & Meyerson, 1996; Butler, Weiss, Stout, & Nemeroff, 1990; Svensson, 1987). The resultant rapid and intensely elevated catecholamine levels trigger a hypermetabolic state within the developing brain. Catecholamines are among the first neurochemicals to respond to stressors in response to perceived threat, and repeated stress triggers their persistent activation (Sabban & Kvetnansky, 2001). Prolonged stress and elevated levels of catecholamines in turn induce high levels of thyroid hormones that accompany hyperarousal (Galton, 1965; Wang, 1997). Thyroid hormones are known to be active agents in brain differentiation and in the regulation of critical period phenomena (Nunez, 1984; Lauder & Krebs, 1986; see Schore, 1994).

Furthermore, increased amounts of vasopressin are expressed, a hypothalamic neuropeptide associated with sympathetic activation (Kvetnansky et al., 1989, 1990). This condition is specifically triggered when an environment is perceived to be unsafe and challenging, and resultant high levels of vasopressin potentiate immobilization responses via sympathetic activation, behaviorally expressed as fear (Porges, 2001). Interestingly, high levels of this neuropeptide are associated with nausea (Koch, Summy-Long, Bingaman, Sperry, & Stern, 1990), a finding that may explain the hyperarousal behaviors observed by Beebe. In addition, when the body of the abused infant is physically assaulted, she is in pain, another state accompanied by sympathetic hyperarousal.

But a second later-forming reaction to infant trauma is seen in dissociation, in which the child disengages from stimuli in the external world and attends to an internal world. The child's dissociation in the midst of terror involves numbing, avoidance, compliance, and restricted affect (the same pattern as adult PTSD). Traumatized infants are observed to be "staring off into space with a glazed look." This behavioral strategy is described by Tronick and Weinberg (1997):

> [W]hen infants' attempts fail to repair the interaction infants often lose postural control, withdraw, and self-comfort. The disengagement is profound even with this short disruption of the mutual regulatory process and break in intersubjectivity. The infant's reaction is reminiscent of the withdrawal of Harlow's isolated monkey or of the infants in institutions observed by Bowlby and Spitz.
>
> *(p. 66)*

This parasympathetic dominant state of conservation-withdrawal occurs in helpless and hopeless stressful situations in which the individual becomes inhibited and strives to avoid attention in order to become "unseen" (Schore, 1994, 2001c). This metabolic shutdown state is a primary regulatory process, used throughout the life span, in which the stressed individual passively disengages in order "to conserve energies . . . to foster survival by the risky posture of feigning death, to allow healing of wounds and restitution of depleted resources by immobility" (Powles, 1992,

p. 213). It is this parasympathetic mechanism that mediates the "profound detach-ment" (Barach, 1991) of dissociation. If early trauma is experienced as "psychic catastrophe" (Bion, 1962), dissociation represents "detachment from an unbearable situation" (Mollon, 1996), "the escape when there is no escape" (Putnam, 1995), and "a last resort defensive strategy" (Dixon, 1998).

Most importantly, the neurobiology of the later-forming dissociative reaction is different than the initial hyperarousal response. In this passive state, pain numbing and blunting endogenous opiates (Fanselow, 1986; Liberzon et al., 2002; Zubieta et al., 2002) and behavior-inhibiting stress hormones, such as cortisol, are elevated. Furthermore, activity of the dorsal vagal complex in the brain stem medulla increases dramatically, decreasing blood pressure, metabolic activity, and heart rate, despite increases in circulating adrenaline. This elevated parasympathetic arousal, a survival strategy (Porges, 1997), allows the infant to maintain homeostasis in the face of the internal state of sympathetic hyperarousal.

It is now known that there are two parasympathetic vagal systems that lower heart rate (Cheng, & Powley, 2000; Cheng, Powley, Schwaber, & Doyle, 1999), a late developing mammalian or "smart" system in the nucleus ambiguous which allows for the ability to communicate via facial expressions, vocalizations, and gestures via contingent social interactions, and a more primitive early developing reptil-lian or "vegetative" system in the dorsal motor nucleus of the vagus that acts to shut down metabolic activity during immobilization, death feigning, and hiding behaviors (Porges, 1997, 2001). Porges described that as opposed to the ventral vagal complex that can rapidly regulate cardiac output to foster engagament and disengagement with the social environment, the dorsal vagal complex "contributes to severe emotional states and may be related to emotional states of 'immobilization' such as extreme terror" (1997, p. 75). Perry and colleagues' (1995) description of the traumatized infant's sudden state switch from sympathetic hyperarousal into parasympathetic dissociation was reflected in Porges's (1997) characterization of:

> the sudden and rapid transition from an unsuccessful strategy of struggling requiring massive sympathetic activation to the metabolically conservative immobilized state mimicking death associated with the dorsal vagal complex.
>
> *(p. 75)*

Meares (1999) also concluded that in all stages "dissociation, at its first occurrence, is a consequence of a 'psychological shock' or high arousal" (p. 1853). Notice that in the traumatic state, and this may be of long duration, both the sympathetic energy-expending and parasympathetic energy-conserving components of the infant's developing ANS are hyperactivated.

Disorganized/disoriented attachment neuropsychology

The next question is, how would the trauma-induced neurobiological and psychobi-ological alterations of the developing right brain be expressed in the socioemotional behavior of an early traumatized toddler? In a classic study, Main and Solomon (1986) studied the attachment patterns of infants who had suffered trauma in the first year of life. This lead to the discovery of a new attachment category, type D, an insecure-disorganized/disoriented pattern, found in 80% of maltreated infants (Carlson, Cicchetti, Barnett, & Braunwald, 1989). Indeed, this group of toddlers exhibits higher cortisol levels and higher heart rates than all other attachment classifications (Hertsgaard, Gunnar, Erickson, & Nachmias, 1995; Spangler & Grossman, 1999).

Main and Solomon concluded that these infants are experiencing low stress tolerance and that the disorganization and disorientation reflect the fact that the infant, instead of finding a haven of safety in the relationship, is alarmed by the parent. They note that because the infant inevitably seeks the parent when alarmed, any parental behavior that directly alarms an infant should place it in an irresolvable paradox in which it can neither approach, shift its attention, or flee. At the most basic level, these infants are unable to generate a coherent behavioral coping strategy to deal with this emotional challenge.

Main and Solomon documented, in some detail, the uniquely bizarre behaviors these 12-month-old infants show in strange situation observations. They note that these episodes of interruptions of organized behavior are often brief, frequently lasting only 10–30 seconds, yet they are highly significant. For example, they show a simultaneous display of contradictory behavior patterns, such as "backing" toward the parent rather than approaching face-to-face.

> The impression in each case was that approach movements were continually being inhibited and held back through simultaneous activation of avoidant tendencies. In most cases, however, proximity-seeking sufficiently "overrode" avoidance to permit the increase in physical proximity. Thus, contradictory patterns were activated but were not mutually inhibited.
>
> *(Main & Solomon, 1986, p. 117)*

Notice the simultaneous activation of the energy-expending sympathetic and energy-conserving parasympathetic components of the ANS.

Maltreated infants also show evidence of apprehension and confusion, as well as very rapid shifts of state during the stress-inducing strange situation:

> One infant hunched her upper body and shoulders at hearing her mother's call, then broke into extravagent laugh-like screeches with an excited forward movement. Her braying laughter became a cry and distress-face without a new intake of breath as the infant hunched forward. Then suddenly she became silent, blank and dazed.
>
> *(Main & Solomon, 1986, p. 119).*

These behaviors generalize beyond just interactions with the mother. The intensity of the baby's dysregulated affective state is often heightened when the infant is exposed to the added stress of an unfamiliar person. At a stranger's entrance, two infants moved away from both mother and stranger to face the wall, and another "leaned fore head against the wall for several seconds, looking back in apparent terror" (p. 120).

These infants exhibit "behavioral stilling" – that is, dazed behavior and depressed affect, behavioral manifestations of dissociation. One infant "became for a moment excessively still, staring into space as though completely out of contact with self, environment, and parent" (p. 120). Another showed "a dazed facial appearance . . . accompanied by a stilling of all body movement, and sometimes a freezing of limbs which had been in motion" (p. 120). Yet another "fell face-down on the floor in a depressed posture prior to separation, stilling all body movements" (p. 120).

Furthermore, Main and Solomon pointed out that the type D behaviors take the form of stereotypes that are found in neurologically impaired infants. These behaviors are overt manifestations of an obviously impaired regulatory system, one that rapidly disorganizes under stress. Notice that these observations are taking place at 12 to 18 months, a critical period of corticolimbic maturation (Schore, 1994), and they reflect a severe structural impairment of the orbitofrontal control system that is involved in attachment behavior and state regulation. The orbitofrontal areas specialize in encoding information (Frey & Petrides, 2000), especially information contained in emotionally expressive faces and voices, including angry and fearful faces (Elliott et al., 2000; Kawasaki et al., 2001).

The mother's face is the most potent visual stimulus in the child's world, and it is well known that direct gaze can mediate not only loving but powerful aggressive messages. In coding the mother's frightening behavior, Hess and Main described "in non-play contexts, stiff-legged 'stalking' of infant on all fours in a hunting posture; exposure of canine tooth accompanied by hissing; deep growls directed at infant" (1999, p. 511). Thus, during the trauma, the infant is presented with an aggressive expression on the mother's face. The image of this aggressive face, as well as the chaotic alterations in the infant's bodily state that are associated with it, are indelibly imprinted into limbic circuits as a "flashbulb memory," and thereby stored in imagistic procedural memory in the visuospatial right hemisphere, the locus of implicit (Hugdahl, 1995) and autobiographical (Fink et al., 1996) memory.

But in traumatic episodes the infant is presented with another affectively overwhelming facial expression, a maternal expression of fear-terror. Main and Solomon noted that this occurs when the mother withdraws from the infant as though the infant were the source of the alarm, and they report that dissociated, trancelike, and fearful behavior is observed in parents of type D infants. Studies have shown a link between frightening maternal behavior and disorganized infant attachment (Schuengel, Bakersmans-Kranenburg, & Van Ijzendoorn, 1999).

I suggest that during these episodes the infant is matching the rhythmic structures of the mother's dysregulated states, and that this synchronization is registered in the firing patterns of the stress-sensitive corticolimbic regions of the infant's brain that are in a critical period of growth. In light of the fact that many of these mothers have suffered from unresolved trauma themselves, this spatiotemporal imprinting of the chaotic alterations of the mother's dysregulated state facilitates the down-loading of programs of psychopathogenesis, a context for the intergenerational transmission of trauma. This represents a fundamental mechanism by which maladaptive parental behavior mediates the association between parental and offspring psychiatric symptoms (Johnson, Cohen, Kasen, Smailes, &Brook, 2001), and parental PTSD and parental trauma exposure impact the child's development of a risk factor for PTSD (Yehuda, Halligan, & Grossman, 2001). PTSD, defined by the *DSM-IV* as "actual or threatened death or serious injury, or threat to the physical integrity of the individual" that invokes "feelings of horror and intense fear"(APA, 1994), thus occurs in the nonverbal infant.

Impact of relational trauma on right brain development

In an early history of traumatic attachment, the developing infant/toddler is too frequently exposed to a massively misattuning primary caregiver who triggers and does not repair long-lasting intensely dysregulated states. These negative states reflect severe biochemical alterations in the rapidly maturing right brain, and because they occur during the brain growth spurt which ends in the second year (Dobbing & Sands, 1973; Ferrie et al., 1999), the effect of ambient cumulative trauma is enduring. In the infant brain, states become traits (Perry et al., 1995), and so the effects of early relational trauma as well as the defenses against such trauma are embedded into the core structure of the evolving personality. According to Bowlby (1969), the effect of an atypical environment is that development is diverted from its adaptive course. This leads to the question, what do we now know about the psychopathomorphogenetic mechanisms that underlie such deflections of normal structural development?

The developing infant is maximally vulnerable to non-optimal environmental events in the period of most rapid brain growth. During these critical periods of genetically encoded synapse overproduction followed by environmentally driven synapse elimination, the organism is sensitive to conditions in the external environment, and if these are outside the normal range a permanent or semi-permanent arrest of development occurs. Of particular importance is the identification of various stressful growth-inhibiting environments that negatively influence the critical period of organization of limbic cortical and subcortical connections that mediate homeostatic self-regulatory and attachment systems. Disruption of attachment bonds in infant trauma leads to a regulatory failure, expressed in an impaired autonomic homeostasis, disturbances in limbic activity, and hypothalamic and reticular formation dysfunction. Intense stress modulates transcriptional regulation of gene expression in the developing brain (Hatalski & Baram, 1997; Mayer et al., 2002). Hyperaroused attachment stressors are correlated with elevated levels of the arousal regulating catecholamines and hyperactivation of the excitotoxic N-methyl-D-aspartate (NMDA)-sensitive glutamate receptor, a critical site of neurotoxicity and synapse elimination in early development (Chaparro-Huerta, Rivera-Cervantes, Torres-Mendoza, & BeasZárate, 2002; Guilarte, 1998; McDonald, Silverstein, & Johnston, 1988).

The relational trauma of infant abuse also triggers significant alterations in the major stress regulating neurochemicals, corticotropin-releasing factor (which induces catecholamines) and the glucocorticoid, cortisol, especially in the right hemisphere that is dominant for the secretion of these hormones (Kalogeras et al., 1996; Wittling & Pfluger, 1990). Yehuda pointed out that the actions of these two systems are synergistic: "where as catecholamines facilitate the availability of energy to the body's vital organs, cortisol's role in stress is to help contain, or shut down sympathetic activation" (1999, p. 257). It is well-established that stress hormones are protective in the short run and yet cause damage when they are overproduced or not shut off when no longer needed (McEwen, 2000). These is a large body of basic research to show that both stress hormones are regulated (for better or worse) within the mother-infant relationship (Gunnar & Donzella, 2002; Schore, 1994).

In situations where the caregiver routinely does not participate in reparative functions that reestablish homeostasis, the resulting psychobiological disequilibrium is expressed in a dysregulated and potentially toxic brain chemistry, especially in limbic areas that are in a critical period of synaptogenesis. Indeed, this same interaction between high levels of catecholamines, excitatory transmitters, and corticosteroids is now thought to mediate programmed cell death, and to represent a primary etiological mechanism for the pathophysiology of neuropsychiatric disorders. (See Schore, 1997a, 2001c for a detailed account of trauma-induced altered calcium metabolism and oxidative stress damage in neurons and astroglia in the developing brain, and Schore, 1994, 1997a for free radical damage of brain mitochondria.)

But in addition, when the attachment trauma exhausts the infant's active coping mechanisms, she shifts into hypoarousal and accesses the ultimate survival strategy, dissociation, "a submission and resignation to the inevitability of overwhelming, even psychically deadening danger" (Davies & Frawley, 1994). If this primary metabolic shutdown becomes a chronic condition, it will have devastating effects on the morphogenesis of limbic structures. Dissociation and conservation-withdrawal, functional expressions of heightened dorsal vagal activity, induce an extreme alteration of the bioenergetics of the developing brain. During critical periods of regional synaptogenesis this would have growth-inhibiting effects, especially in the right brain which specializes in withdrawal and contains a vagal circuit of emotion regulation (Davidson & Hugdahl, 1995; Porges, Doussard-Roosevelt, & Maiti, 1994). This is because the biosynthetic processes that mediate the proliferation of synaptic connections in the postnatally developing brain demand, in addition to sufficient quantities of essential nutrients, massive amounts of energy (Schore, 1994, 1997a, 2000b). An infant brain that is chronically shifting into hypometabolic survival modes and decreased heart rate has little energy available for brain growth.

In describing the dorsal vagal complex, Porges (2001) stated that when all else fails, the nervous system elects a metabolically conservative course; this strategy may be adaptive in the short-term, but lethal if maintained. He also noted that high levels of dorsal vagal activation are associated with potentially life-threatening bradycardia, apnea, and cardiac arrhythmias. This may describe stresses on the infant's cardiovascular during and after relational trauma. I have suggested that in the developing brain this "lethality' is expressed in intensified apoptotic cell death in "affective centers" in the limbic system (Schore, 1997a, 2001c). The neonatal brain is much more prone to excitoxicity than the adult brain, and apoptotic neurodegeneration following trauma is markedly enhanced in the immature brain (Bittigau et al., 1999; Johnston, 2001; Portera-Cailliau, Price, & Martin, 1997).

As opposed to the excitotoxic cell death associated with elevated levels of corticosteroids, prolonged and intense dorsal vagal activity may be associated with profoundly low corticosteroid levels, also known to impair brain development in limbic structures (Gould, Wooley, & McEwen, 1991). Hypocortisolism develops subsequent to extended periods of elevated cortisol in response to trauma, and adverse conditions in early life that induce elevated levels of cortisol are now proposed to contribute to the development of hypocortisolism in adulthood (Gunnar & Vazquez, 2001), a known predictor of PTSD (Yehuda, McFarlane, & Shalev, 1998). Recall that abused type D infants show higher cortisol levels than all other attachment classifications (Hertsgaard, Gunnar, Erickson, & Nachmias, 1995). It should be pointed out that infants raised in a neglectful environment show a low cortisol pattern of circadian cortisol production (Gunnar & Vazquez, 2001). This suggests different neurobiological impairments and neurophysiological deficits in the two types of infant trauma – abuse and neglect.

In other words, a caregiver's dysregulating effect on the infant's internal state, and her poor capacity to psychobiologically regulate excessive levels of high and/or low arousal negative affect, defines a pathomorphogenetic influence. Structural limitations in the mother's emotion processing right brain are reflected in a poor ability to comfort and regulate her child's affective states, and these experiences, central to the intergenerational transmission of psychopathology, are stamped into the insecurely attached infant's right orbitofrontal system and its cortical and subcortical connections. Stuss and Alexander (1999) described that experiences are "affectively burnt in" the right frontal lobe. Harkness and Tucker (2000) stated that the early traumatic experiences of childhood abuse literally kindle limbic areas. In this manner, severe early adverse developmental experiences may imprint "neurological scars" (Poeggel et al., 1999) that leave behind a permanent physiological activity in limbic areas of the brain (Post, Weiss, & Leverich, 1994), thereby inhibiting its capacity to cope with future stressors.

In light of the fact that males, due to delayed rates of cerebral maturation, are more susceptible than females to a large number of conditions that impair the developing brain, and that the limbic system of males and females show different connectivity patterns, gender differences in developmental traumatology must be considered. These factors indicate that by nature of their CNS and ANS immaturity, males may be more susceptible to relational abuse, and that the dysregulation of early abused males is psychobiologically biased more toward hyperarousal, while females are biased more toward dissociation. These would endure as permanent limbic reactivities that underlie gender predispositions to externalizing and internalizing disorders.

The infant PTSD episodes of hyperarousal and dissociation imprint the template for later childhood, adolescent, and adult PTSDs, all of which show disturbances of autonomic arousal (Prins, Kaloupek, & Keane, 1995), abnormal catecholaminergic function (Geracioti et al., 2001; Southwick et al., 1993), neurologic soft signs (Gurvits et al., 2000), and dissociation (Schore, 2001c). This would be symptomatically expressed as a cycling between intrusive hypersympathetically driven terrifying flashbacks and traumatic images and parasympathetically driven dissociation, avoidance, and numbing. More recent models of PTSD refer to stressor-induced oscillations between traumatic and avoidant states, and cycling between the bidirectional symptoms of emotional re-experiencing and emotional constrictedness (Antelman et al., 1997).

Trauma-induced excessive pruning of right brain circuits

Even more specifically, social-emotional environments that provide traumatizing attachment histories retard the experience-dependent development of frontolimbic regions, especially the right cortical areas that are prospectively involved in affect regulating functions. These descending projections from the prefrontal cortex to subcortical structures are known to mature during infancy (Bouwmeester, Smits, & van Ree, 2002; Nair, Berndt, Barrett, & Gonzalez-Lima, 2001), and relational traumatic experiences could induce a severe and extensive pruning of higher limbic connections (orbitofrontal, anterior cingulate, and amygdala) into the arousal centers in the reticular formation and autonomic centers in the hypothalamus via a "kindling" (Post & Weiss, 1997) mechanism.

Relational trauma-induced developmental overpruning of a corticolimbic system, especially one that contains a genetically encoded underproduction of synapses, represents a scenario for high-risk conditions. It is now established that psychological factors "prune" or "sculpt" neural networks in the postnatal brain. In earlier works, I have suggested that excessive pruning of hierarchical cortical-subcortical circuits operates in the etiology of a vulnerability to later extreme disorders of affect regulation (Schore, 1994, 1996, 1997a, 2001c). In the last decade, a growing body of neurobiological research on PTSD has uncovered dysfunctional frontal-subcortical systems (Sutker, Vasterling, Brailey, & Allain, 1995; Uddo, Vasterling, Brailey, & Sutker, 1993), and altered functional activity of the orbitofrontal cortex (Berthier et al., 2001; Bremner et al., 1997; Galletly et al., 2001; Koenen et al., 2001; Shin et al., 1999), anterior cingulate (Bremner et al., 1999; Hamner, Lorberbaum, & George, 1999; Lanius et al., 2001; Schin et al., 2001), and amygdala (Rauch et al., 1996). This represents an uncoupling of components of the rostral limbic system.

An extensive parcellation of axonal-dendritic connections between orbitofrontal and catecholaminergic areas of the midbrain and medullary reticular formation would lead to a predisposition for arousal dysregulation under stress. At the same time, severe pruning of its hypothalamic connections would lead to inefficient regulation of the ANS by higher centers in the CNS (Schore 1997c, 2001c), functionally expressed in a dissociation of central regulation of sympathetic and hypothalamic-pituitary-adrenal systems (Young, Rosa, & Landsberg, 1984). The orbitofrontal cortex, in normal circumstances, represents the apex of a hierarchy of control of autonomic functions. Recall that this system is specialized to show a flexible response in stressful contexts of uncertainty. A loss of these functions means that under stress a coupled reciprocal mode of autonomic control would give way to a coupled nonreciprocal mode of autonomic control, resulting in an intensely high state of sympathetic plus parasympathetic arousal. Severe dysregulation of both central and autonomic arousal is a hallmark of PTSDs.

The right orbitofrontal cortex is thought to act as the neural basis by which humans control their instinctive emotional responses through cognitive processes, and the emotional disturbances of PTSD are now proposed to have their origins in the inability of the right prefrontal cortex to modulate amygdala functions (Hariri et al., 2000). What could be the origin of a defective "rostral limbic system"? The answer may lie in early development. Amygdala-driven aversive conditioning has been shown to operate in the early attachment to an abusive caregiver (Sullivan, Landers, Yeaman, & Wilson, 2000).

Over the course of postnatal development, connections between the orbitofrontal cortex and amygdala increase (Bouwmeester, Wolterink, & van Ree, 2002), and this hierarchical organization allows this prefrontal system to take over amygdala functions (Rolls, 1996), and for the right frontotemporal cortex to maintain inhibitory control over intense emotional arousal (Kinsbourne & Bemporad, 1984). But early traumatic attachment intensifies the parcellation of these right-lateralized connections, and so in PTSDs, when orbitofrontal inhibitory control is lost, activity of the right amygdala (Adamec, 1999), known to nonconsciously process frightening faces (Whalen et al., 1998) and "unseen fear" (Morris et al., 1999), drives the right brain system. Work on the neurobiology of stress suggests that chronic stress contributes to atrophy of specifically the prefrontal cortex and amygdala (McEwen, 2000).

It is established that a pathological response to stress reflects the functions of a hyperexcitable amygdala (Halgren, 1992), that fear-potentiation of startle is mediated through the amygdala (Angrilli et al., 1996), which directly projects to the brainstem startle center (Davis, 1989), and that the memory processes of the amygdala are amplified by extreme stress (Corodimas, LeDoux, Gold, & Schulkin, 1994). These amygdala-driven startle and fear-freeze responses would be intense, because they are totally unregulated by the orbitofrontal (and medial frontal) areas that are unavailable for the correction and adjustment of emotional responses. Loss of modulating function of the right anterior cingulate, anterior and inferior to the amygdala, would interfere with its known role in inducing a relaxation of bodily states of sympathetic arousal (Critchley, Melmed, Featherstone, Mathias, & Dolan, 2001). In poorly evolved right brain systems of PTSD vulnerable personalities, even low intensity interpersonal stressors could activate unmodulated terrifying and painful bodily-based dysregulated experiences of the individual's early history that are imprinted into amygdala-hypothalamic limbic-autonomic circuits. According to Valent (1998), early handling and misattunements may be deeply remembered physiologically in later life in the form of disconnected physiological responses, emotions, and acting out, a description that mirrors Van der Kolk's (1996) assertion that "the body keeps the score."

In light of the findings that autonomic changes in the body are evoked when angry facial expressions are subliminally presented at levels beneath awareness to the right and not the left hemisphere (Johnsen & Hugdahl, 1991), and that the right amygdala is preferentially activated by briefly presented, subliminal faces (Morris et al., 1998) and specialized for the expression of memory of aversively motivated experiences (Coleman-Mensches & McGaugh, 1995), I suggest that subliminal (Mogg, Bradley, Williams, & Mathews, 1993) visual and auditory stressors emanating from faces, processed in an inefficient right hemisphere, the locus of the startle mechanism (Bradley, Cuthbert, & Lang, 1996), are potent triggers of dysregulation and dissociation in early traumatized patients. Of special importance is the very rapid right brain perception (Braeutigam, Bailey, & Swithenby, 2001; Funayama, Grillon, Davis, & Phelps, 2001; Nakamura et al., 1999) and memory retrieval (Funnell, Corballis, & Gazzaniga, 2001; Keil et al., 2002; Simons, Graham, Owen, Patterson, & Hodges, 2001) of visual images and prosodic tones of voice that emanate from subjectively perceived threatening and humiliating faces (Schore, 1994, 2001c, 2002a).

These neuropsychological deficits in social cognition underlie the severe interpersonal difficulties in PTSD patients. It is often overlooked that such individuals experience severe social-emotional deficits, including problems in self-disclosure, intimacy, and affection, as well as in the control of interpersonal hostility and aggression (Beckham et al., 1996; Calhoun, Beckham, & Bosworth, 2002; Carroll, Foy, Cannon, & Zwier, 1991). The orbital frontolimbic cortex is centrally involved in not only the regulation of interpersonal behavior (Eslinger, 1999) but also in the regulation of aggression (Schore, 1994). Impairments of the right orbitofrontal region are known to be associated with violence (Blair & Cipolotti, 2000; Raine et al., 2001). The rapid shifts in mood, aggressive impulses, and interpersonal violence (Beckham, Feldman, Kirby, Hertzberg, & Moore, 1997; Savarese, Suvak, King, & King, 2001; Yehuda, 1999) in PTSD patients thus may trace back to early relational trauma-induced limbic dysfunction.

Furthermore, the right, as opposed to the left, amygdala is activated when the individual is not consciously aware of the aversive nature of a nonverbal eliciting stimulus, one that still triggers an immediate negative representation (Phelps et al., 2001). Loss of function of the right anterior cingulate would preclude its function in attentional processes (Casey et al., 1997). Loss of higher orbital corticolimbic regulation would lead to a deficit in distinguishing between mental representations of ongoing reality and currently irrelevant memories (Schnider, Treyer, & Buck, 2000). When dissociated from these "top-down" influences, an "exaggerated amygdala" response to masked facially expressed fearful reminders of traumatic events occurs in PTSD patients (Rauch et al., 2000).

It is well-established that individuals with PTSD show a selective memory and attention for trauma-related experiences (Reynolds & Brewin, 1998). Much has been written about the memory mechanisms of PTSD, and until recently the focus has been upon deficits in hippocampal function and impairments of conscious explicit memory. Stress-induced elevations of cortisol impair declarative memory

(Kirschbaum, Wolf, May, Wippich, & Hellhammer, 1996). But PTSD models are shifting from the later-developing hippocampus to the early developing amygdala, from "cool" to "hot" memory systems (Metcalfe & Jacobs, 1998), from the explicit memory of places to the implicit memory of faces. Very recent research demonstrates that chronic stress induces contrasting patterns of dendritic remodeling in hippocampal and amygdaloid neurons, leading to a loss of hippocampal inhibitory control as well as a gain of excitatory control by the amygdala, and thereby an imbalance in HPA axis function (Vyas, Mitra, Shankaranarayana Rao, & Chattarji, 2002).

This work is complemented by current neuropsychological models of PTSD which suggest that amygdala inhibition of hippocampal function at high levels of arousal mediates the diminution of conscious explicit memory in peritraumatic events (Layton & Krikorian, 2002). These neurobiological mechanisms may account for the retention of implicit memory yet amnesia for the explicit memory of the traumatic event (Krikorian & Layton, 1998). Indeed, the amygdala is centrally involved in the consolidation of the traumatic experience and in the storage of perceptual implicit memory for trauma-related information (McNally & Amir, 1996). Recall that the right amygdala is activated in experiences of "unseen fear" (Morris et al., 1999) and that this hemisphere is specialized for the processing of implicit memory (Hugdahl, 1995).

Thus, in peritraumatic flashback moments, a right subcortically-driven traumatic re-enactment encoded in implicit memory would occur in the form of a strong physiological autonomic dysregulation and highly aversive motivational state for "no apparent reason." In other words, the person would not be aware that his fear has any origin in space, place, and time. This bears upon McFarlane and Yehuda's observation, "Essentially, the core of traumatic syndromes is the capacity of current environmental triggers (real or symbolic), to provoke the intense recall of affectively charged traumatic memory structures, which come to drive current behaviour and perception" (2000, p. 900). I would add that a focus on cumulative relational instead of "single-hit" trauma emphasizes that the traumatic event of the PTSD patient originated as a personal and social process, thereby suggesting that the "affectively charged traumatic memory" is not of a specific overwhelming experience with the physical environment as much as a reevocation of a prototypical disorganized attachment transaction with the misattuning social environment that triggers an intense arousal dysregulation. The right brain, at nonconscious levels, both appraises trauma-related conditioned social stimuli and (re-)organizes the traumatic "conditioned emotional response" (Kolb & Multipassi, 1982).

Indeed, there is evidence that early relational trauma is particularly expressed in right hemisphere deficits. Studies revealed that maltreated children diagnosed with PTSD manifest right-lateralized metabolic limbic abnormalites (De Bellis, Casey, et al., 2000; De Bellis et al., 2002a) and smaller right temporal lobe volumes (De Bellis et al., 2002b), and that right brain impairments associated with severe anxiety disorders are expressed in childhood (De Bellis, Casey, et al., 2000). Adults severely abused in childhood (Raine et al., 2001) and diagnosed with PTSD (Galletly et al., 2001) show reduced right hemisphere activation during a working memory task. Neurological studies of adults confirmed that dysfunction of the right frontal lobe is involved in PTSD symptomatology (Freeman & Kimbrell, 2001) and dissociative flashbacks (Berthier et al., 2001). Neuropsychiatric research indicated that the paralimbic areas of the right hemisphere are preferentially involved in the storage of traumatic memories (Schiffer, Teicher, & Papanicolaou, 1995), that right-lateralized activation occurs during acquisition of conditioned fear (Fisher, Andersson, Furmark, Wik, & Fredrikson, 2002), that altered right-sided activity occurs in panic and social phobic anxiety states (Davidson, Marshall, Tomarken, & Henriques, 2000; Galderisi et al., 2001), and that dissociation is associated with a deficiency of the right brain (Lanius et al., 2002; Weinberg, 2000). Neurobiological research thus suggests a continuity in the expression of the stress coping deficits of PTSDs over the course of the life span.

Continuity among infant, childhood, and adult PTSD

In parallel work, clinical researchers described a continuity in infant and adult coping deficits:

> The stress responses exhibited by infants are the product of an immature brain processing threat stimuli and producing appropriate responses, while the adult who exhibits infantile responses has a mature brain that, barring stress-related abnormalities in brain development, is capable of exhibiting adult response patterns. However, there is evidence that the adult brain may regress to an infantile state when it is confronted with severe stress.
>
> *(Nijenhuis, Vanderlinden, & Spinhoven, 1998, p. 253)*

This "infantile state" is a disorganized-disoriented state of insecure attachment. As in infancy, children, adolescents, and adults with PTSDs cannot generate an active coherent behavioral coping strategy to confront subjectively perceived overwhelming, dysregulating events, and thus they quickly access the passive survival strategy of disengagement and dissociation.

Indeed, the type D attachment classification has been observed to utilize dissociative behaviors in later stages of life (van Ijzendoorn et al., 1999), and to be implicated in the etiology of the dissociative disorders (Liotti, 1992). The characterological use of dissociation over developmental stages is discussed by Allen and Coyne (1995):

> Although initially they may have used dissociation to cope with traumatic events, they subsequently dissociate to defend against a broad range of daily stressors, including their own posttraumatic symptoms, pervasively undermining the continuity of their experience.
>
> *(p. 620)*

These initial traumatic events are embedded in the abuse and neglect experienced by type D infants, the first relational context in which dissociation is used to autoregulate massive stress. In developmental research, Sroufe and his colleagues concluded that early trauma more so than later trauma has a greater impact on the development of dissociative behaviors (Ogawa, Sroufe, Weinfield, Carlson, & Egeland, 1997). Dissociation, like hyperarousal and elevated heart rate, is a common symptom in PTSD patients, and their occurrence at the time of a trauma is a strong predictor of the disorder (Bremner et al., 1992; Koopman, Classen, & Spiegel, 1994; Shalev, Peri, Canetti, & Schreiber, 1996, 1998). Although initially an acute response, a chronic pattern of dissociation to even minor stressors develops in these individuals (Bremner & Brett, 1997).

The fact that dissociation becomes a trait in PTSDs has devastating effects on self, and therefore psychobiological functions. In neurological studies of trauma Scaer referred to somatic dissociation, and concluded, "Perhaps the least appreciated manifestations of dissociation in trauma are in the area of perceptual alterations and somatic symptoms" (2001, p. 104). He further pointed out that distortion of proprioceptive awareness of the trauma patient's body is a most common dissociative phenomenon. Similarly, in clinical psychiatric studies Nijenhuis (2000) described not just psychological (e.g., amnesia) but "somatoform dissociation," which is associated with early onset traumatization, often involving physical abuse and threat to life by another person. Somatoform dissociation is expressed as a lack of integration of sensorimotor experiences, reactions, and functions of the individual and his/her self-representation.

Clinical research suggests a link between childhood traumatic experiences and somatoform dissociation in chronic PTSD (and borderline and somatoform disorders) (Waller et al., 2000). The dissociation is manifest as a suppression of autonomic physiological responses (e.g., heart rate and skin conductance), especially when recalling traumatic experiences (Carrey, Butter, Pessinger, & Bialek, 1995; Griffin, Resick, & Mechanic, 1997; Lanius et al., 2002). A study of psychophysiological reactivity in adults with childhood abuse demonstrated a significant decline in heart rate and diastolic blood pressure in a PTSD patient, while she was dissociating (Schmahl, Elzinga, & Bremner, 2002). Recall that in the previous description of early relational trauma, the infant's dissociative response is mediated by heightened dorsal vagal activity that dramatically decreases heart rate and blood pressure. These data suggest that somatic dissociation ontogenetically precedes psychological dissociation.

This shift from the cognitive to the affective-somatic aspects of dissociation is echoed in the neuroscience literature, which describes "a dissociation between the emotional evaluation of an event and the physiological reaction to that event, with the process being dependent on intact right hemisphere function" (Crucian et al., 2000, p. 643). PTSDs therefore reflect a severe dysfunction of the right brain's role in attachment, regulatory functions, the stress response, and in maintaining a coherent, continuous, and unified sense of self. Although the right brain's growth spurt is maximal in the first two years, it continues to enter into experience-dependent growth (Thatcher, 1994) and forms connections with the later-developing left, which would be impacted by later relational trauma such as sexual abuse in childhood (e.g., Teicher et al., 1997). It is thought that the effectiveness of newly formed and pruned networks in these later stages is limited by the adequacy of already formed, underlying networks, and therefore maturation is optimal only if the preceding stages were installed optimally (Epstein, 2001).

Traumatic attachment experiences negatively impact the early organization of the right brain, and thereby produce deficits in its adaptive functions of emotionally understanding and reacting to bodily and environmental stimuli, identifying a corporeal image of self and its relation to the environment, distinguishing the self from the other, and generating self-awareness (Devinsky, 2000; Keenan et al., 2001; Ruby & Decety, 2001; Schore, 1994). Optimal attachment experiences allow for the emergence of self-awareness, the adaptive capacity to sense, attend to, and reflect upon the dynamic changes of one's subjective self-states, but traumatic attachments in childhood lead to self-modulation of painful affect by directing attention away from internal emotional states.

From a psychoneurobiological perspective, dissociation reflects the inability of the right brain cortical-subcortical system to recognize and coprocess (integrate) external stimuli (exteroceptive information coming from the environment) and internal stimuli (interoceptive information from the body, the corporeal self). According to van der Kolk and McFarlane (1996), a central feature of PTSD is a loss of the ability to physiologically modulate stress responses which leads to a reduced capacity to utilize bodily signals as guides to action, and this alteration of psychological defense mechanisms is associated with an impairment of personal identity.

These deficits are the expression of an malfunctioning orbitofrontal cortical-subcortical system, the senior executive of the right brain (Schore, 1994, 1996, 1998a, 2000b, 2000c, 2001a). In light of the finding that the orbitofrontal cortex is involved in critical human functions that are crucial in defining the "personality" of an individual (Cavada & Schultz, 2000), personality organizations that characterologically access dissociation can be described as possessing an inefficient orbital frontolimbic regulatory system and a developmentally immature coping mechanism. And because adequate limbic function is required to allow the brain to adapt to a rapidly changing environment and organize new learning (Mesulam, 1998), a metabolically altered orbitofrontal system would interfere with ongoing social-emotional development. Early failures in attachment thus skew the developmental trajectory of the right brain over the rest of the life span, thereby engendering what Bowlby described as a diverting of development from its adaptive course, and precluding what Janet called an "enlargement" of personality development.

De-evolution of right brain limbic cicuits and PTSD pathogenesis

According to Krystal (1988), the long-term effect of infantile psychic trauma is the arrest of affect development. Because emotions involve rapid nonconscious appraisals of events that are important to the individual (Frijda, 1988) and represent reactions to fundamental relational meanings that have adaptive significance (Lazarus, 1991a), this enduring developmental impairment is expressed in a variety of critical dysfunctions of the right brain. PTSD patients, especially when stressed, show severe deficits in the preattentive reception and expression of facially expressed emotion, the processing of somatic information, the communication of emotional states, the maintaining of interactions with the social environment, the use of higher level more efficient defenses, the capacity to access an empathic stance and a reflective function, and the psychobiological ability to regulate, either by autoregulation or interactive regulation, and thereby recover from stressful affective states. Most of these dysfunctions represent pathological alterations of implicit, unconscious mechanisms. Note that they also describe the deficits of borderline personality disorders, a condition that correlates highly with PTSD and shares both a history of early attachment trauma and orbitofrontal and amygdala dysfunction (see Schore, 2001c).

Furthermore, the observations that in human infancy, the right brain, the neuro-biological locus of the stress response, organizes in an affective experiencedependent fashion, and that the emotion processing and stress coping limbic system evolves in stages, from the amygdala, to anterior cingulate, to orbitofrontal cortex (Schore, 1994, 2001a), supports the concept of de-evolution as a mechanism of symptom generation in PTSD. Wang, Wilson, and Mason (1996) described "stages of decompensation" in chronic PTSD, reflected in incremental impairments in amplified hyperarousal symptoms and defensive dissociation, decreased range of spontaneity and facial expression, heightened dysregulation of self-esteem, deepening loss of contact with the environment, reduced attachment and insight, and increased probability of destruction and suicide. Intriguingly, they posited the existence of specifically three stages beneath a level of good to maximum functioning, and suggest each stage is physiologically distinct.

The concept of "decompensation" describes a condition in which a system is rapidly disorganizing over a period of time. This construct derives from Jackson's (1931) classic principle that pathology involves a "dissolution," a loss of inhibitory capacities of the most recently evolved layers of the nervous system that support higher functions (negative symptoms), as well as the release of lower, more automatic functions (positive symptoms). This principle applies to the dissolution or disorganization of the brain's complex circuit of emotion regulation of orbital frontal cortex, anterior cingulate, and amygdala (Davidson et al., 2000; Schore, 2000b, 2001a).

And so it is tempting to speculate that the stage model of Wang and her colleagues describes a Jacksonian de-evolution of the "rostral limbic system" (Devinsky et al., 1995), in reverse developmental order, from orbitofrontal loss, to anterior cingulate loss, and finally to amygdala dysfunction. At a certain threshold of stress, the frontolimbic systems of PTSD patients would be unable to perform a higher regulatory function over lower levels, thereby releasing lower level right amygdala activity, without the adaptive capacity of flexibly reinitiating higher control functions. Heightened baseline right amygdala metabolism is found in patients with major depressive disorder (Abercombie et al., 1998). The amygdala is activated in states of helplessness (Schneider et al., 1996), and thus may be the key brain system that triggers the onset of conservation-withdrawal.

In addition, in light of the fact that the orbitofrontal, anterior cingulate, and amygdala systems each connect into the ANS (Schore, 2001a), the mechanism of devolution dynamics would also apply to the hierarchical disorganization of the ANS. This would be manifest in long-lasting episodes of a coupled nonreciprocal mode of autonomic control, in which concurrent increases (or decreases) occur in both sympathetic and parasympathetic components, or uncoupled nonreciprocal mode of autonomic control, in which responses in one division of the ANS occur in the absence of change in the other. In other words, the ANS would too easily be displaced from a state of autonomic balance, and once displaced, have difficulty in re-establishing balance, that is, show a poor capacity for vagal rebound and recovery from psychological stress (Mezzacappa, Kelsey, Katkin, & Sloan, 2001).

This de-evolution would also be manifest in a stress-associated shift down from the higher ventral vagal complex (which is known to be defective in PTSD; Sahar, Shalev, & Porges, 2001) to the dorsal vagal complex that mediates severe emotional states of terror, immobilization, and dissociation. Ultimately, higher vagal functions would be metabolically compromised, and dorsal vagal activity would predominate even in a resting state. This lowest level may be seen in infants raised in a neglectful environment (Gunnar & Vazquez, 2001) , mothers of child cancer survivors with PTSD (Glover & Poland, 2002), chronic PTSD patients with low cortisol levels (Mason, Kosten, Southwick, & Giller, 1990, 2001), suicidal patients with severe right brain deficiencies experiencing intense despair (Weinberg, 2000), and Wang and colleagues' (1996) final stage of depression – hopelessness. I suggest low levels are also found in coronary patients showing "vital exhaustion" (Kop, Appels, Mendes de Leon, de Swart, & Bär, 1994). This conception therefore suggests qualitative physiological as well as symptomatic differences between acute and chronic PTSD populations, and it relates developmental models of early organization to later clinical models of disorganization.

At the beginning of the this chapter, I suggested that a developmental psycho-neurobiological perspective can deepen our understanding of the deficits of mind and body seen in chronic PTSD. I then outlined how early physical abuse and relational trauma induce central and autonomic hyperarousal, the latter associated with severe states of bodily dysregulation and subjective pain. It is established that the child's reactivity and the parenting context contribute to changes in the infant's pain response (Sweet, McGrath, & Symons, 1999), that non-optimal parenting contributes to chronic pain patterns in certain children who have experienced prolonged or repeated pain as neonates (Grunau, Whitfield, Petrie, & Fryer, 1994), and that persistent pain experiences during the early neonatal period, a critical period for the organization of nociceptive neuronal circuits, rewires immature pain circuits, and leads to lasting and potentially detrimental alterations in the individual's response to pain in adulthood (Ruda, Ling, Hohmann, Peng, & Tachibana, 2000).

These effects may reflect an alteration of the experience-dependent maturation of the right hemisphere, specifically the right insular cortex that is dominant for the representation of somatic sensation and pain (Ostrowsky et al., 2002), the right anterior cingulate that plays a central role in the sensorial/affective aspect of pain (Hsieh et al., 1995; Price, 2000), and the right lateral orbitofrontal regions that modulate distant processing of pain and therefore coping with a painful stimulus

(Petrovic, Petersson, Ghatan, Stone-Elander, & Ingvar, 2000). This relational trauma-induced structural limitation of right limbic circuits in processing pain may be exposed under later stress, and play a critical role in PTSD pathogenesis. Indeed, there is extensive documentation that persistent pain is frequently associated with symptoms of PTSD (Benedikt & Kolb, 1986; Chibnall & Duckro, 1994; Geisser, Roth, Bachman, & Eckert, 1996; Perry, Cella, Falkenberg, Heidrich, & Gaudwin, 1987; Smith, Egert, Winkel, & Jacobson, 2002).

The endpoint of chronically experiencing catastrophic states of relationalinduced trauma in early life is a progressive impairment of the ability to adjust, take defensive action, or act on one's own behalf, and a blocking of the capacity to register affect and pain, all critical to survival. These individuals perceive themselves as different from other people and outside of, as well as unworthy of, meaningful attachments (Lansky, 1995). Henry (cited in Wang, 1997) echoed this conclusion:

> The ability to maintain personally relevant bonds is vital for our evolutionary survival. The infant's tie to the mother's voice and odor is recognized even by the newborn (van Lancker, 1991), yet this personal relevance and recognition of the familiar can be impaired by anxious insecurity resulting from difficult early experiences or traumatic stress. The vital task of establishing a personally relevant universe and the solace derived from it depend on right hemispheric functioning. If this function is indeed lost in the insecurely attached, much has been lost.
>
> *(p. 168)*

These survival limitations may negatively impact not just psychological but also essential organismic functions in coping with physical disease. Studies are linking attachment, stress, and disease (Maunder & Hunter, 2001; Schmidt, Nachtigall, Wuethrich-Martone, & Strauss, 2002) and childhood attachment and adult cardiovascular and cortisol function (Luecken, 1998), as well documenting effects of childhood abuse on multiple risk factors for several of the leading causes of death in adults (Felitti et al., 1998).

This developmental neurobiological model has significant implications for psychiatry and the other mental health professions. The organization of the brain's essential coping mechanisms occurs in critical periods of infancy. The construct of critical periods implies that certain detrimental early influences lead to particular irreversible or only partially reversible enduring effects. But the flip side of the critical period concept emphasizes the extraordinary sensitivity of developing dynamic systems to their environment, and asserts that these systems are most plastic in these periods. The development of the right brain is experience-dependent, and this experience is embedded in the attachment relationship between caregiver and infant.

Attachment researchers in association with infant mental health workers are devising interventions that effectively alter the affect-communicating capacities of mother-infant systems, and thereby the attachment experiences of high-risk dyads.

Early interventions that are timed to critical periods of development of the right brain, the locus of the human stress response, can facilitate the maturation of neuro-biologically adaptive stress coping systems, and thereby have lifelong effects on the adaptive capacities of a developing self. Early treatment and prevention programs, if expanded onto a societal scale, could significantly diminish the number of individuals who develop pathological reactions of mind and body to catastrophic life events. These efforts could, in turn, make deep inroads into not only altering the intergenerational transmission of PTSDs but improving the quality of many lives throughout all stages of human development.

References

Abercombie, H. C., Schaefer, S. M., Larson, C. L., Oakes, T. R., Lindgren, K. A., & Holden, J. E. (1998). Metabolic rate in the right amygdala predicts negative affect in depressed patients. *NeuroReport*, 9, 3301–3307.

Adamec, R. E. (1997). Transmitter systems involved in neural plasticity underlying increased anxiety and defense – implications for understanding anxiety following traumatic stress. *Neuroscience and Biobehavioral Reviews*, 21, 755–765.

Adamec, R. E. (1999). Evidence that limbic neural plasticity in the right hemisphere mediates partial kindling induced lasting increases in anxiety-like behavior: Effects of low frequency stimulation (quenching?) on long-term potentiation of amygdala efferents and behavior following kindling. *Brain Research*, 839, 133–152.

Adolphs, R. (2002). Recognizing emotion from facial expressions: Psychological and neurological mechanisms. *Behavioral and Cognitive Neuroscience Reviews*, 1, 21–62.

Adolphs, R., Damasio, H., Tranel, D., Cooper, G., & Damasio, A. R. (2000). A role for somatosensory cortices in the visual recognition of emotion as revealed by three-dimensional lesion mapping. *Journal of Neuroscience*, 20, 2683–2690.

Adolphs, R., Damasio, H., Tranel, D., & Damasio, A. R. (1996). Cortical systems for the recognition of emotion in facial expressions. *Journal of Neuroscience*, 23, 7678–7687.

Adolphs, R., Tranel, D., & Damasio, H. (2001). Emotion recognition from faces and prosody following temporal lobectomy. *Neuropsychology*, 15, 396–404.

Allen, J. G., & Coyne, L. (1995). Dissociation and vulnerability to psychoticexperience: The dissociative experiences scale and theMMPI-2. *Journal of Nervous and Mental Disease*, 183, 615–622.

Angrilli, A., Mauri, A., Palomba, D., Flor, H., Birbaumer, N., Sartori, G., & de Paola, F. (1996). Startle reflex and emotion modulation impairment after a right amygdala lesion. *Brain*, 119, 1991–2000.

Anisman, H., Zaharia, M. D., Meaney, J., & Merali, Z. (1998). Do early-life events permanently alter behavioural and hormonal responses to stressors? *International Journal of Developmental Neuroscience*, 16, 149–164.

Antelman, S. M., Caggiula, A. R., Gershon, S., et al. (1997). Stressor-induced oscillation: A possible model of the bidirectional symptoms in PTSD. *Annals of the New York Academy of Sciences*, 821, 296–304.

American Psychiatric Association. (1994). *Diagnostic and statistical manual of Mental Disorders – DSM-IV-TR*. Washington, DC: APA.

AstonJones, G., Valentino. R. J., Van Bockstaele, E. J., & Meyerson, A. T. (1996). Locus coeruleus, stress, and PTSD: Neurobiological and clinical parallels. In M. M. Marburg (Ed.), *Catecholamine function in PTSD*, 17–62. Washington, DC: American Psychiatric Press.

Barach, P. M. M. (1991). Multiple personality disorder as an attachment disorder. *Dissociation*, 4, 117–123.

Bargh, J. A., & Chartrand, T. L. (1999). The unbearable automaticity of being. *American Psychologist*, 54, 462–479.

Basch, M. F. (1976). The concept of affect: A re-examination. *Journal of the American Psychoanalytic Association*, 24, 759–777.

Beckham, J. C., Feldman, M. E., Kirby, A. G., Hertzberg, M. A., & Moore, S. D. (1997). Interpersonal violence and its correlates in Vietnam veterans with chronic posttraumatic stress disorder. *Journal of Clinical Psychology*, 53, 859–869.

Beckham, J. C., Roodman, A. A., Barefoot, J. C., Haney, T. L., Helms, M. J., Fairbank, J. A., Hertzberg, M. A., & Kudler, H. S. (1996). Interpersonal and self-reported hostility among combat veterans with and without posttraumatic stress disorder. *Journal of Traumatic Stress*, 9, 335–342.

Beebe, B. (2000). Coconstructing mother-infant distress: The microsychrony of maternal impingement and infant avoidance in the face-to-face encounter. *Psychoanalytic Inquiry*, 20, 412–440.

Beers, S. R., & De Bellis, M. D. (2002). Neuropsychological function in children with maltreatment-related posttraumatic stress disorder. *American Journal of Psychiatry*, 159, 483–486.

Benedikt, R., & Kolb, L. (1986). Preliminary findings on chronic pain and posttraumatic stress disorder. *American Journal of Psychiatry*, 143, 908–910.

Berntson, G. G., Cacioppo, J. T., & Quigley, K. S. (1991). Autonomic determinism: The modes of autonomic control, the doctrine of autonomic space, and the laws of autonomic contraint. *Psychological Review*, 98, 459–487.

Berthier, M. L., Posada, A., & Puentes, C. (2001). Dissociative flashbacks after right frontal injury in a Vietnam veteran with combat-related posttraumatic stress disorder. *Journal of Neuropsychiatry and Clinical Neuroscience*, 13, 101–105.

Bion, W. R. (1962). *Learning from experience*. London: Heinemann.

Bittigau, P., Sifringer, M., Pohl, D., Stadhaus, D., Ishimaru, M., Shimizu, H., Ikeda, M., Lang, D., Speer, A., Olney, J. W., & Ikonomidou, C. (1999). Apoptotic neurodegeneration following trauma is markedly enhanced in the immature brain. *Annals of Neurology*, 45, 724–735.

Blair, R. J. R., & Cipolotti, L. (2000). Impaired social response reversal: A case of acquired sociopathy. *Brain*, 123, 1122–1141.

Blonder, L. X., Bowers, & D., Heilman, K. M. (1991). The role of the right hemisphere in emotional communication. *Brain*, 114, 1115–1127.

Borod, J., Cicero, B. A., Obler, L. K., et al. (1998). Right hemisphere emotional perception: Evidence across multiple channels. *Neuropsychology*, 12, 446–458.

Borod, J., Haywood, C. S., & Koff, E. (1997). Neuropsychological aspects of facial asymmetry during emotional expression: A review of the adult literature. *Neuropsychology Review*, 7, 41–60.

Bouwmeester, H., Smits, K., & van Ree, J. (2002). Neonatal development of projections to the basolateral amygdala from prefrontal and thalamic structures in the rat. *Journal of Comparative Neurology*, 450, 241–255.

Bouwmeester, H., Wolterink, G., & van Ree, J. (2002). Neonatal development of projections from the basolateral amygdala to prefrontal, striatal, and thalamic structures in the rat. *Journal of Comparative Neurology*, 442, 239–249.

Bowlby, J. (1969). *Attachment and loss: Vol. 1. Attachment.* New York: Basic Books.

Bowlby, J. (1978). Attachment theory and its therapeutic implications. *Adolescent Psychiatry*, 6, 5–33.

Bradley, M., Cuthbert, B. N., & Lang, P. J. (1996). Lateralized startle probes in the study of emotion. *Psychophysiology*, 33, 156–161.

Braeutigam, S., Bailey, A. J., & Swithenby, S. J. (2001). Task-dependent early latency (30–60ms) visual processing of human faces and other objects. *Neuroreport*, 12, 1531–1536.

Brake, W. G., Sullivan, R. M., & Gratton, A. (2000). Perinatal distress leads to lateralized medial prefrontal cortical dopamine hypofunction in adult rats. *Journal of Neuroscience*, 20, 5538–5543.

Braun, K., & Poeggel, G. (2001). Recognition of mother's voice evokes metabolic activation in the medial prefrontal cortex and lateral thalamus of octodon degus pups. *Neuroscience*, 103, 861–864.

Bremner, J. D. (1999). Acute and chronic responses to psychological trauma: Where do we go from here? *American Journal of Psychiatry*, 156, 349–351.

Bremner, J. D., & Brett, E. (1997). Trauma related dissociative states and long-term psychopathology in posttraumatic stress disorder. *Journal of Traumatic Stress*, 10, 37–50.

Bremner, J. D., Innis, R. B., Ng, C. K., et al. (1997). Positron emissiontomography measurement of cerebral metabolic correlates of yohimbe administration in combat-related posttraumatic stress disorder. *Archives of General Psychiatry*, 54, 246–254.

Bremner, J. D., Southwick, S., Brett, E., Fontana, A., Rosenheck, R., & Charney, D. S. (1992). Dissociation and posttraumatic stress disorder in Vietnam combat veterans. *American Journal of Psychiatry*, 149, 328–332.

Bremner, J. D., Staib, L. H., Kaloupek, D., Southwick, S. M., Soufer, R., & Charney, D. S. (1999). Neural correlates of exposure to traumatic pictures and sound in combat veterans with and without posttraumatic stress disorder: A positron emission tomography study. *Biological Psychiatry*, 45, 806–818.

Brown, M. R., Fisher, L. A., Rivier, J., Spiess, J., Rivier, C., & Vale, W. (1982). Corticotropin-releasing factor: Effects on the sympathetic nervous system and oxygen consumption. *Life Sciences*, 30, 207–219.

Butler, P. D., Weiss, J. M., Stout, J. C., & Nemeroff, C. B. (1990). Corticotropin-releasing factor produces fear-enhancing and behavioral activating effects following infusion into the locus coeruleus. *Journal of Neuroscience*, 10, 176–183.

Calhoun, P. S., Beckham, J. C., & Bosworth, H. B. (2002). Caregiver burden and psychological distress in partners of veterans with chronic posttraumatic stress disorder. *Journal of Traumatic Stress*, 15, 205–212.

Carlson, V., Cicchetti, D., Barnett, D., & Braunwald, K. (1989). Disorganized/disoriented attachment relationships in maltreated infants. *Developmental Psychology*, 25, 525–531.

Carmichael, S. T., & Price, J. L. (1995). Limbic connections of the orbital and medial prefrontal cortex in macaque monkeys. *Journal of Comparative Neurology*, 363, 615–641.

Carrey, N. J., Butter, H. J., Pessinger, M. A., & Bialek, R. J. (1995). Physiological and cognitive correlates of child abuse. *Journal of the American Academy of Child and Adolescent Psychiatry*, 34, 1067–1075.

Carrion, V. G., Weems, C. F., Eliez, S., Patwardhan, A., Brown, W., Ray, R. D., & Reiss, A. L. (2001). Attenuation of frontal asymmetry in pediatric posttraumatic stress disorder. *Biological Psychiatry*, 50, 943–951.

Carrion, V. G., Weems, C. F., Ray, R. D., Glaser, B., Hessl, D., & Reiss, A. L. (2002). Diurnal salivary cortisol in pediatric posttraumatic stress disorder. *Biological Psychiatry*, 51, 575–582.

Carroll, E. M., Foy, D. W., Cannon, B. J., & Zwier, G. (1991). Assessment issues involving families of trauma victims. *Journal of Traumatic Stress*, 4, 25–40.

Casey, B. J., Trainor, R., Giedd, J., Vauss, Y., Vaituzis, C. K., Hamburger, S., Kozuch, P., & Rapoport, J. L. (1997). The role of the anterior cingulate in automatic and controlled processes: A developmental neuroanatomical study. *Developmental Psychobiology*, 30, 61–69.

Cavada, C., Company, T., Tejedor, J., Cruz-Rizzolo, R. J., & Reinoso-Suarez, F. (2000). The anatomical connections of the macaque monkey orbitofrontal cortex: A review. *Cerebral Cortex*, 10, 220–242.

Cavada, C., & Schultz, W. (2000). The mysterious orbitofrontal cortex. *Foreword, Cerebral Cortex*, 10, 205.

Chambers, R. A., Bremner, J. D., Moghaddam, B., Southwick, S. M., Charney, D. S., & Krystal, J. H. (1999). Glutamate and post-traumatic stress disorder: Toward a psychobiology of dissociation. *Seminars in Clinical Neuropsychiatry*, 4, 274–281.

Chaparro-Huerta, V., Rivera-Cervantes, M. C., Torres-Mendoza, B. M., & BeasZárate, C. (2002). Neuronal death and tumor necrosis factor-α response to glutamate-induced excitotoxicity in the cerebral cortex of neonatal rats. *Neuroscience Letters*, 333, 95–98.

Charney, D. S., Deutch, A. Y., Southwick, S. M., & Krystal, J. H. (1995). Neuralcircuits and mechanisms of post-traumatic stress disorder. In M. J. Friedman & D. S. Charney (Eds.), *Neurobiological and clinical consequences of stress: From normal adaptation to posttraumatic stress disorder*. Philadelphia: Lippincott Williams & Wilkins, 291–314.

Cheng, Z., & Powley, T. L. (2000). Nucleus ambiguus projections to cardiac ganglia of rat atria: An anterograde tracing study. *Journal of Comparative Neurology*, 424, 588–606.

Cheng, Z., Powley, T. L., Schwaber, J. S., & Doyle, F. J. (1999). Projections of the dorsal motor nucleus of the vagus to cardiac ganglia of rat atria: An anterograde tracing study. *Journal of Comparative Neurology*, 401, 320–341.

Chibnall, J. T., & Duckro, P. N. (1994). Post-traumatic stress disorder in chronic post-traumatic headache patients. *Headache*, 34, 257–361.

Chiron, C., Jambaque, I., Nabbout, R., Lounes, R., Syrota, A., & Dulac, O. (1997). The right brain hemisphere is dominant in human infants. *Brain*, 120, 1057–1065.

Coghill, R. C., Gilron, I., & Iadorola, M. J. (2001). Hemispheric lateralization of somatosensory processing. *Journal of Neurophysiology*, 85, 2602–2612.

Coleman-Mensches, K., & McGaugh, J. L. (1995). Differential involvement of the right and left amygdalae in expression of memory for aversively motivated training. *Brain Research*, 670, 75–81.

Corodimas, K. P., LeDoux, J. E., Gold, P. W., & Schulkin, J. (1994). Corticosterone potentiation of learned fear. *Annals of the New York Academy of Sciences*, 746, 392–393.

Craig, A. D. (2002). How do you feel? Interoception: The sense of the physiological condition of the body. *Nature Neuroscience*, 3, 655–666.

Critchley, H. D., Melmed, R. N., Featherstone, E., Mathias, C. J., & Dolan, R. J. (2001). Brain activity during biofeedback relaxation: A functional neuroimaging investigation. *Brain*, 124, 1003–1012.

Crittenden, P. M., & Ainsworth, M. D. S. (1989). Child maltreatment and attachment theory. In D. Cicchetti & V. Carlson (Eds.), *Child maltreatment: Theory and research on the causes and consequences of child abuse and neglect*, 432–463. New York: Cambridge University Press.

Crucian, G. P., Hughes, J. D., Barrett, A. M., et al. (2000). Emotional and physiological responses to false feedback. *Cortex*, 36, 623–647.

Cutting, J. (1992). The role of right hemisphere dysfunction in psychiatric disorders. *British Journal of Psychiatry*, 160, 583–588.

Damasio, A. R. (1994). *Descartes' error*. New York: Grosset/Putnam.

Davidson, J. R. T., & Foa, E. (1993). *Post traumatic stress disorder: DSM-IV and beyond*. Washington: American Psychiatric Press.

Davidson, R. J. T., & Hugdahl, K. (1995). *Brain asymmetry*. Cambridge, MA: MIT Press.

Davidson, R. J. T., Marshall, J. R., Tomarken, A. J., & Henriques, J. B. (2000). While aphobic waits: Regional brain electrical and autonomic activity in social phobics during anticipation of public speaking. *Biological Psychiatry*, 47, 85–95.

Davies, J. M., & Frawley, M. G. (1994). *Treating the adult survivor of childhood sexual abuse: A psychoanalytic perspective.* New York: Basic Books.

Davis, M. (1989). The role of the amygdala and its efferent projections in fear and anxiety. In P. Tyrer (Ed.), *Psychopharmacology of anxiety*, 52–39. Oxford: Oxford University Press.

De Bellis, M. D. (2001). Developmental traumatology: The psychobiological development of maltreated children and its implications for research, treatment, and policy. *Development and Psychopathology*, 13, 539–564.

De Bellis, M. D., Baum, A. S., Birmaher, B., et al. (1999). Developmental traumatology: Teil 1, biological stress systems. *Biological Psychiatry*, 45, 1259–1270.

De Bellis, M. D., Casey, B. J., Dahl, R. E., et al. (2000). A pilot study of amygdala volume in pediatric generalized anxiety disorder. *Biological Psychiatry*, 48, 51–57.

De Bellis, M. D., Keshavan, M. S., Clark, D. B., Casey, B. J., Giedd, J. N., Boring, A. M. Frustaci, K., & Ryan, N. D. (1999). Developmental traumatology Part II: *Brain Development. Biological Psychiatry*, 45, 1271–1284.

De Bellis, M. D., Keshavan, M. S., Frustaci, K., Shifflett, H., Iyengar, S., Beers, S. R., & Hall, J. (2002a). Superior temporal gyrus volumes in maltreated children and adolescents with PTSD. *Biological Psychiatry*, 51, 544–552.

De Bellis, M. D., Keshavan, M. S., Shifflett, H., Iyengar, S., Beers, S. R., & Hall, J., & Mortiz, G. (2002b). Brain structures in pediatric maltreatment-related posttrraumtic stress disorder: A socio demographically matched study. *Biological Psychiatry*, 52, 1066–1078.

De Bellis, M. D., Keshaven, M. S., Spencer, S., & Hall, J. (2000). N-acetylaspartate concentration in anterior cingulate with PTSD. *American Journal of Psychiatry*, 157, 1175–1177.

Deutch, A. Y., & Young, C. D. (1995). A model of the stress-induced activation of prefrontal cortical dopamine systems: Coping and the development of post-traumatic stress disorder. In M. J. Friedman & D. S. Charney (Eds.), *Neurobiological and clinical consequences of stress: From normal adaptation to post-traumatic stress disorder*, 163–175. Philadelphia: Lippincott Williams & Wilkins.

Devinsky, O. (2000). Right cerebral hemisphere dominance for a sense of corporeal and emotional self. *Epilepsy & Behavior*, 1, 60–73.

Devinsky, O., Morrell, M. J., & Vogt, B. A. (1995). Contributions of anterior cingulate cortex to behaviour. *Brain*, 118, 279–306.

Dimberg, U., & Petterson, M. (2000). Facial reactions to happy and angry facial expressions: Evidence for right hemisphere dominance. *Psychophysiology*, 37, 693–696.

Dixon, A. K. (1998). Ethological strategies for defense in animals and humans: Their role in some psychiatric disorders. *British Journal of Medical Psychology*, 7, 417–445.

Dobbing, J., & Sands, J. (1973). Quantitative growth and development of human brain. *Archives of Disease in Childhood*, 48, 757–767.

Draijer, N., & Langeland, W. (1999). Childhood trauma and perceived parental dysfunction in the etiology of dissociative symptoms in psychiatric patients. *American Journal of Psychiatry*, 156, 379–385.

Elliott, R., Dolan, R. J., & Frith, C. D. (2000). Dissociable functions in themedial and lateral orbitofrontal cortex: Evidence from human neuroimaging studies. *Cerebral Cortex*, 10, 308–317.

Epstein, H. T. (2001). An outline of the role of brain in human cognitive development. *Brain and Cognition*, 45, 44–51.

Erciyas, A. H., Topaktas, S., Akyuz, A., & Dener, S. (1999). Suppression of cardiac parasympathetic functions in patients with right hemispheric stroke. *European Journal of Neurology*, 6, 685–690.

Erickson, M. F., Egeland, B., & Pianta, R. (1989). The effects of maltreatment on the development of young children. In D. Cicchetti & V. Carlson (Eds.), *Child maltreatment: Theory and research on the causes and consequences of child abuse and neglect*, 647–684. New York: Cambridge University Press.

Eslinger, P. J. (1999). Orbital frontal cortex: Historical and contemporary views about its behavioral and physiological significance: An introduction to special topic papers: Part I. *Neurocase*, 5, 225–229.

Essex, M. J., Klein, M. H., Cho, E., & Kalin, N. H. (2002). Maternal stress beginning in infancy may sensitize children to later stress exposure: Effects on cortisol and behavior. *Biological Psychiatry*, 52, 776–784.

Falk, D., Hildebolt, C., Cheverud, J., Vannier, M., Helmkamp, R. C., & Konigsberg, L. (1990). Cortical asymmetries in frontal lobes of Rhesus monkeys (Macacamulatta). *Brain Research*, 512, 40–45.

Fanselow, M. S. (1986). Conditioned fear-induced opiate analgesia: A compelling motivational state theory of stress analgesia. In D. D. Kelly (Ed.), *Stress-induced analgesia*, 40–54. New York: The New York Academy of Sciences.

Felitti, V. J., Anda, R. F., Nordenberg, D., Williamson, D. F., Spitz, A. M., Edwards, V., Koss, M. P., & Marks, J. S. (1998). Relationship of childhood abuse and household dysfunction to many of the leading causes of death in adults: The adverse childhood experiences (ACE) study. *American Journal of Preventive Medicine*, 14, 245–258.

Ferrie, J. C., Barantin, L., Saliba, E., Akoka, S., Tranquart, F., Sirinelli, D., & Pourcelot, L. (1999). MR assessment of the brain maturation during the perinatal period: Quantitative T_2 MR study in premature newborns. *Magnetic Resonance Imaging*, 17, 1275–1288.

Fink, G. R., Markowitsch, H. J., Reinkemeier, M., Bruckbauer, T., Kessler, J., & Heiss, W.-D. (1996). Cerebral representation of one's own past: Neural networks involved in autobiographical memory. *Journal of Neuroscience*, 16, 4275–4282.

Fisher, H., Andersson, J. L. R., Furmark, T. Wik, G., & Fredrikson, M. (2002). Right-sided human prefrontal brain activation during acquisition of conditioned fear. *Emotion*, 2, 233–241.

Fonagy, P., & Target, M. (2002). Early intervention and development of self-regulation. *Psychoanalytic Inquiry*, 22, 307–335.

Francis, D. D., & Meaney, M. J. (1999). Maternal care and the development of stress responses. *Current Opinion in Neurobiology*, 9, 128–134.

Freeman, T. W., & Kimbrell, T. (2001). A "cure" for chronic combat-related posttraumatic stress disorder secondary to a right frontal lobe infarct: A case report. *Journal of Neuropsychiatry and Clinical Neuroscience*, 13, 106–109.

Frey, S., & Petrides, M. (2000). Orbitofrontal cortex: A key prefrontal region for encoding information. *Proceedings of the National Academy of Sciences of the United States of America*, 97, 8723–8727.

Freyd, J. J. (1996). *Betrayal trauma theory: The logic of forgetting childhood abuse*. Cambridge, MA: Harvard University Press.

Frijda, N. H. (1988). The laws of emotion. *American Psychologist*, 43, 349–358.

Funayama, F. S., Grillon, C., Davis, M., & Phelps, E. A. (2001). A double dissociation in the affective modulation of startle in humans: Effects of unilateral temporal lobectomy. *Journal of Cognitive Neuroscience*, 13, 721–729.

Funnell, M. G., Corballis, P. M., & Gazzaniga, M. S. (2001). Hemispheric processing asymmetries: Implications for memory. *Brain and Cognition*, 46, 135–139.

Gaensbauer, T. J. (2002). Representations of trauma in infancy: Clinical and theoretical implications for the understanding of early memory. *Infant Mental Health Journal*, 23, 259–277.

Galderisi, S., Bucci, P., Mucci, A., Bernardo, A., Koenig, T., & Maj, M. (2001). Brain electrical microstates in subjects with panic disorder. *Psychophysiology*, 54, 427–435.

Galletly, C., Clark, C. R., McFarlane, A. C., & Weber, D. L. (2001). Working memory in posttraumatic stress disorder – an event-related potential study. *Journal of Traumatic Stress*, 14, 295–309.

Galton, V. A. (1965). Thyroid hormone-catecholamine relationships. *Endocrinology*, 77, 278–284.

Garavan, H., Ross, T. J., & Stein, E. A. (1999). Right hemisphere dominance of inhibitory control: An event-related functional MRI study. *Proceedings of the National Academy of Sciences of the United States of America*, 96, 8301–8306.

Geisser, M. E., Roth, S. R., Bachman, J. E., & Eckert, T. A. (1996). The relationship between symptoms of post-traumatic stress disorder and pain, affective disturbance and disability among patients with accident and non-accident related pain. *Pain Augmentation*, 66, 207–214.

George, C., & Solomon, J. (1996). Representational models of relationships: Links between caregiving and attachment. *Infant Mental Health Journal*, 17, 198–216.

Geracioti, T. D., Baker, D. G., Ekhator, N. N., et al. (2001). CSF norepinephrine concentrations in posttraumatic stress disorder. *American Journal of Psychiatry*, 158, 1227–1330.

Glover, D. A., & Poland, R. E. (2002). Urinary cortisol and catecholamines in mothers of child cancer survivors with and without PTSD. *Psychoneuroendocrinology*, 27, 805–819.

Gould, E., Wooley, C. S., & McEwen, B. S. (1991). Adrenal steroids regulate postnatal development of the rat dentate gyrus: Effects of glucocorticoids on cell death. *Journal of Comparative Neurology*, 313, 479–485.

Graham, Y. P., Heim, C., Goodman, S. H., Miller, A. H., & Nemeroff, C. B. (1999). The effects of neonatal stress on brain development: Implications for psychopathology. *Development and Psychopathology*, 11, 545–565.

Griffin, M. G., Resick, P. A., & Mechanic, M. B. (1997). Objective assessment of peritraumatic dissociation: Psychophysiological indicators. *American Journal of Psychiatry*, 15, 1081–1088.

Grunau, R. V. E., Whitfield, M. F., Petrie, J. H., & Fryer, E. L. (1994). Early pain experience, child and family factors, as precursors of somatization: A prospective study of extremely premature and full-term children. *Pain*, 56, 353–359.

Guilarte, T. R. (1998). The N-methyl-D-aspartate receptor: Physiology and neurotoxicology in the developing brain. In W. Slikker & L. W. Chang (Eds.), *Handbook of developmental neurotoxicology*, 285–304. San Diego: Academic Press.

Gunnar, M. R., & Donzella, B. (2002). Social regulation of the cortisol levels in early human development. *Psychoneuroendocrinology*, 27, 199–220.

Gunnar, M. R., & Vazquez, D. M. (2001). Low cortisol and a flattening of expected daytime rhythm: Potential indices of risk in human development. *Development and Psychopathology*, 13, 515–538.

Gurvits, T. V., Gilbertson, M. W., Lasko, N. B., et al. (2000). Neurologic softsigns in chronic posttraumatic stress disorder. *Archives of General Psychiatry*, 57, 181–186.

Halgren, E. (1992). Emotional neurophysiology of the amygdala within the context of human cognition. In J. P. Aggleton (Eds.), *The amygdala: Neurobiological aspects of emotion, memory, and mental dysfunction*, 191–228. New York: Wiley-Liss.

Hamner, M. B., Lorberbaum, J. P., & George, M. S. (1999). Potential role of the anterior cingulate cortex in PTSD: Review and hypothesis. *Depression and Anxiety*, 9, 1–14.

Hariri, A. R., Bookheimer, S. Y., & Mazziotta, J. C. (2000). Modulating emotional responses: Effects of a neocortical network on the limbic system. *Neuro Report*, 11, 43–48.

Harkness, K. L., & Tucker, D. M. (2000). Motivation of neural plasticity: Neural mechanisms in the self-organization of depression. In M. D. Lewis & I. Granic (Eds.), *Emotion, development, and self-organization*, 186–208. New York: Cambridge University Press.

Hatalski, C. G., & Baram, T. Z. (1997). Stress-induced transcriptional regulation in the developing rat brain involves increased cyclic adenosine 3:5'-monophosphate-regulatory element binding activity. *Molecular Endocrinology*, 11, 2016–2024.

Helmeke, C., Ovtscharoff, W. Jr., Poeggel, G., & Braun, K. (2001). Juvenile emotional experience alters synaptic inputs on pyramidal neurons in anterior cingulate cortex. *Cerebral Cortex*, 11, 717–727.

Helmeke, C., Poeggel, G., & Braun, K. (2001). Differential emotional experience induces elevated spine densities on basal dentrites of pyramidal neurons in the anterior cingulate of *Octodon degus*. *Neuroscience*, 104, 927–931.

Hennessy, M. B. (1997). Hypothalamic-pituitary-adrenal responses to brief social separation. *Neuroscience & Behavioral Reviews*, 21, 11–29.

Henry, J. P. (1993). Psychological and physiological responses to stress: The right hemisphere and the hypothalamo-pituitary-adrenal axis, an inquiry into problems of human bonding. *Integrative Physiological and Behavioral Science*, 28, 369–387.

Henry, J. P., & Wang, S. (1998). Effects of early stress on adult affiliative behavior. *Psychoneuroendocrinology*, 23, 863–875.

Hertsgaard, L., Gunnar, M., Erickson, M. F., & Nachmias, M. (1995). Adrenocortical responses to the strange situation in infants with disorganized/disoriented attachment relationships. *Child Development*, 66, 1100–1106.

Hess, E., & Main, M. M. (1999). Second-generation effects of unresolved trauma in nonmal treating parents: Dissociated, frightened, and threatening parental behavior. *Psychoanalytic Inquiry*, 19, 481–540.

Hilz, H. W., Tarnowski, W., & Arend, P. (1963). Glucose polymerisation and cortisol. *Biochemical and Biophysical Research Communications*, 10, 492–502.

Hsieh, J.-C., Belfrage, M., Stone-Elander, S., Hansson, P., & Ingvar, M. (1995). Central representation of chronic ongoing neuropathic pain studied by positron emission tomography. *Pain*, 63, 225–236.

Hugdahl, K. (1995). Classical conditioning and implicit learning: The right hemisphere hypothesis. In R. J. Davidson & K. Hugdahl (Eds.), *Brain asymmetry*, 235–267. Cambridge, MA: MIT Press.

Jackson, J. H. (1931). *Selected writings of John Hughlings Jackson*, Vols. 1 & 2. London: Hodder & Stoughton.

Janet, P. (1889). *L'Automatisme psychologique*. Paris: Alcan.

Janet, P. (1911). *L'etat mental des hystériques* (2nd ed.). Paris: Alcan.

Johnsen, B. H., & Hugdahl, K. (1991). Hemispheric asymmetry in conditioning to facial emotional expressions. *Psychophysiology*, 28, 154–162.

Johnson, J. G., Cohen, P., Kasen, S., Smailes, E., & Brook, J. S. (2001). Association of maladaptive parental behavior with psychiatric disorder among parents and their offspring. *Archives of General Psychiatry*, 58, 453–460.

Johnston, M. V. (2001). Excitotoxicity in neonatal hypoxia. *Mental Retardation and Developmental Disabilities Research Reviews*, 7, 229–234.

Kalogeras, K. T., Nieman, L. K., Friedman, T. C., Doppman, J. L., Cutler, G. B. Jr., Chrousos, G. P., Wilder, R. L., Gold, P. W., & Yanovski, J. A. (1996). Inferior petrosal sinus sampling in healthy human subjects reveals a unilateral corticotropin-releasing hormone-induced arginine vasopressin release associated with ipsilateral adrenocorticotropin secretion. *Journal of Clinical Investigation*, 97, 2045–2050.

Kaufman, J., Plotsky, P. M., Nemeroff, C. B., & Charney, O. S. (2000). Effects of early adverse experiences on brain structure and function: Clinical implications. *Biological Psychiatry*, 48, 778–790.

Kawasaki, H., Adolphs, R., Kaufman, O., et al. (2001). Single-neuron responses to emotional visual stimuli recorded in human ventral prefrontal cortex. *Nature Neuroscience*, 4, 15–16.

Keenan, J. P., Nelson, A., O'Connor, M., & Pascual-Leone, A. (2001). Self-recognition and the right hemisphere. *Nature*, 409, 305.

Kehoe, P., Shoemaker, W. J., Triano, L., Hoffman, J., & Arons, C. (1996). Repeated isolation in the neonatal rat produces alterations in behavior and ventral striatal dopamine release in the juvenile after amphetamine challenge. *Behavioral Neuroscience*, 110, 1435–1444.

Keil, A., Bradley, M. M., Hauk, O., Rockstroh, B., Elbert, T., & Lang, P. J. (2002). Large-scale neural correlates of affective picture processing. *Psychophysiology*, 39, 641–649.

Kessler, D. C., Sonnega, A., Bromet, E., Hughes, M., & Nelson, C. B. (1995). Posttraumatic stress disorder in the National Comorbidity Survey. *Archives of General Psychiatry*, 52, 1048–1060.

Kinsbourne, M., & Bemporad, B. (1984). Lateralization or emotion: A model and the evidence. In N. A. Fox & R. J. Davidson (Eds.), *The psychobiology of affective development*, 259–291. Hillsdale, NJ: Erlbaum.

Kirschbaum, C., Wolf, O. T., May, M., Wippich, W., & Hellhammer, D. H. (1996). Stress- and treatment-induced elevations of cortisol levels associated with impaired declarative memory in healthy adults. *Life Sciences*, 58, 1475–1483.

Koch, K. L., Summy-Long, J., Bingaman, S., Sperry, N., & Stern, R. M. (1990). Vasopressin and oxytocin responses to illusory self-motion and nausea in man. *Journal of Clinical and Endocrinological Metabolism*, 71, 1269–1275.

Koenen, K. C., Driver, K. L., Oscar-Berman, M., et al. (2001). Measures of prefrontal system dysfunction in posttraumatic stress disorder. *Brain and Cognition*, 45, 64–78.

Kolb, L. C., & Multipassi, L. R. (1982). The conditioned emotional response: A subclass of the chronic and delayed posttraumatic stress disorder. *Psychiatric Annals*, 12, 979–987.

Koopman, C., Classen, C., & Spiegel, D. (1994). Predictors of posttraumatic stress symptoms among survivors of the Oakland/Berkeley, California, firestorm. *American Journal of Psychiatry*, 151, 888–894.

Kop, W. J., Appels, P. W. M., Mendes de Leon, C. F., de Swart, H. B., & Bär, F. W. (1994). Vital exhaustion predicts new cardiac events after successful coronary angioplasty. *Psychosomatic Medicine*, 56, 281–287.

Korfman, O. (2002). The role of prenatal stress in the etiology of developmental behavioural disorders. *Neuroscience and Biobehavioral Reviews*, 26, 457–470.

Korte, S. M. (2001). Corticosteroids in relation to fear, anxiety and psychopathology. *Neuroscience and Biobehavioral Reviews*, 25, 117–142.

Krikorian, R., & Layton, B. S. (1998). Implicit memory in posttraumatic stress disorder with amnesia for the traumatic event. *Journal of Neuropsychiatry and Clinical Neuroscience*, 10, 359–362.

Krystal, H. (1988). *Integration and self-healing: Affect-trauma-alexithymia*. Hillsdale, NJ: Analytic Press.

Kuhn, C. M., & Schanberg, S. M. (1998). Responses to maternal separation: Mechanisms and mediators. *International Journal of Developmental Neuroscience*, 16, 261–270.

Kvetnansky, R., Dobrakovova, M., Jezova, D., Oprsalova, Z., Lichardus, B., & Makara, G.B (1989). Hypothalamic regulation of plasma catecholamine levels during stress: Effect of vasopressin and CRF. In G. R. Van Loon, R. Kvetnansky, R. McCarty & J. Axelrod (Eds.), Stress: Neurochemical and humoral mechanisms, 549–570. New York: Gordon and Breach Science.

Kvetnansky, R., Jezova, D., Oprsalova, Z., Foldes, O., Michjlovskij, N., Dobrakovova, M., Lichardus, B., & Makara, G.B. (1990). Regulation of the sympathetic nervous system by circulating vasopressin. In J.C. Porter & D. Jezova (Eds.), *Circulating regulatory factors and neuroendocrine function,* 113–134. New York: Plenum.

La Bar, K. S., Gatenby, J. C., Gore, J. C., Le Doux, J. E., & Phelps, E. A. (1998). Human amygdala activation during conditioned fear acquisition and extinction: A mixed-trial MRI study. *Neuron*, 20, 937–945.

Lanius, R. A., Williamson, P. C., Boksman, K., Densmore, M., Gupta, M., Neufeld, R. W. J., Gati, J. S., & Menon, R. S. (2002). Brain activation during script-driven imagery induced dissociative, responses in PTSD: A functional magnetic resonance imaging investigation. *Biological Psychiatry*, 52, 305–311.

Lanius, R. A., Williamson, P. C., Densmore, M., Boksman, K., Gupta, M. A., Neufeld, R. W., Gati, J. S., & Menon, R. S. (2001). Neural correlates of traumatic memories in posttraumatic stress disorder: A functional MRI investigation. *American Journal of Psychiatry*, 158, 1920–1922.

Lansky, M. R. (1995). *Posttraumatic nightmares: Psychodynamic explorations.* New York: Analytic Press.

Lauder, J. M., & Krebs, H. (1986). Do neurotransmitters, neurohumors, and hormones specify critical periods? In W. T. Greenough & J. M. Juraska (Eds.), *Developmental neuropsychobiology*, 119–174. Orlando, FL: Academic Press.

Layton, B., & Krikorian, R. (2002). Memory mechanisms in posttraumatic stress disorder. *Journal of Neuropsychiatry and Clinical Neuroscience*, 14, 254–261.

Lazarus, R. S. (1991a). Progress on a cognitive-motivational-relational theory of emotion. *American Psychologist*, 46, 819–834.

LeDoux, J. E. (2002). *Synaptic self: How our brains become who we are.* New York: Viking.

Levine, S. (1994). The ontogeny of the hypothalamic-pituitary-adrenal axis: The influence of maternal factors. *Annals of the New York Academy of Sciences*, 746, 275–288.

Liberzon, I., Zubieta, J. K., Fig, L. M., Phan, K. L., Koeppe, R. A., & Taylor, S. F. (2002). μ-opioid receptors and limbic responses to aversive emotional stimuli. *Proceedings of the National Academy of Sciences of the United States of America*, 99, 7084–7089.

Liotti, G. (1992). Disorganized/disoriented attachment in the etiology of the dissociative disorders. *Dissociation*, 4, 196–204.

Lipton, P. A., Alvarez, P., & Eichenbaum, H. (1999). Crossmodal associative memory representations in rodent orbitofrontal cortex. *Neuron*, 22, 349–359.

Luecken, L. J. (1998). Childhood attachment and loss experiences affect adult cardiovascular and cortisol function. *Psychosomatik Medicine*, 60, 765–772.

Luu, P., & Tucker, D. M. (1996). Self-regulation and cortical development: Implications for functional studies of the brain. In R. W. Thatcher, G. R. Lyon, J. Rumsey & N. Krasnegor (Eds.), *Developmental neuroimaging: Mapping the development of brain and behavior*, 297–305. San Diego: Academic.

MacLean, P. D. (1985). Evolutionary psychiatry and the triune brain. *Psychological Medicine*, 15, 219–221.

Main, M. (1996). Introduction to the special section on attachment and psychopathology: Overview of the field of attachment. *Journal of Consulting and Clinical Psychology*, 64, 237–243.

Main, M., & Solomon, J. (1986). Discovery of an insecure-disorganized/disoriented attachment pattern: Procedures, findings and implications for the classification of behavior. In T. B. Brazelton & M. W. Yogman (Eds.), *Affective development in infancy*, 95–124. Norwood, NJ: Ablex.

Mason, J. W., Kosten, T. R., Southwick, S., & Giller, E. L. (1990). The use of psychoendocrine strategies in posttraumatic stress disorder. *Journal of Applied Social Psychology*, 20, 1822–1746.

Mason, J. W., Wang, S., Yehuda, R., Riney, S., Charney, D. S., & Southwick, S. M. (2001). Psychogenic lowering of urinary cortisol levels linked to increased emotional numbing and a shame-depressive syndrome in combat-related posttraumatic stress disorder. *Psychosomatic Medicine*, 63, 387–401.

Matsuzawa, J., Matsui, M., Konishi, T., Noguchi, K., Gur, R. C., Bilker, W., & Miyawaki, T. (2001). Age-related changes of brain gray and white matter in healthy infants and children. *Cerebral Cortex*, 11, 335–342.

Maunder, R. G., & Hunter, J. J. (2001). Attachment and psychosomatic medicine: Developmental contributions to stress and disease. *Psychosomatic Medicine*, 63, 556–567.

Mayer, P., Ammon, S., Braun, H., Tischmeyer, H., Riechert, U., Kahl, E., & Höllt, V. (2002). Gene expression profile after intense second messenger activation in cortical primary neurones. *Journal of Neurochemistry*, 82, 1077–1086.

McDonald, J. W., Silverstein, F. S., & Johnston, M. V. (1988). Neurotoxicity of N-methyl-D-aspartate is markedly enhanced in developing rat central nervous system. *Brain Research*, 459, 20–203.

McEwen, B. S. (2000). The neurobiology of stress: From serendipity to clinical relevance. *Brain Research*, 886, 172–189.

McFarlane, A. C., & Yehuda, R. (2000). Clinical treatment of posttraumatic stress disorder: Conceptual challenges raised by recent research. *Australian and New Zealand Journal of Psychiatry*, 34, 940–953.

McNally, R. J., & Amir, N. (1996). Perceptual implicit memory for trauma-related information in post-traumatic stress disorder. *Cognition and Emotion*, 10, 551–556.

Meares, R. (1999). The contribution of Hughlings Jackson to an understanding of dissociation. *American Journal of Psychiatry*, 156, 1850–1855.

Mesulam, M.-M. (1998). From sensation to cognition. *Brain*, 121, 1013–1052.

Metcalfe, J., & Jacobs, W. (1998). Emotional memory: The effects of stress on "cool" and "hot" memory systems. *Psychology of Learning and Motivation*, 38, 187–222.

Mezzacappa, E. S., Kelsey, R. M., Katkin, E. S., & Sloan, R. P. (2001). Vagal rebound and recovery from psychological stress. *Psychosomatic Medicine*, 63, 650–657.

Mogg, K., Bradley, B. P., Williams, R., & Mathews, A. (1993). Subliminal processing of emotional information in anxiety and depression. *Journal of Abnormal Psychology*, 102, 304–311.

Mollon, P. (1996). *Multiple selves, multiple voices: Working with trauma, violation and dissociation.* Chichester: John Wiley.

Morgan, C. A., III, Wang, S., Rasmusson, A., Hazlett, G., Anderson, G., & Charney, D. S. (2001). Relationship among plasma cortisol, catecholamines, neuropeptide Y, and human performance during exposure to uncontrollable stress. *Psychosomatic Medicine*, 63, 412–422.

Morgan, M. A., & LeDoux, J. E. (1995). Differential acquisition of dorsal and ventral medial prefrontal cortex to the acquisition and extinction of conditioned fear in rats. *Behavioral Neuroscience*, 109, 681–688.

Morgan, M. A., Romanski, L. M., & LeDoux, J. E. (1993). Extinction of emotional learning: Contribution of medial prefrontal cortex. *Neuroscience Letters*, 163, 109–113.

Morris, J. S., Ohman, A., & Dolan, R. J. (1998). Conscious and unconscious emotional learning in the human amygdala. *Nature*, 393, 467–470.

Morris, J. S., Ohman, A., & Dolan, R. J. (1999). A subcortical pathway to the right amygdala mediating "unseen" fear. *Proceedings of the National Academy of Sciences of the United States of America*, 96, 1680–1685.

Nachmias, M., Gunnar, M. R., Mangelsdorf, S., Parritz, R., & Buss, K. (1996). Behavioral inhibition and stress reactivity: Moderating role of attachment security. *Child Development*, 67, 508–522.

Nair, H. P., Berndt, J. D., Barrett, D., & Gonzalez-Lima, F. (2001). Maturation of extinction behavior in infant rats: Large-scale regional interactions with medial prefrontal cortex, and anterior cingulate. *Journal of Neurscience*, 21, 4400–4407.

Nakamura, K., Kawashima, R., Sato, N., Nakamura, A., Sugiura, M., Kato, T., Hatano, K., Ito, K., Fukuda, H., Schorman, T., & Zilles, K. (2000). Functional delineation of the human occipito-temporal areas related to face and scene processing: A PET study. *Brain*, 123, 1903–1912.

Nakamura, K., Kawashima, R., Sugiura, M., Kato, T., Nakamura, A., Hatano, K., Nagumo, S., Kubota, K., Fukuda, H., & Kojima, S. (1999). Activation of the right inferior frontal cortex during assessment of facial emotion. *Journal of Neurophysiology*, 82, 1610–1614.

Neafsey, E. J. (1990). Prefrontal cortical of the autonomic nervous system: Anatomical and physiological observations. *Progress in Brain Research*, 85, 147–166.

Nijenhuis, E. R. S. (2000). Somatoform dissociation: Major symptoms of dissociative disorders. *Journal of Trauma and Dissociation*, 1, 7–32.

Nijenhuis, E. R. S., Vanderlinden, J., & Spinhoven, P. (1998). Animal defensive reactions as a model for trauma-induced dissociative reactions. *Journal of Traumatic Stress*, 11, 242–260.

Northoff, G., Richter, A., Gessner, M., Schlagenhauf, F., Fell, J., Baumgart, F., Kaulisch, T., Kotter, R., Stephan, K. E., Leschinger, A., Hagner, T., Bargel, B., Witzel, T., Hinrichs, H., Bogerts, B., Scheich, H., & Heinze, H.-J. (2000). Functional dissociation between medial and lateral prefrontal cortical spatiotemporal activation in negative and positive emotions: A combined fMRI/MEG study. *Cerebral Cortex*, 10, 93–107.

Nunez, J. (1984). Effects of thyroid hormones during brain differentiation. *Molecular and Cellular Endocrinology*, 37, 125–132.

Ogawa, J. R., Sroufe, L. A., Weinfield, N. S., Carlson, E. A., & Egeland, B. (1997). Development and the fragmented self: Longitudinal study of dissociative symptomatology in an on clinical sample. *Development and Psychopathology*, 9, 855–879.

Ostrowsky, K., Magnin, M., Ryvlin, P., Isnard, J., Guenot, M., & Mauguière, F. (2002). Representation of pain and somatic sensation in the human insula: A study of responses to direct electrical cortical stimulation. *Cerebral Cortex*, 12, 376–385.

Ovtsharoff, W. Jr., & Braun, K. (2001). Maternal separation and social isolation modulate the postnatal development of synaptic composition in the infralimbic cortex of *octodon degus*. *Neuroscience*, 104, 33–40.

Perry, B. D., Pollard, R. A., Blakely, T. L., Baker, W. L., & Vigilante, D. (1995). Childhood trauma, the neurobiology of adaptation, and "use-dependent" development of the brain: How "states" become "traits". *Infant Mental Health Journal*, 16, 271–291.

Perry, S., Cella, D., Falkenberg, J., Heidrich, G., & Gaudwin, C. (1987). Pain perception in burn patients with stress disorders. *Journal of Pain and Symptom Management*, 2, 29–33.

Petrovic, P., Petersson, K. M., Ghatan, P. H., Stone-Elander, S., & Ingvar, M. (2000). Pain-related cerebral activation is altered by a distracting cognitive task. *Pain*, 85, 19–30.

Phelps, E. A., O'Connor, K. J., Gatenby, J. C., Gore, J. C., Grillon, C., & Davis, M. (2001). Activation of the left amygdala to a cognitive representation of fear. *Nature Neuroscience*, 4, 437–441.

Pizzagalli, D. A., Lehmann, D., Hendrick, A. M., Regard, M., Pascual-Marqui, R. D., & Davidson, R. J. (2002). Affective judgments of faces modulate early activity (~160 ms) with the fusiform gyri. *Neuro Image*, 16, 663–677.

Poeggel, G., & Braun, K. (1996). Early auditory filial learning in degus (*octodon degus*): Behavioural and autoradiographic studies. *Brain Research*, 743, 162–170.

Poeggel, G., Lange, E., Hase, C., Metzger, M., Gulyaeva, N., & Braun, K. (1999). Maternal separation and early social deprivation in *octodon degus*: Quantitative changes of nicotinamide adenine dinucleotide phosphate-diasporase.-reactive neurons in the prefrontal cortex and nucleus accumbens. *Neuroscience*, 94, 497–504.

Porges, S. W. (1997). Emotion: An evolutionary by-product of the neural regulation of the autonomic nervous system. *Annals of the New York Academy of Sciences*, 807, 62–77.

Porges, S. W. (2001). The polyvagal theory: Phylogenetic substrates of asocial nervous system. *International Journal of Psychophysiology*, 42, 123–146.

Porges, S. W., Doussard-Roosevelt, J. A., & Maiti, A. K. (1994). Vagal tone and the physiological regulation of emotion. *Monographs of the Society for Research in Child Development*, 59, 167–186.

Portera-Cailliau, C., Price, D. L., & Martin, L. J. (1997). Excitotoxic neuronal death in the immature brain is an apoptosis-necrosis morphological continuum. *Journal of Comparative Neurology*, 378, 70–87.

Post, R. M., Weiss, R. B., & Leverich, G. S. (1994). Recurrent affective disorder: Roots in developmental neurobiology and illness progression based on changes in gene expression. *Development and Psychopathology*, 6, 781–813.

Post, R. M., & Weiss, S. (1997). Emergent properties of neural systems: How focal molecular neurobiological alterations can affect behaviour. *Development and Psychopathology*, 9, 907–929.

Powles, W. E. (1992). *Human development and homeostasis*. Madison, CT: International Universities Press.

Pribram, K. H. (1981). Emotions. In S. B. Filskov & T. J. Boll (Eds.), *Handbook of clinical neuropsychology*, 102–134. New York: Wiley.

Price, D. D. (2000). Psychological and neural mechanisms of the affective dimension of pain. *Science*, 288, 1769–1772.

Price, J. L., Carmichael, S. T., & Drevets, W. C. (1996). Networks related to the orbital and medial prefrontal cortex: A substrate for emotional behavior? *Progress in Brain Research*, 107, 523–536.

Prins, A., Kaloupek, D. G., & Keane, T. M. (1995). Psychophysiological evidence for autonomic arousal and startle in traumatized adult populations. In M. J. Friedman & D. S. Charney (Eds.), *Neurobiological and clinical consequences of stress: From normal adaptation to post-traumatic stress disorder*, 291–314. Philadelphia: Lippincott Williams & Wilkins.

Putnam, F. W. (1995). Development of dissociative disorders. In D. Cicchetti & D. J. Cohen (Eds.), *Developmental psychopathology: Vol. 2. Risk, disorder, and adaptation*, 581–608. New York: Wiley.

Pynoos, R. S. (1993). Traumatic stress and developmental psychopathology in children and adolescents. In J. M. Oldham, M. B. Riba & A. Tasman (Eds.), *Review of psychiatry*, 239–272. Washington: American Psychiatric Press.

Raine, A., Park, S., Lencz, T., et al. (2001). Reduced right hemisphere activation in severely abused violent offenders during a working memory task: A fMRI study. *Aggressive Behavior*, 27, 111–129.

Rapoport, S. (2000). The development of neurodevelopmental psychiatry. *American Journal of Psychiatry*, 157, 159–161.

Rauch, S. L., van der Kolk, B. A., Fisler, R. E., et al. (1996). A symptom provocation study of posttraumatic stress disorder using positrone mission tomography and script-driven imagery. *Archives of General Psychiatry*, 53, 380–387.

Rauch, S. L., Whalen, P. J., Shin, L. M., et al. (2000). Exaggerated amygdale response to masked facial stimuli in posttraumatic stress disorder: A functional MRI study. *Biological Psychiatry*, 47, 769–776.

Reynolds, M., & Brewin, C. R. (1998). Intrusive cognitions, coping strategies, and emotional responses in depression, post-traumatic stress disorder and a non-clinical population. *Behavior Research and Therapy*, 36, 135–147.

Rinaman, L., Levitt, P., & Card, J. P. (2000). Progressive postnatal assembly of limbic-autonomic circuits revealed by central transneuronal transport of pseudorabies virus. *Journal of Neuroscience*, 20, 2731–2741.

Rolls, E. T. (1996). The orbitofrontal cortex. *Philosophical Transactions of the Royal Society of London*, 351, 1433–1444.

Ross, E. D., Homan, R. W., & Buck, R. (1994). Differential hemispheric lateralization of primary and social emotions. Implications for developing a comprehensive neurology for emotions, repression, and the subconscious. *Neuropsychiatry, Neuropsychology, and Behavioral Neurology*, 7, 1–19.

Ruby, P., & Decety, J. (2001). Effect of subjective perspective taking during simulation of action: A PET investigation of agency. *Nature Neuroscience*, 4, 546–550.

Ruda, M. A., Ling, Q.-D., Hohmann, A. G., Peng, Y. B., & Tachibana, T. (2000). Altered, nociceptive neuronal circuits after neonatal peripheral inflammation. *Science*, 289, 628–630.

Ryan, R. M., Kuhl, J., & Deci, E. L. (1997). Nature and autonomy: An organizational view of social and neurobiological aspects of self-regulation in behavior and development. *Development and Psychopathology*, 9, 701–728.

Sabban, E. L., & Kvetnansky, R. (2001). Stress-triggered activation of gene expression in catecholaminergic systems: Dynamics of transcriptional events. *Trends in Neuroscience*, 24, 91–98.

Sahar, T., Shalev, A. Y., & Porges, S. W. (2001). Vagal modulation of responses to mental challenge in posttraumtic stress disorder. *Biological Psychiatry*, 49, 637–643.

Savage, C. R., Deckersbach, T., Heckers, S., Wagner, A. D., Schacter, D. L., Alpert, N. M., Fischman, A. J., & Rauch, S. L. (2001). Prefrontal regions supporting spontaneous and directed application of verbal learning strategies: Evidence from PET. *Brain*, 124, 219–231.

Savarese, V. W., Suvak, M. K., King, L. A., & King, D. W. (2001). Relationships among alcohol use, hyperarousal, and marital abuse and violence in Vietnam veterans. *Journal of Traumatic Stress*, 14, 717–732.

Scaer, R. C. (2001). *The body bears the burden: Trauma, dissociation, and disease.* New York: Haworth.

Scheeringa, M. S., & Zeanah, C. H. (2001). A relational perspective on PTSD in early childhood. *Journal of Traumatic Stress*, 14, 799–815.

Schiffer, F., Teicher, M. H., & Papanicolaou, A. C. (1995). Evoked potential evidence for right brain activity during the recall of traumatic memories. *Journal of Neuropsychiatry and Clinical Neurosciences*, 7, 169–175.

Schmahl, C. G., Elzinga, B. M., & Bremner, J. D. (2002). Individual differences in psychophysiological reactivity in adults with childhood abuse. *Clinical Psychology and Psychotherapy*, 9, 271–276.

Schmidt, S., Nachtigall, C., Wuethrich-Martone, O., & Strauss, B. (2002). Attachment and coping with chronic disease. *Journal of Psychosomatic Research*, 53, 763–773.

Schneider, F., Gur, R. E., Alavi, A., Seligman, M. E., Mozley, L. H., Smit, R. V., Mozley, P. D., & Gur, R. C. (1996). Cerebral blood flow changes in limbic regions induced by unsolvable anagram tasks. *American Journal of Psychiatry*, 153, 206–212.

Schnider, A., Treyer, V., & Buck, A. (2000). Selection of currently relevant memories by the human posterior medial orbitofrontal cortex. *Journal of Neuroscience*, 20, 5880–5884.

Schnurr, P. P., & Friedman, M. J. (1997). An overview of research findings on the nature of posttraumatic stress disorder. *In Session: Psychotherapy in Practice*, 3, 11–25.

Schore, A. N. (1991). Early superego development: The emergence of shame and narcissistic affect regulation in the practicing period. *Psychoanalysis and Contemporary Thought*, 14, 187–250.

Schore, A. N. (1994). *Affect regulation and the origin of the self: The neurobiology of emotional development.* Mahwah, NJ: Erlbaum.

Schore, A. N. (1996). The experience-dependent maturation of a regulatory system in the orbital prefrontal cortex and the origin of developmental psychopathology. *Development and Psychopathology*, 8, 59–87.

Schore, A. N. (1997a). A Century after Freud's Project – is a rapprochement between psychoanalysis and neurobiology at hand? *Journal of the American Psychoanalytic Association*, 45, 1–34.

Schore, A. N. (1997b). Early organization of the nonlinear right brain and development of a predisposition to psychiatric disorders. *Development and Psychopathology*, 9, 595–631.

Schore, A. N. (1997c). Interdisciplinary developmental research as a source of clinical models. In M. Moskowitz, C. Monk, C. Kaye & S. Ellman (Eds.), *The neurobiological and developmental basis for psychotherapeutic intervention*, 1–71. Northvale, NJ: Aronson.

Schore, A. N. (1998a). Early shame experiences and infant brain development. In P. Gilbert & B. Andrews (Eds.), *Shame: Interpersonal behavior, psychopathology, and culture*, 57–77. New York: Oxford University Press.

Schore, A. N. (1998b). The experience-dependent maturation of an evaluative system in the cortex. In K. H. Pribram (Ed.), *Fifth appalachian conference on behavioral neurodynamics, "brain and values"*, 337–358. Mahwah, NJ: Erlbaum.

Schore, A. N. (1998c). *Early trauma and the development of the right brain.* Unveröffentl, Vortrag. Royal Australian and New Zealand College of Psychiatrists, Faculty of Child and Adolescent Psychiatry, 11. Annual Conference. Sydney, Australia.

Schore, A. N. (1998d). *Early trauma and the development of the right brain.* Unveröffentl, Vortrag. C. M. Hincks Institute Conference. Traumatized Parents and Infants: The Long Shadow of Early Childhood Trauma, Toronto, Canada: University of Toronto.

Schore, A. N. (1998e). *The relevance of recent research on the infant brain to clinical psychiatry.* Keynote address at the 11th Annual Conference of the Royal Australian and New Zealand College of Psychiatrists, Sydney, Australia.

Schore, A. N. (1998f). *Early trauma and the development of the right brain.* Keynote address, C. M. Hincks Institute Conference on "Traumatized Parents and Infants: The Long Shadow of Early Childhood Trauma", University of Toronto, Canada.

Schore, A. N. (1999a). Commentary on emotions: Neuropsychoanalytic views. *Neuro-Psychoanalysis*, 1, 49–55.

Schore, A. N. (1999b). *The right brain, the right mind, and psychoanalysis (on-line) Neuro-Psychoanalysis.* Retrieved from www.neuropsa.com/schore.htm.

Schore, A. N. (1999c). *Early trauma and the development of the right brain.* Unveröffentl, Vortrag. School of Medicine Conference. Psychological trauma: Maturational processes and therapeutic interventions. Boston, MA: Boston University.

Schore, A. N. (1999d). *The enduring effects of early trauma on the right brain.* Unveröffentl. Vortrag. Annual Meeting of the American Academy of Child and Adolescent Psychiatry, Symposium, "Attachment, trauma, and the developing mind". Chicago, IL.

Schore, A. N. (1999e, April). *Early trauma and the development of the right brain.* Invited address presented at the Boston University School of Medicine conference, "Psychological Trauma: Maturational Processes and Therapeutic Interventions," Boston, MA.

Schore, A. N. (1999f). *The right brain, the right mind, and psychoanalysis.* Retrieved January 30, 2003, from www.neuro-psa.com/schore.htm.

Schore, A. N. (2000a). Attachment and the regulation of the right brain. *Attachment & Human Development*, 2, 23–47.

Schore, A. N. (2000b). Attachment, the right brain, and empathic processes within the therapeutic alliance. *Psychologist Psychoanalyst*, 20(4), 8–11.

Schore, A. N. (2000c). *Foreword to the reissue of Attachment and loss: Vol. 1. Of John Bowlby*, 49–73. New York: Basic Books.

Schore, A. N. (2000d). Plenary address: Parent-infant communications and the neurobiology of emotional development. In F. Lamp-Parker, J. Hagan & R. Robinson (Eds.), *Proceedings of Head Start's Fifth National Research Conference, Developmental and Contextual Transitions of Children and Families. Implications for Research, Policy, and Practice*, 49–73 Washington, DC: Department of Health and Human Service.

Schore, A. N. (2001a). Contributions from the decade of the brain to infant mental health: An overview. *Infant Mental Health Journal*, 22, 1–6.

Schore, A. N. (2001b). The effects of a secure attachment relationship on right brain development, affect regulation, and infant mental health. *Infant Mental Health Journal*, 22, 7–66.

Schore, A. N. (2001c). The effects of relational trauma on right brain development, affect regulation, and infant mental health. *Infant Mental Health Journal*, 22, 201–269.

Schore, A. N. (2001d). The right brain as the neurobiological substratum of Freud's dynamic unconscious. In D. Scharff (Ed.), *The psychoanalytic century: Freud's legacy for the future*, 61–88. New York: The Other Press.

Schore, A. N. (2001e). *Early relational trauma and the development of the right brain*. Unpublished Keynote Address. Joint Annual Conference. Australian Centre for Posttraumatic Mental Healthand the Australasian Society for Traumatic Stress Studies. Canberra, Australia.

Schore, A. N. (2001f). The seventh annual John Bowlby memorial lecture, Minds in the making: Attachment, the self-organizing brain, and developmentally-oriented psychoanalytic psychotherapy. *British Journal of Psychotherapy*, 17, 299–328.

Schore, A. N. (2002a). Clinical implications of a psychoneurobiological model of projective identification. In S. Alhanati (Ed.), *Primitive mental states: Vol. 3. Pre-and peri-natal influences on personality development*. London: Karnac, 1–65.

Schore, A. N. (2002b). The neurobiology of attachment and early personality organization. *Journal of Prenatal & Perinatal Psychology and Health*, 16, 249–263.

Schore, A. N. (2002c). Dysregulation of the right brain: A fundamental mechanism of traumatic attachment and the psychopathogenesis of posttraumatic stress disorder. *Australian and New Zealand Journal of Psychiatry*, 36, 9–30.

Schore, A. N. (2003a). *Affect regulation and the repair of the self*. New York, London: Norton.

Schore, A. N. (2003b). *Affect dysregulation and the disorder of the self*. New York, London: Norton.

Schore, A. N. (2005). Attachment, affect regulation, and the developing right brain: Linking developmental neuroscience to pediatrics. *Pediatrics in Review*, 26(6), 204–217.

Schore, A. N. (2008, 12, April). *The paradigm shift: The right brain and the relational unconscious*. Vortrag bei der Division 39 Spring Conference in New York.

Schore, A. N. (2012). *The science of the art of psychotherapy*. New York/London: Norton.

Schore, A. N., & McIntosh, J. (2011). Family law and the neuroscience of attachment, Part 1. *Family Court Review*, 49, 501–512.

Schore, A. N., & Newton, R. P. (2012). Using modern attachment theory to guide clinical assessments of early attachment relationships. In A. N. Schore (Ed.) (2012), *The science of the art of psychotherapy*. New York/London: Norton, 383–427.

Schore, J. R. (1983). *A study of the superego: The relative proneness to shame or guilt as related to psychological masculinity and femininity in women*. Unveröffentl. Dissertation, California Institute for Clinical Social Work, Berkeley.

Schore, J. R., & Schore, A. N. (2008). Modern attachment theory: The central role of affect regulation in development and treatment. *Clinical Social Work*, 36, 9–20.

Schuengel, C., Bakersmans-Kranenburg, M. J., & Van Ijzendoorn, M. H. (1999). Frightening maternal behavior linking unresolved loss and disorganized infant attachment. *Journal of Consulting and Clinical Psychology*, 67, 54–63.

Schuff, N., Marmar, C. R., Weiss, D. S., et al. (1997). Reduced hippocampal volume and n-acetyl aspartate in posttraumatic stress disorder. *Annals of the New York Academy of Sciences*, 821, 516–520.

Semple, W. E., Goyer, P., McCormick, R., et al. (1992). Increased orbital frontal cortex blood flow and hippocampal abnormality in PTSD: A pilot PET study. *Biological Psychiatry*, 31, 129A.

Sgoifo, A., Koolhaas, J., De Boer, S., Musso, E., Stilli, D., Buwalda, B., & Meerlo, P. (1999). Social stress, autonomic neural activation, and cardiac activity in rats. *Neuroscience and Biobehavioral Reviews*, 23, 915–923.

Shalev, A. Y., Peri, T., Canetti, L., & Schreiber, S. (1996). Predictors of PTSD in injured trauma survivors: A prospective study. *American Journal of Psychiatry*, 153, 219–225.

Shalev, A. Y., Sahar, T., Freedman, S., Peri, T., Glick, N., Brandes, D., Orr, S., & Pitman, R. K. (1998). A prospective study of heart rate response following trauma and the subsequent development of posttraumatic stress disorder. *Archives of General Psychiatry*, 55, 553–559.

Shimazu, T. (1971). Regulation of glycogen metabolism in live by the autonomic nervous system: IV. Activation of glycogen synthetase by vagal stimulation. *Biochemica Biophysica Acta*, 252, 28–38.

Shimazu, T., & Amakawa, A. (1968). Regulation of glycogen metabolism in liver by the autonomic nervous system: II. Neural control of glycogenolytic enzymes. *Biochemica Biophysica Acta*, 165, 335–348.

Shin, L. M., McNally, R. J., Kosslyn, S. M., et al. (1999). Regional cerebral blood flow during script-driven imagery in childhood sexual abuse-related PTSD: A PET investigation. *American Journal of Psychiatry*, 156, 575–584.

Schin, L. M., Whalen, P. J., Pitman, R. K., Bush, G., Macklin, M. L., Lasko, N. B., Orr, S. P., Melnerney, S. C., & Rauch, S. L. (2001). An fMRI study of anterior cingulate function in posttraumatic stress disorder. *Biological Psychiatry*, 50, 932–942.

Siegel, D. J. (1999). *The developing mind: Toward a neurobiology of interpersonal experience*. New York: Guilford Press.

Simons, J. S., Graham, K. S., Owen, A. M., Patterson, K., & Hodges, J. R. (2001). Perceptual and semantic components of memory for objects and faces: A PET study. *Journal of Cognitive Neuroscience*, 13, 430–443.

Smith, M. Y., Egert, S., Winkel, G., & Jacobson, J. (2002). The impact of PTSD on pain experience in persons with HIV/AIDS. *Pain*, 98, 9–17.

Southwick, S. M., Krystal, J. H., Morgan, A., et al. (1993). Abnormal noradrenergic function in posttraumatic stress disorder. *Archives of General Psychiatry*, 50, 266–274.

Spangler, G., & Grossman, K. (1999). Individual and physiological correlates of attachment disorganization in infancy. In J. Solomon & C. George (Eds.), *Attachment disorganization*, 95–125. New York: Guilford.

Spangler, G., Schieche, M., Ilg, U., Maier, U., & Ackerman, C. (1994). Maternal sensitivity as an organizer for biobehavioral regulation in infancy. *Developmental Psychobiology*, 27, 425–437.

Spence, S., Shapiro, D., & Zaidel, E. (1996). The role of the right hemisphere in the physiological and cognitive components of emotional processing. *Psychophysiology*, 33, 112–122.

Spivak, B., Segal, M., Mester, R., & Weizman, A. (1998). Lateral preference in posttraumatic stress disorder. *Psychological Medicine*, 28, 229–232.

Sroufe, L. A. (1996). *Emotional development: The organization of emotional life in the early years*. New York: Cambridge University Press.

Stern, D. N. (1985). *The interpersonal world of the infant*. New York: Basic Books.

Streeck-Fischer, A., & van der Kolk, B. A. (2000). Down will come baby, cradle and all: Diagnostic and therapeutic implications of chronic trauma on child development. *Australian and New Zealand Journal of Psychiatry*, 34, 903–918.

Stuss, D. T., & Alexander, M. P. (1999). Affectively burnt in: A proposed role of the right frontal lobe. In E. Tulving (Ed.), *Memory, consciousness, and the brain: The Talin conference*, 215–227. Philadelphia: Psychology Press.

Suchecki, D., Nelson, D. Y., Van Oers, H., & Levine, S. (1995). Activation and exhibition of the hypothalamic-pituitary-adrenal axis of the neonatal rat: Effects of maternal deprivation. *Psychoneuroendocrinology*, 20, 169–182.

Sullivan, R. M., & Gratton, A. (1999). Prefrontal cortical regulation of hypothalamic-pituitary-adrenal function of the rat and implications for psychopathology: Side matters. *Psychoneuroendocrinology*, 27, 99–114.

Sullivan, R. M., Landers, M., Yeaman, B., & Wilson, D. A. (2000). Good memories of bad events in infancy. *Nature*, 407, 38–39.

Suomi, S. J. (1995). Influence of attachment theory on ethological studies of biobehavioral development in nonhuman primates. In S. Goldberg, R. Muir & J. Kerr (Eds.), *Attachment theory: Social, developmental and clinical perspectives*, 185–201. Hillsdale, NJ: Analytic Press.

Sutker, P. B., Vasterling, J. J., Brailey, K., & Allain, A. N. Jr. (1995). Memory attention, and executive deficits in POW survivors: Contributing biological and psychological factors. *Neuropsychology*, 9, 118–125.

Svensson, T. H. (1987). Peripheral autonomic regulation of locus coeruleus noradrenergic neurons in brain: Putative implications for psychiatry and psychopharmacology. *Psychopharmacology*, 92, 1–7.

Sweet, S. D., McGrath, P. J., & Symons, D. (1999). The roles of child reactivity and parenting context in infant pain responses. *Pain*, 80, 655–661.

Taylor, G. J., Bagby, R. M., & Parker, J. D. A. (1997). *Disorders of affect regulation: Alexithymia in medical and psychiatric illness*. Cambridge: Cambridge University Press.

Teicher, M. H., Glod, C. A., Surrey, J., & Swett, C. Jr. (1993). Early childhood abuse and limbic system ratings in adult psychiatric conditions. *Journal of Neuropsychiatry and Clinical Neuroscience*, 5, 301–306.

Teicher, M. H., Ito, Y., Gold, C. A., Andersen, S. L., Dumont, N., & Ackerman, E. (1997). Preliminary evidence for abnormal cortical development in physically and sexually abused children using EEG coherence and MRI. *Annals of the New York Academy of Sciences*, 821, 160–175.

Terr, L. C. (1988). What happens to early memories of trauma? *Journal of the American Academy of Child and Adolescent Psychiatry*, 1, 96–104.

Thatcher, R. W. (1994). Cyclical cortical reorganization: Origins of human cognitive development. In G. Dawson & K. W. Fischer (Eds.), *Human behavior and the developing brain*, 232–266. New York: Guilford.

Thompson, R. A. (1990). Emotion and self-regulation. In R. A. Thompson (Ed.), *Nebraska symposium on motivation*, 367–467. Lincoln: University of Nebraska Press.

Thompson, R. A. (1990). The legacy of early attachment. *Child Development*, 71, 145–152.

Toth, S. C., & Cicchetti, D. (1998). Remembering, forgetting, and the effects of trauma on memory: A developmental psychopathologic perspective. *Developmental and Psychopathology*, 10, 580–605.

Tronick, E. Z., & Weinberg, M. K. (1997). Depressed mothers and infants: Failure to form dyadic states of consciousness. In L. Murray & P. J. Cooper (Eds.), *Postpartum depression in child development*, 54–81. New York: Guilford.

Tucker, D. M. (1992). Developing emotions and cortical networks. In M. R. Gunnar & C. A. Nelson (Eds.), *Minnesota symposium on child psychology: Vol. 24. Developmental behavioral neuroscience*, 75–128. Hillsdale, NJ: Erlbaum.

Uddo, M., Vasterling, J. J., Brailey, K., & Sutker, P. B. (1993). Memory and attention in combat-related post-traumatic stress disorder (PTSD). *Journal of Psychopathology and Behavioral Assessment*, 15, 43–52.

Valent, P. (1998). *From survival to fulfillment: A framework for the life-trauma dialectic*. Philadelphia, PA: Brunner/Mazel.

van der Kolk, B. A. (1996). The body keeps the score. Approaches to the psychobiology of posttraumatic stress disorder. In. B. A. van der Kolk, A. C. McFarlane & L. Weisaeth (Eds.), *Traumatic stress: The effects of overwhelming experience on mind, body, and society*, 214–241. New York: Guilford.

van der Kolk, B. A., & Fisler, R. E. (1994). Childhood abuse and neglect and loss of self-regulation. *Bulletin of the Menninger Clinic*, 58, 145–168.

van der Kolk, B. A., & McFarlane, A. C. (1996). The black hole of trauma. In B. A. van der Kolk, A. C. McFarlane & L. Weisaeth (Eds.), *Traumatic stress: The effects of overwhelming experience on mind, body, society*, 3–23. New York: Guilford.

van Ijzendoorn, M. H., Schuengel, C., & Bakermans-Kranenburg, M. J. (1999). Disorganized attachment in early childhood: Meta-analysis of pre cursors, concomitants, and sequelae. *Development and Psychopathology*, 11, 225–249.

van Lancker, D. (1991). Personal relevance and the human right hemisphere. *Brain and Cognition*, 17, 64–92.

Vasterling, J. J., Brailey, K., & Sutker, P. B. (2000). Olfactory identification in combat-related posttraumatic stress disorder. *Journal of Traumatic Stress*, 13, 241–253.

Vermetten, E., & Bremner, J. D. (2002). Circuits and systems in stress: II. Applications to neurobiology and treatment in posttraumatic stress disorder. *Depression and Anxiety*, 16, 14–38.

Vyas, A., Mitra, R., Shankaranarayana Rao, B. S., & Chattarji, S. (2002). Chronic stress induces contrasting pattern of dendritic remodeling in hippocampal and amygdaloid neurons. *Journal of Neuroscience*, 22, 6810–6818.

Wang, S. (1997). Traumatic stress and attachment. *Acta Physiologica Scandinavica*, 640(Suppl.), 164–169.

Wang, S., Wilson, J. P., & Mason, J. W. (1996). Stages of decompensation in combat-related posttraumatic stress disorder: A new conceptual model. *Integrative Physiological and Behavioral Science*, 31, 237–253.

Weinberg, I. (2000). The prisoners of despair: Right hemisphere deficiency and suicide. *Neuroscience and Biobehavioral Reviews*, 24, 799–815.

Whalen, P. J., Rauch, S. L., Etcoff, N., McInerney, S. C., Lee, M. B., & Jenike, M. A. (1998). Masked presentations of emotional facial expressions modulate amygdala activity without explicit knowledge. *Journal of Neuroscience*, 18, 411–418.

Wittling, W. (1997). The right hemisphere and the human stress response. *Acta Physiologica Scandinavica*, 640(Suppl.), 55–59.

Wittling, W., Block, A., Schweiger, E., & Genzel, S. (1998). Hemisphere asymmetry in sympathetic control of the human myocardium. *Brain and Cognition*, 38, 17–35.

Wittling, W., & Pfluger, M. (1990). Neuroendocrine hemisphere asymmetries: Salivary cortisol secretion during lateralized viewing of emotion-related and neutral films. *Brain and Cognition*, 14, 243–265.

Yehuda, R. (1999). Managing anger and aggression in patients with posttraumatic stress disorder. *Journal of Traumatic Stress*, 12, 1–517.

Yehuda, R., Halligan, S. L., & Grossman, R. (2001). Childhood trauma and risk for PTSD: Relationship to intergenerational effects of trauma, parental PTSD, and cortisol excretion. *Development and Psychopathology*, 13, 733–753.

Yehuda, R., McFarlane, A. C., & Shalev, A. Y. (1998). Predicting the development of posttraumatic stress disorder from the acute response to a traumatic event. *Biological Psychiatry*, 44, 1305–1313.

Yoon, B.-W., Morillo, C. A., Cechetto, D. F., & Hachinski, V. (1997). Cerebral hemispheric lateralization in cardiac autonomic control. *Archives of Neurology*, 54, 741–744.

Young, J. B., Rosa, R. M., & Landsberg, L. (1984). Dissociation of sympathetic nervous system and adrenal medullary responses. *American Journal of Physiology*, 247, E35–E40.

Zald, D. H., & Kim, S. W. (1996). Anatomy and function of the orbital frontal cortex, II: Function and relevance to obsessive-compulsive disorder. *Journal of Neuropsychiatry*, 8, 249–261.

Zlotnick, C., Warshaw, M., Shea, M. T., Allsworth, J., Pearlstein, T., & Keller, M. B. (1999). Chronicity in posttraumatic stress disorder (PTSD) and predictors of course of comorbid PTSD in patients with anxiety disorders. *Journal of Traumatic Stress*, 12, 89–100.

Zubieta, J.-K., Smith, Y. R., Bueller, J. A., Yu, Y., Kilbourn, M. R., Jewett, D. M., Meyer, C. R., Koeppe, R. A., & Stohler, C. S. (2002). μ-opioid receptor-mediated anti nociceptive responses differ in men and women. *Journal of Neuroscience*, 22, 5100–5107.

3.5 Looking back and looking forward: our professional and personal journey – UCLA Interpersonal Neurobiology Conference 2014

The past three days have been amongst the most special in my life. They've been special because this occasion provides me with the extraordinary experience of receiving direct tangible feedback from my colleagues and peers on this stage and across the country, people I highly value, about the impact of my studies on their own. What a unique and wonderful gift. Despite what on the surface looks like different areas of work, all of these presenters share an intention to use rapidly accumulating scientific and clinical knowledge in order to more deeply understand and indeed better the human condition – no small goal. And I admire the dedication and the courage of each of them. But this occasion is also special because it's happening here at UCLA, with an audience of so many colleagues and friends. I've presented here 13 times since 1998, the end of the last century, and this conference has allowed me to share the continued development of my ideas and get audience feedback even before they were published, a valuable context for the ongoing development of the body of my work.

This weekend also heightens my awareness of the passage of time, along the course of living one's life. Last month, somehow, without my permission, I turned 71, which to ease the shock my mind turned into a "dyslexic 17." One of the conscious goals that runs throughout my life is to remain emotionally and intellectually open to the future, what Bob Dylan calls "forever young." But I'm now at a stage in which there is even more looking backward, into the past, especially in light of the 20th anniversary of a central moment in my life. In that spirit I'd like to share with you some personal thoughts about the creation of *Affect Regulation and the Origin of the Self* in 1994, and the events even before it that set the foundation of the path that has guided everything from that point of origin.

Earlier, in a stage when looking forward was intense, in my late 30s, as a husband and a father of two young children, I set out to "write something." Even before that something had a specific shape, I intuitively understood, at both a surface and a deeper level, that the time had come to actively begin the venture. And so in 1980 I began what would turn out to be a ten-year period of independent study, ten years before I would put pen to paper (note the late 20th century now almost obsolete reference). In the preceding decade, the '70s, a time when I had the valuable experience of being the patient in a psychotherapeutic process, I dutifully put in my 10,000 hours of clinical work and had developed some expertise and confidence in the professions in which I was trained: clinical psychology and clinical neuropsychology.

But in parallel my up close therapeutic work with patients fueled a rapidly growing intense curiosity about the relational processes of psychotherapy – which at the time took the form of the question, "How do minds and brains touch and shape other minds and brains?" In order to clear out the substantial amounts of time for this continuing education and self study I left my clinical position at the Psychiatry Department at Kaiser Permanente and cut back my private practice from five to three days. All with Judy's support – even more than emotional support, hard cash financial support. We switched income responsibilities and for the entire decade of the '80s my period of independent study was financed by a Judy Schore grant.

Judy has told you something about my visits to the Cal State Northridge library, just a mile from our home. For about three out of four Saturdays for ten years I roamed through the stacks, in a state of pleasurable exploration, like a child in a candy store (again pardon the mid-20th century reference), back and forth between sections of psychological, psychiatric, biological, chemical, and even physical sciences. When Beth and David were old enough they'd come along, riding their bicycles on the campus while I immersed myself in journal after journal, and doling out huge numbers of quarters into voracious copying machines. What is most important is that I brought the knowledge back to my home, which is where the careful analysis and synthesis of the knowledge took place. Another 10,000 hours, expanding the evolving science of my earlier education, but this time not at a university but in my home.

Meanwhile I continued to see patients, many of them in long-term psycho-therapeutic explorations. What I was learning from them (and about myself) was developing in parallel to my second scientific education. The process of extended "self study" involved not only the independent, solitary processing of large amounts of external knowledge, but also reflecting upon the increasing knowledge about my own internal emotional world. And perhaps an even greater source was my ongoing development as a husband, father, son, and friend. It is no coincidence that my application of science to the understanding of the most personal and deepest aspects of the human condition was created in the intimate context of my home, and not in an academic institution. Everything I have created about development, and attachment, about subjectivity and intersubjectivity, about shame and joy, about brain and mind has occurred in the close quarters of my life – which is why my work had to explore subjective emotions and close relationships, at both the conscious and unconscious levels.

Led almost entirely by my curiosity (a personal trait that had been nurtured from my early beginnings under the watchful eye of my loving mother, Barbara Schore) and absolutely trusting my intuition in deciding what to read beyond the fields in which I was trained, for ten years I enjoyed long states of play, out there in the library and back at my home office. I was acting out in daily life my long-held wish to become a scholar. But a particular kind of scholar. And here I looked backward. My father George Schore, my role model in so many areas of my life, was a chemical engineer, an applied scientist, an international expert in metal finishing and water pollution, and had numerous patents on electroplating copper and gold recovery processes. In 1976, he received an award from the *Environmental Protection Agency*

Office of Research Applied Science and Technology "in recognition of having contributed major efforts and demonstrated a significant advancement in our nation's continuing struggle for environmental pollution abatement." The plaque hangs in my office. His work was always at the cutting-edge, and even ahead of its time. His career, like mine, significantly changed at several points in his life. So I was exposed to the mind of a creative scientist who was continually translating advances in basic chemical science into practical applications.

When I was 21 years old, between college graduation and my postgraduate education, I spent about a year working with my father. At that time he was designing and building the first automated metal finishing systems, and sold them to, amongst others, General Electric, General Motors, and IBM. I continued to learn from him. But on one particular occasion he taught me something that was to become invaluable. I went with him to Tampa Florida, where he was giving a sales presentation to build an automation system for Honeywell, the manufacturer of thermostats (yes, temperature regulators). I have a strong visual memory of the room, of my father in the center of a long table, facing seven scientists and executives. I watched him effortlessly field questions posed by an electrical engineer, a chemical engineer, a mechanical engineer, a water pollution expert and vice presidents from three different departments. He was going back and forth answering each of their technical questions, talking about the automation system in terms of its impact on all of these different fields, and then integrating that information into a system specifically tailored to their needs.

In that "Aha" moment of recognition and insight I saw my father in the role of a polymath, and I thought, that's the professional mind that I admired and needed to nurture in myself, one that knows the language of and can communicate with a number of different professions. An ability to fluidly move between disciplines would become the prototype for my burgeoning career as a scholar. This synthetic, integrative approach was opposed to the then (and still) dominant role of specialization and an increased narrowing into one's field. This affectively imprinted autobiographical memory later naturally evolved into an interdisciplinary perspective which pervades all my work. And so I would create a theoretical model that could not only describe but integrate various scientific disciplines – that would chart the points of contact between psychology and psychiatry, biology and chemistry. Early development and emotion would turn out to be a common factor.

So in 1980 as I began the independent study, I had a theoretical perspective to process and understand the various literatures I would encounter. But on a practical level I had to create a structure that self-organized my time, and an environment that could support and allow for the growth of my creativity. The routine I came up with was to visit the library on the weekend, return with 30–40 xeroxed articles, and then spend the weekdays taking notes on each in 100-sheet 8½x 11 legal pads. Every third or fourth notebook I found myself recording repeating patterns across fields and began to integrate different research literatures, especially developmental biology, developmental neurochemistry, and developmental psychology. And meanwhile I'm shuttling between my study and consulting room, where I'm focusing more and more on the relational processes that lie at the core of psychotherapy.

The work expanded my skills as a clinician-scientist, a term that best fit the professional identity I was creating. The scientist part was expressed in careful observations about the patient's and my own subjectivities, especially about the emotional interactions between us, including our internal worlds. But the emerging scientist was also extremely careful about the kinds of evidence that I found convincing and would later use to develop an interdisciplinary theoretical model. My focus was on the boundaries between fields, and the commonalities that lie beneath what appear on the surface to be unrelated phenomena. I became especially confident putting my money on certain organizing principles and theoretical concepts that cut across different sciences. And so when I found the construct of regulation to lie at the core of chemistry, physics, and biology, I knew that any overarching developmental or clinical model could be centered in that.

For ten years I was frequently and routinely in a positive state of play, of flow, both intellectually and emotionally. I became very adept at transitioning between different scientific and clinical literatures, at moving between brain and mind, and by five years in I became absolutely confident that by creating a theoretical model of emotion and human relationships that integrated psychology and biology I could alter the course of clinical practice, and indeed science. That was the phrase that literally came to mind. And even though my self-image is basically to be a modest man, again something I learned from my father, I became comfortable with that explicit sense of conviction and confidence, even certainty in the power of the model my mind was creating.

I should mention that over the decade I engaged in one other activity, in order to create an environment that could support my creativity and imagination. At the very outset I chose to return to the piano. When I was a child I dabbled with the piano for a couple of years. Now in my late 30s, I took lessons, as an adult. I wanted to not just listen to but create music, and thereby bring music into my homemade ivory tower. I was aware that the music would allow me to understand something in my fingers, in my body, and not just in my mind. I was learning that science, and emotions in particular, were not apprehended just through logical understanding. I also wanted to learn how to visualize what I was learning, to think in images as well as thoughts. Later I realized my intent was to involve myself in exercises that tapped specifically into my right brain, the source of creative processing. And along the way I was able to give a pretty good imitation of a cocktail pianist. Again exercises for shoring up (probably no pun intended) my right brain.

In order to come up with a fresh solution to the problems I was addressing, I realized that my right brain implicit learning processes played an even larger role than my familiar left brain approaches. From the outset I decided never to explicitly memorize anything. And then I found that I had to expand my tolerance for the uncertainty of not knowing, to allow my mind to stay open long enough rather than prematurely closing down the exploratory process with what appeared to be a quick solution. In order to foster the creative process I never deliberately attempted to solve anything in particular. Rather, I would just take in large amounts of salient information, with an intuitive bodily-based knack for knowing what is meaningful and essential information to the phenomenon I was attempting to understand. Ultimately my right brain unconscious mind would recognize patterns, which then my left brain conscious mind would describe verbally. Frequently these solutions took a visual form. More than just describing data, at the most fundamental level I was attempting not only to understand different fields but to integrate them, and ultimately to describe underlying mechanisms.

By the end of the decade the hundreds of legal pads stacked well over six feet high, and they contained long sections of detailed notes on research common to and overlapping different disciplines. So after ten years, I made the decision, again intuitively, to end the period of solitary, independent study (as well as the piano). My plan was to write a psychoneurobiological formulation of emotional development, both in early life and in the therapeutic process I was observing in my practice. And now the next set of questions. How was I going to transport the work of science I had created in my garage (family room and study) into the real world? How could I establish my credentials in order to be offered a publishing contract for a book? I decided to write an article. But on what, and where would it appear?

Coincidentally, in the '80s, Judy returned to academia for her PhD in clinical social work, on a relatively unexplored clinical phenomenon, the emotion of shame. Now when it came to emotions I found that the kind of work that I was doing with my patients, especially early disturbed patients, was all about emotion. Their interpersonal deficits were fundamentally deficits in coping with a wide array of emotions. So I became very interested in the early forming nonverbal emotion of shame, which then lead me to the early development of emotions *per se*, a then unchartered landscape in both the clinical and scientific literatures. In addition to becoming acquainted with the (meager) literature on bodily-based shame, I was also studying it clinically, in my work with narcissistic patients, and became convinced that working with this affect was essential to the treatment of all developmental disorders.

So Judy and I wrote an article together, on shame and gender development. We submitted it to the *Journal of the American Psychoanalytic Association* (JAPA) and they would have none of it. However, there was another psychoanalytic journal, one related to JAPA, *Psychoanalysis and Contemporary Thought*. With a sense of relief I noticed that on its editorial board were developmental psychoanalysts like Erik Erikson, Bob Emde, and Fred Pine. When I saw their names I knew immediately that this journal would be a good fit. I wrote "Early superego development: the emergence of shame and narcissistic affect regulation in the practicing period" and submitted it to that journal. The paper ended with neurobiological speculations about the early development of the right hemisphere. It was accepted immediately. As I look back I view it as my first articulation of developmental neuropsychoanalysis, the study of the early development of the unconscious mind, as well as a regulation model of the neurobiology of attachment, themes that would become central in not only the 1994 book all my subsequent writings.

But I wanted more than to publish a paper – I wanted to come into direct contact and dialogue with the minds I admired. As soon as the shame paper came out I sent reprints to 40 authors cited in it, and along with it a letter introducing my work and carefully tying it into their own. Incidentally, many of these were child and adult psychiatrists trained in psychoanalysis, like Stan Greenspan, Dan Stern, Jim Masterson, Henry Krystal, and especially Jim Grotstein, who helped me get established here in LA. And later in that summer, this was about '91, I got back about 35 letters, and I knew that I had connected into a group of peers, clinicians and theoreticians who were also convinced of the centrality of the developmental perspective. The psychoanalytic article succeeded because the reviewers and readers could evaluate evidence that was familiar to them, observations from both psycho-analytic clinicians and researchers about the early developing mind and inner world.

But now I needed to find out how neuroscientists would respond, and what types of "evidence" were meaningful for them. I needed their feedback, and so I decided to submit to a peer-reviewed neuroscience journal an expanded version of how the early mother-infant relationship was affecting the neurobiology of the developing brain. To get this feedback I submitted an article to *Behavioural and Brain Sciences*. Although three of the reviewers accepted it, the editor-in-chief rejected it. But one reviewer, Carol Izard, a major developmental psychologist who had worked with Sylvan Tomkins, an early pioneer in the study of emotions, told me to focus less on psychoanalysis and more on John Bowlby's attachment theory, which was more palatable to scientists because of its connections to ethology. At the time I wasn't aware of the fact that three months before I offered that article there was a severe critique of psychoanalysis in that journal.

But even the sting of the rejection was a learning experience. The emotional disappointment led me into parts of myself that I would later describe in my work. Instead of rationalizing the pain or avoiding the risk, or even using Judy to help booster me against the injury to my self-esteem, I became aware that I just needed to allow myself to deflate and sink deeper into the momentary defeat. That became helpful to me. In other words, I allowed myself to experience not only the accelerat-ing high arousal play states, but also the decelerating low arousal painful deflations. And I found that implicit processes, other than my conscious mind, would operate down there, and when they had run their course I'd come back up and continue forward. These experiences highlighted the fact that the ability to tolerate both positive and negative emotions was a fundamental aspect of emotional growth and development.

And so now at age 50, with a single journal publication under my belt, I sent a book proposal to a psychoanalytic publisher, Analytic Press, who then passed it along to their scientific division, Lawrence Erlbaum. As it went into the mail I had the clear thought that everything I had accomplished in my life up to then would have little meaning unless this product of my mind would find a home at a pub-lisher. They immediately accepted the book, although they had severe reservations that it would not sell because they felt that the people who were interested in the biology would not be interested in the psychology, the people who were interested in the psychiatry wouldn't care about the neuroscience, and so on. Remember, the positive valence of the term "interdisciplinary" was not yet established when the book came out in 1994. Even so, my initial reaction was one of great relief. I felt that the previous decade had paid off, and that I had said exactly what I wanted to say in the book. Indeed not one word was changed by the copy editor in what turned out to be 700 pages, including 105 pages of 2,500 references.

In the spring of 1994 I got my hands on the book, and that summer I again used the feedback–communication device and wrote 60 letters, sending out many copies at my own expense. But this time in addition to psychiatrists and psychoanalysts, I wrote to neuroanatomists, neurochemists, brain researchers, cell biologists, developmental psychologists etc., literally around the world. And again at the end of the summer I got back about 50 letters which I still have. I knew even before the book had "hit the streets" that it would get a good reception. The format of the book included citing a quotation from a major figure in each field at the beginning of every chapter. It was these experts I sent letters to, and when they responded so quickly I knew that it was a done deal. So, soon after its birth, I remember thinking I could die now and have the satisfaction of knowing that I had accomplished what I set out to do, to "write something." And then the very positive journal reviews started to come in. The *British Journal of Psychiatry* called me "a polymath," something that had special meaning, and described the book as a "superb integrative work" with a depth and breadth that was "staggering." That brightened up my day.

The "Green Book" in essence was an argument for the power of integrating the psychological and the biological, the scientific and the clinical. The opening paragraph was meant at the time to be groundbreaking, if not revolutionary:

> The understanding of early development is one of the fundamental objectives of science. The beginnings of living systems set the stage for every aspect of an organism's internal and external functioning throughout the life span. Events that occur during infancy, especially transactions with the social environment, are indelibly imprinted into the structures that are maturing in the first years of life. The child's first relationship, the one with the mother, acts as a template, as it permanently molds the individual's capacities to enter into all later emotional relationships. These early experiences shape the development of a unique personality, its adaptive capacities as well as its vulnerabilities and resistances against particular forms of future pathologies. Indeed, they profoundly influence the emergent organization of an integrated system that is both stable and adaptable, and thereby the formation of the self.

I remember knowing that the book was about ten years ahead of the field, some parts 20 years, especially in terms of scientific research. What I didn't know was if other people would find "the first relationship," the maturation of the infant's brain, emotional development, and an affective description of the baby's emerging consciousness, to be as fascinating as I did. I was also surprised that the book, which was written in the language of science, appealed to clinicians. This may be a surprise to some of you, but the book was not an easy read.

The year after the book was born, in 1995, I was invited to join a small group, mostly faculty at UCLA, who were studying how neuroscience could be integrated into psychiatry, psychology, psychoanalysis, and linguistics. And so for the next two years this group focused intently on just one volume – my Green Book. The other members of this seminal peer group – Dan Siegel, Lou Cozzolino, Regina Paley, and John Schumann – were to write their own books on interpersonal neuroscience and neuropsychoanalysis by the end of the decade. In 1996 I joined the clinical faculty at the UCLA Medical School, and also began my first in a number of study groups in Los Angeles, Seattle, Berkeley, Portland, Boulder, and Austin. These groups have since become important sources of feedback from experienced clinicians, as well as of new questions that I later addressed in my writings. The groups have also been a context in which I mentored numerous other professionals. Many began their own writing careers, and a number became Norton authors.

But from the beginning, the book brought another instant bonus – invitations from influential journal editors in a number of different fields. These invitations from high-level developmental, psychiatric, psychoanalytic, and neuroscience peer-reviewed journals allowed me to impact a much larger readership than the book itself and gave me exposure across a wide range of disciplines. This single work also brought me invitations to be a reviewer or on the editorial boards of dozens of journals, which in turn allowed me to influence the direction of both experimental research and clinical models. It also was the generator of numerous invitations to lecture nationally and internationally, and thereby an opportunity to offer my ideas to audiences both here and around the world. If the problem of emotion had been ignored by science for most of the century, by the end of the '90s the clinical audiences I was addressing became aware and indeed very interested in how to apply the new information about bodily-based affect and affect regulation into their work with patients.

As "the decade of the brain" progressed, a rapidly expanding interest in the neurobiology of attachment and in early brain development allowed me to present to dozens of conferences, where I could share ideas with a large number of leading neuroscientists and prominent clinical writers. Many of these people later presented at this UCLA Lifespan Conference. Thanks to Marion Solomon, these UCLA conferences have attained an international reputation for cutting-edge themes and for presenting an intellectual context that allows for an ongoing dialogue between leading neuroscientists, prominent clinicians, and an extremely well-informed audience. But perhaps the most unexpected bonus of the work was the creation, at a later stage of life, of deep friendships with so many colleagues of not only like minds, but like hearts (including many people here in the audience).

Over the last 20 years my daily life has been profoundly changed, yet in some important ways remains the same. I continue to set aside large amounts of time every day for reading and poring over new studies over a broad spectrum of disciplines. Sitting at my desk I have instant access to every University of California

Library. The fact that the body of my work has been cited in Google Scholar in well over 12,000 publications over a broad range of scientific and clinical disciplines is a source of great pride. I still see patients in my home office because everything I create in science must ring true clinically. This homemade ivory tower has become the context that allows for the collaborative research with colleagues in different disciplines, some of whom have presented this weekend. It also is the locus of my work as editor of the Norton Series, as well as a reviewer of dozens of journals. Through these various activities, my conscious and unconscious minds are continuously stimulated, challenged and surprised by novel and intrinsically interesting information.

What I learned early on about the organic needs of my imagination continues to be expressed. Looking forward, my curiosity is now turning to, amongst other problems, the early assessment of both attachment and infantile autism, the lifelong impact of love on the right brain, the development of the deep unconscious and the survival functions of the right amygdala, the central role of mitochondrial energy systems in brain functioning, and continued studies of the subtle yet fundamental mechanisms that underlie the psychotherapeutic healing of the self. In regard to my recent appointment to the Honorary Scientific Committee and the co-chair of the Child Section of the next Psychodynamic Diagnostic Manual (PDM-2), I look forward to helping to establish this alternative to the DSM, a clinically relevant, integrative, science-based in-depth approach to personality assessment that addresses both nonconscious and conscious psychological functioning.

Along the course of my personal journey things have dramatically changed, yet remain constant. In addition to the work, the greatest constancy comes from my relationship with Judy. The essential nature of the support that she provides continues to sustain my intellectual and emotional needs. The "Green Book" and everything that has naturally evolved from it has taken us to most of the states in this country, and around the world many, many times. Our early investment has paid off nicely, in a tremendously exciting "quiet life." In the acknowledgements of the 1994 book I said of her, "Through her intellectual keenness and emotional honesty, she continues to reflect and reveal to me those reciprocal emotional processes that are, willingly and unwillingly, most clearly exposed in an intimate human relationship." As I look back I see this as an attempt to describe the loving bond we've created. In dedicating one of my 2003 volumes to Judy I quoted Robert Frost, "Wing to wing, oar to oar." This weekend has been an extraordinary "wing to wing" experience for Judy and me. We thank you, colleagues and friends, for this special gift.

Notes

1 *Affect Regulation and the Origin of the Self*, 1994, pp. XXIX–XXXI.
2 *Affect Regulation and the Repair of the Self*, 1994, pp. 3–8.

4

DEVELOPMENTALLY ORIENTED PSYCHOTHERAPY

Central mechanisms of the psychotherapy change process

Over the course of his extensive work, Schore has provided interdisciplinary evidence to show that implicit right-brain-to-right-brain attachment transactions occur in both the caregiver-infant and the therapist-patient relationship (the therapeutic alliance). The central theme in all his writing is the essential function of implicit affect regulation in the organization of the self; that is why special attention must be paid to affect regulation in the therapeutic process. Indeed, the inability to implicitly regulate the intensity of emotions is a major outcome of early relational trauma, a common history of a large number of psychiatric disorders.

In two essays, "Minds in the Making: Attachment, the Self-Organizing Brain, and Developmentally Oriented Psychoanalytic Psychotherapy" (2001) and "The Right Brain Implicit Self: A Central Mechanism of Psychotherapy Change Process" (2010), Schore has detailed a psychotherapeutic approach which elaborates a neurobiologically informed psychodynamic psychotherapy based on the concepts of attachment and affect regulation theory. A summary of the evidence-based clinical approach outlined in these two papers will be offered in the following section.

Schore suggests that it is not left brain verbal explicit patient-therapist discourse but right brain nonverbal affect-laden communication that directly represents the attachment dynamic embedded within the alliance. Therefore the empathic therapist is consciously, explicitly attending to the patient's verbalizations in order to objectively diagnose and rationalize the patient's dysregulating symptomatology. But the therapist has also to listen and attend at another level, an experience near subjective level, one that implicitly processes moment-to-moment socioemotional information at levels beneath awareness. His/her attentiveness focuses on barely perceptible cues that signal a change of state (Sander, 1992) in both patient and therapist, and on nonverbal behaviors and shifts in affects (McLaughlin, 1996). Studies show that 60% of human communication is nonverbal (Burgoon, 1985). Hutterer and Liss (2006) state that nonverbal variables such as tone, tempo, rhythm, timbre, prosody and amplitude of speech, as well as body language signals may need to be re-examined as essential aspects of therapeutic technique. Nonverbal transference-countertransference interactions at preconscious-unconscious levels represent implicit right brain-to-right-brain, face-to-face nonverbal communications of fast acting, automatic regulated and especially dysregulated bodily-based stressful emotional states between patient and therapist. Countertransferential reactions include the clinician's "visceral reaction to the patient's material" (Loewald, 1986, p. 278).

This dyadic psychobiological mechanism allows for the detection of unconscious affects, and underlies the premise that "an enactment, by patient or analyst, could be evidence of something which has not yet been 'felt' by them" (Zanocco, De Marchi, & Pozzi, 2006, p. 153). Ginot (2007) concludes that enactments are understood as powerful manifestations of the intersubjective process and as inevitable expressions of complex, though largely unconscious self-states and relational patterns which bring to life and consequently alter implicit memories and attachment styles. Ginot states that such intense manifestations of transference-countertransference entanglements "generate interpersonal as well as internal processes eventually capable of promoting integration and growth" (pp. 317–318). Schore stresses the fact that the relational mechanism of enactments is especially prominent during stressful ruptures of the therapeutic alliance. They occur at the edges of the regulatory boundaries of affect tolerance. An enactment can be the turning point in a psychotherapy in which the relationship is characterized by a mode of resistance/counterresistance (Zanocco et al., 2006), and these moments call for the most complex clinical skills of the therapist. Such heightened affective moments induce the most stressful countertransference responses, including the clinician's implicit coping strategies that are formed in his/her own attachment history. Plakun (1999) observes that the therapist's refusal of the transference, particularly the negative transference is an early manifestation of an enactment. The therapist's refusal, his/her need for self-protection and restoring an internal equilibrium, is expressed implicitly and spontaneously in nonverbal communications, not explicitly in the verbal narrative. These "communications" are therefore right brain primary process emotional and not left brain rational logical secondary process communications. "An interpretative stance . . . not only is thereby useless during an enactment, but also escalates the enactment and rigidifies the dissociation" (Bromberg, 2006, p. 8). Interpretation is limited in effectiveness in pathologies arising from the verbal phase, related to explicit memories, with no affect in the preverbal phase where implicit memories are to be found.

"Interpretation – the method used to the exclusion of all others for a century – is only partial; when used in isolation it does not meet the demands of modern broad-based-spectrum psychoanalysis" (Andrade, 2005, p. 677). But if not an explicit analytic response, what type of implicit cognition should the therapist use in order to guide him through stressful negative affective states? What implicit right brain coping strategies could not only autoregulate the patient's dysregulating intense affective communication but at the same time allow the *clinician* to maintain an attunement to the unacknowledged affective shifts in his/her own and the patient's self-states? Schore proposes that the therapist's moment-to-moment navigation through *these* heightened affective moments occurs by implicit nonverbal primary process clinical intuition. Intuition is defined as "the subjective experience associated with the use of knowledge gained through implicit learning" (Lieberman, 2000, p. 109). And, as Bowlby speculated in his last work (1991a), "clearly the best therapy is done by a therapist who is naturally intuitive and although guided by the appropriate theory" (p. 16).

There are direct commonalities between the spontaneous responses of the maternal intuition of a psychobiologically attuned primary caregiver and the intuitive therapist's sensitive countertransferencial responsiveness to the patient's unconscious nonverbal affective bodily-based implicit communications. Schore suggests that the intuitive psychobiological attuned therapist, on a moment-to-moment basis, implicitly tracks and resonates with the patterns of rhythmic crescendos/decrescendos of the patient's regulated and dysregulated states of affective arousal. Rather than the therapist's technical explicit skills, the clinician's intuitive implicit capacities are responsible for the outcome of an affectively charged enactment, and may dictate the depth of change process. It is the regulation of stressful and disorganizing high or low levels of affective-automatic arousal that allows for the repair and the reorganization of the right-lateralized implicit self, the biological substrate of the human unconscious. Effective psychotherapy of attachment pathologies and severe personality disorders must focus on unconscious affect and the survival defense of pathological dissociation.

Indeed, long-term psychotherapy can positively alter the developmental trajectory of the right brain as the growth-facilitating expansion of interconnectivity within the unconscious system also promotes an increased complexity of defenses and right brain strategies for regulating stressful affects that are more flexible and adaptive than pathological dissociation. Schore points out that the work of psychotherapy is not defined by what the therapist explicitly, objectively does for the patient, or says to the patient. Rather, the key mechanism is how to implicitly and subjectively be with the patient, especially during affectively stressful moments when the "going-on-being" of the patient's implicit self is dis-integrating in real time.

It is important to note that the right hemisphere cycles back into growth phases throughout the life span (Thatcher, 1994) and the orbitofrontal cortex retains a capacity for plasticity in later life (Barbas, 1995), thereby allowing for the continuing experience-dependent maturation of a more efficient and flexible right brain regulatory system within the growth- facilitating environment of an affect regulation therapeutic relationship. Bowlby (1991b) described the therapeutic process as a "joint exploration." An attachment model grounded in both biology and psychoanalysis thus accounts for how a successful therapeutic relationship can act as an interactive affect regulating context that optimizes the growth of two "minds in the making", that is, increases in complexity in both the patient's and the therapist's continually developing unconscious right minds.

References

Andrade, V. M. (2005). Affect and the therapeutic action in psychoanalysis. *International Journal of Pschoanalysis*, 86, 677–697.

Barbas, H. (1995). Anatomic basis of cognitive-emotional interactions in the primate prefrontal cortex. *Neuroscience and Biobehavioral Reviews*, 19, 499–510.

Bowlby, J. (1991a). *Charles Darwin*. New York: Norton.

Bowlby, J. (1991b, autumn). The role of the psychotherapist's personal resources in the therapeutic situation. *Tavistock Gazette*.

Bromberg, P. M. (2006). *Awakening the dreamer: Clinical journeys*. Mahweh NJ: Analtic Press.

Burgoon, J. K. (1985). Nonverbal signals. In M. L. Knapp & C. R. Miller (Eds.), *Handbook of interpersonal communication*, 344–390. Beverly Hills, CA: Sager Publications.

Ginot, E. (2007). Intersubjectivity and neuroscience: Understanding enactments and their therapeutic significance within emerging paradigms. *Psychoanalytic Psychology*, 24, 317–332.

Lieberman, M. D. (2000). Intuition: A social neuroscience approach. *Psychological Bulletin*, 126, 109–137.

Loewald, H. (1986). Transference-countertransference. *Journal of the American Psychoanalytic Association*, 34, 275–287.

McLaughlin, J. T. (1996). Power, authority, and influence in the analytic dyad. *Psychoanalytic Quarterly*, 63, 201–235.

Plakun, E. M. (1999). Making the alliance and taking the transference in work with suicidal patients. *Journal of Psychotherapy Practice and Research*, 10f, 269–276.

Sander, L. W. (1992). Letter to the editor. *International Journal of Psycho-Analysis*, 73, 582–584.

Schore, A. N. (2001). Minds in the making: Attachment, the self organizing brain, and developmentally oriented psychoanalytic psychotherapy. *British Journal of Psycho-Therapy*, 17, 299–328.

Schore, A. N. (2010). The right brain implicit self: A central mechanism of the psychotherapy change process. In J. Petrucelli (Ed.) (2010), *Knowing, not-knowing and sort-of-knowing: Psychoanalyis and the experience of uncertainty*, 177–202. London: Karnac.

Thatcher, R. W. (1994). Cyclical cortical reorganization: Origins of human cognitive development. In G. Dawson & K. W. Fischer (Eds.), *Human behavior and the developing brain*. New York: Guilford Press, 232–266.

Zanocco, G., De Marchi, A., & Pozzi, F. (2006). Sensory empathy and enactment. *International. Journal of Psychoanalysis*, 87, 145–158.

5

DEVELOPMENTAL ORIGINS OF HEALTH AND DISEASE

The neurobiology of childhood attachment trauma

5.1 Review of the Conference of the German Association for Pediatricians (2011)

In 2005 Allan Schore published the article "Attachment, Affect Regulation and the Developing Right Brain: Linking Developmental Neuroscience to Pediatrics" in the journal *Pediatrics in Review*. In this paper, Schore integrated a substantial amount of recent technical information directly relevant to the practicing pediatrician. Schore argued that research in developmental biology and physiology strongly supported a model of the developmental origins of health and disease. It has become clear that genes do not specify behavior entirely, as prenatal and postnatal environmental factors play critical roles in their developmental expressions. The newer interdisciplinary models detail the mechanisms by which "mother nature meets mother nurture." The social environment, particularly the one created together by mother and infant, directly affects gene-environment interactions and, thereby, has long-enduring effects.

These published findings caused the German Association of Pediatricians to invite Schore for a keynote address and workshop for the 107th Annual Conference of the German Association for Pediatricians on the issue of the developmental origins of health and disease. The following is a summary of those presentations.

Schore referenced the work of Leckman and March (2011) who described the phenomenal progress of the past three decades in developmental neuroscience. According to these authors it is now abundantly clear that the *in utero* environment and the dyadic relations between the child and caregivers within the early years of life have direct and enduring effects on the child's brain development and behavior. Indeed, they conclude that the enduring impact of early maternal care and the role of epigenetic modification of the genome during critical periods in early brain development are "one of the most important discoveries in all of science," and have major implication for the pediatric field. A scientific consensus has emerged that the origin of adult disease can often be found due to developmental and biological disruptions occurring during the prenatal and perinatal periods of life. Schore stated that current interdisciplinary models which integrate developmental psychology, developmental biology, and child psychiatry have direct relevance to pediatrics' interest in the normal and abnormal functions of the developing child's mind and body. The medical specialty of pediatrics specializes in diseases that are commonly found in the early stages of human development, a period marked by active states of body and brain growth.

The biology of growing tissues and the psychology of an immature yet evolving mind and body are qualitatively different than a mature organism. The infant's immature immune system is particularly vulnerable to pathogens that may adversely effect developing organs, as well as to psychopathological forces that threaten developing brain-mind-body systems. Despite different origins of these stressors both trigger common adaptive and maladaptive alterations of an immature organism's evolving psychobiological coping mechanism in order to respond to internal pathogenic organisms and external psychopathogenic forces. The definition of the medical specialty of pediatrics takes essential interest in not just diseases of children but in "childhood" – the stage of development before maturation, before adulthood. This means that normal healthy processes of development are also an essential part of basic pediatric knowledge. Therefore research in developmental biology and physiology strongly supports a model of developmental origins of health and disease (Gluckman & Adler, 2004).

The recent information on developmental origins of health and disease can be translated directly into clinical practice. The rapid advances in knowledge in the developmental sciences can strengthen the ties of pediatrics to allied fields that border it – such as pediatric neurology, child psychiatry and psychology, developmental psychology, and infant mental health. This expanding knowledge is generating a paradigm shift across disciplines.

This ongoing paradigm shift in basic and applied sciences may be expressed in three converging themes. The first arises from the wealth of neurobiological data available since the last decade. Contemporary neuroscience is very interested in the brain growth spurt from the last trimester of pregnancy through the 2nd year as this early development fosters the growth of the right brain in this critical period. The second theme of the paradigm shift can be seen in transformations within psychology, psychiatry, and neuroscience from cognition to emotion, which means that after three decades of the dominance of cognitive approaches, motivational and emotional processes have emerged in the limelight of science research. Interdisciplinary developmental research suggests that the evolutionary mechanism of the creation of an attachment bond and of social-emotional communication, the maturation of affects, and the attainment of adaptive capacity for the self-regulation of affects represent the key events in early childhood. The third theme of paradigm shift revolves around one of the few theoretical constructs that lies at the core of literally every biological and psychological discipline, self-regulation.

This process of development represents a progression of stages in which emergent adaptive self-regulatory structures and functions enable qualitatively new and more complex interactions between the individual and the social environment. Self-regulation is directly tied to affect regulation. These trends of the paradigm shift – studies of early right brain development, emphasis on attachment and processing of social-emotional information, and focus on self-regulation – converge to produce clinical models that are absolutely relevant to pediatrics, specifically, models of the origins of the development of childhood mental health and mental illness.

Schore emphasized in his presentation that out of the perspective of regulation theory self-regulation is central to the emergence of infant social-emotional, mental and physical health. A complex, dynamic unfolding of evolutionarily-conserved epigenetic programs that guide brain development shape our *in utero* and postnatal interpersonal worlds, molding the individuals we are to become. Prenatal and postnatal epigenetic factors in the social environment impact genome influenced by the mother-infant attachment relationship.

From birth onwards, an infant is plunged into a world of other human beings in which conversation, gestures, and faces are omnipresent during the infant's waking hours. These harbingers of social information are dynamic, multimodal, and reciprocal. In this context it is important to state that in infancy the maturation of the right hemisphere precedes the left, and that the right hemisphere can be considered dominant for the type of visual and acoustic communication relevant for the prelinguistic child. The self-organization of the developing brain occurs in the context of another self, another brain. In these right-brain-to-right-brain experiences the infant becomes securely attached to a psychobiologically attuned caregiver who minimizes negative affect and maximizes positive affect. Research indicates that the right hemisphere is more involved than the left in the social and biological functions activated in the infant-caregiver attachment emotional bond. Referring to McGilchrist (2009), Schore stressed that the right hemisphere is more closely in touch with emotion and the body, and thereby with the more ancient subcortical regions of the CNS.

In 1986 Winnicott emphasized that the main issue between mother and child is a communication between the anatomy and physiology of living bodies – more specifically, touch, gesture, prosody. To regulate the infant's brain, the crescendos/decrescendos of the mother's affective state have to be in resonance with similar crescendos/decrescendos of the infant's internal states of positive and negative arousal. The dyadic interaction between the infant and the mother constantly controls and modulates the baby's exposure to environment stimuli and thereby serves as a regulator of the developing individual's internal homeostasis. The regulatory function of the infant-mother interaction is also an essential promotor of the normal development and maintenance of synaptic connections during the establishment of functional brain circuits. The infant's brain volumes increases by 101% in the first year, followed by a 15% increase in the second. This clearly represents a robust growth of the human brain in the first two years of life. The attachment relationship thus strongly impacts the structure of the developing right hemisphere, the functions of which are crucial to the most precious interpersonal and intrapersonal needs of the mother and infant. The earlier maturation of the nonverbal right hemisphere than the verbal left is supported by both anatomical and neuroimaging evidence. Bodily-based attachment transactions leave their indelible mark on the right brain which is deeply connected to the emotion processing limbic circuits system and the ANS. Therefore the functional maturation of limbic circuits is significantly influenced by early social-emotional experience (Helmeke, Ovtscharoff, Poeggel, & Braun, 2001). Even the infant's HPA axis is shaped through the maternal attachment relationship. The right hemisphere regulates the HPA and mediates the human stress response, and thus the emotional dialogue right hemisphere is central to the control of vital functions supporting survival and enabling the organism to cope with stress and challenges.

Subsequent to the child's formation of an attachment to the mother in the first year, he/she will form another to the father in the second. The biorhythmicity of man with infant and woman with infant enables the child to have interactive, state-sharing, and state-attuning experiences with two different kinds of caregivers. Studies demonstrate that paternal care also affects synaptic development of the developing brain. Fathers are critically involved in male and female toddler's aggression regulation while mothers are more involved in the regulation of fear and sorrow. In all later interpersonal functioning this right hemisphere (RH) representation of attachment, acting at levels beneath conscious awareness, is accessed to appraise, interpret, and regulate socioemotional information and thereby guide future action in familiar and novel interpersonal environments. For the rest of the life span, attachment models and stress coping strategies are right hemispherically encoded in implicit-procedural memory. To have a secure attachment at one's disposal allows for an adaptive capacity to resiliently regulate emotional states through interactions with others in interconnected contexts. Parallel to this interactive regulation the individual is also equipped with the ability for autoregulation – the capacity to regulate internal psychobiological states in autonomous contexts without others. Schore emphasized the advantage of being able to adaptively shift between the two modes depending upon context. There is a tension between the two regulatory strategies responsible for conflict between interconnectness and autonomy.

Positive or negative emotional experiences may carve a permanent trace into a still developing neuronal network of immature synaptic connections, and thereby can extend or limit the functional capacity of the brain during later phases of life. Early relational trauma such as abuse/neglect are associated with severe attachment stressors and an impaired right brain development. The right hemisphere's growth spurt ends in the middle/end of the second year when the left hemisphere begins its own. Early relational traumata, which are associated with severe attachment disruptions, impair the healthy development of the right hemisphere. Therefore it is important to keep in mind that most mental illness begins far earlier in life than was previously believed. The history of relational trauma is not only a risk for psychiatric but for medical disorders too. An avoidant attachment style is associated with a lower natural killer cell cytotoxicity and with elevated antibody levels to herpes simplex virus type 1.

With an eye to childhood impairments, recent models of early life trauma are altering their focus from deficits in later maturing conscious, verbal, explicit and voluntary behavioral functions, to impairments of early maturing nonconscious, nonverbal, implicit and automatic adaptive social-emotional functions. Developmental neuroscience is moving from studies of later maturing left brain conscious verbal cognitive processes into the early preverbal development of adaptive emotion processing right brain systems in pre- and postnatal periods. Assessments of infant mental health and social-emotional development in the first year must evaluate the right brains of both members of the attachment dyad. The secure attachment is a resilience factor for coping with psychobiological stressors in later stages of the life cycle. An insecure attachment is a risk factor for interruptions of development processes and a vulnerability to the coping deficits that define later-forming pathologies.

This knowledge allows pediatrics to more deeply understand the system of nonverbal communication and interactive regulation that lies at the core of the mother-infant relationship, the fundamental interpersonal element of a healthy child's brain/mind/body developmental matrix. Therefore early social-emotional development should lie at the core of pediatric's commitment to the attainment of optimal physical, mental and social health for all infants, children, adolescents, and young adults. Recent advances in the developmental sciences allow pediatrics a position to update its models of early intervention and prevention.

In the ensuing workshop, Schore placed special emphasis on the fact that updated modern attachment theory provides interpersonal neurobiological modes of psychopathogenesis and early forming disorders of self-regulation. Once again he stressed that positive and negative emotional experience may carve a permanent trace into a still developing neuronal network of immature synaptic connections, and thereby can extend or limit the functional capacity of the brain during the later stages of life. Schore cited studies which indicate that the full expression of an individual's potentialities depend on multiple genetic and environmental factors that could cancel or potentiate the former, due to socialcultural conditions or due to the early potential being cancelled following exposure to unwanted health or child-rearing hazards during gestation and/or early childhood, or a lack of an adequate child-raising environment. Schore referred to LeDoux (2002) who stated that if a significant proportion of the early emotional experiences one has is due to the activation of the fear system rather than the positive emotional systems then a characteristic personality begins to build up from the parallel learning processes coordinated by the emotional state which is characterized by pessimism or hopelessness rather than affection and optimism. Furthermore research suggests that during acute stressful life episodes all mothers are less sensitive, more irritable, critical and punitive, and show less warmth and flexibility in the relational dialogue with their children. On the other hand, mothers who manifest chronic stress, often a product of their own experiences of early abuse and attachment disruption in abusive relationships, can be re-enacted with their own infants. This re-enactment occurs in episodes of a relational trauma – not as a singular event but ambient and cumulative. Insecure-disorganized/disoriented attachment patterns were found in 80% of maltreated infants. In the strange situation, this group shows the highest cortisol levels and heart rates.

Schore also described the subjective state of these traumatized infants. During early relational trauma, the raw impact of non-articulated, unsymbolized experience hits the child's mental system like a bolt of lightning hits the electrical panel of a house. Without a human transformor that can regulate this high-voltage overwhelming affect, all the circuits can be blown. Citing De Bellis (2002), Schore worked out that in the developing brain, elevated levels of catecholamines and cortisol may lead to adverse brain development through the mechanisms of accelerated loss of neurons, delays in myelination, abnormalities in developmentally appropriate pruning, and by inhibited neurogenesis. These alterations may provide the biological substrate for a panoply of psychiatric consequences including affective instability, limited stress tolerance, dissociative disturbances, and memory impairment. Perhaps the least known manifestation of dissociation in trauma is in the field of perceptual alteration and somatic symptoms.

Schore once again stressed the importance of early pediatric intervention and prevention. Referring to Knickmeyer (2008), he emphasized that the large increase of total brain volume in the first year of life suggests that this is a critical period in which disruptions in the developmental processes, as the result of innate genetic abnormalities or as a consequence of environmental insults, may have long-lasting or permanent effects on brain structure and function. Although the beginning of life may be a period of developmental vulnerability, it may also be a period in which therapeutic interventions would have the greatest positive effect. As an example, interpersonal disjunctions between the caregiver and borderline child-to-be are already apparent in the first six months. Due to the primary caregiver's severely limited capacity to act as a psychobiological regulator of the infant's maturing nervous system, the attachment system develops poorly.

In the last part of the workshop, Schore described an infant-mother-psychotherapy model based on neurobiologically informed modern attachment theory that can guide assessments of early attachment relationships (Schore & Newton, 2012). Visual-facial, auditory-prosodic, and tactile-gestural communications are of overriding importance as the observation of the dyadic interchange allows for the appraisal of the ongoing status of emotional and social development. Clinicians have to access their own right hemispheres to use their instincts to see, feel, and react on this bodily-based intersubjective level, as there is no verbal interaction between the caregiver and therapist. As a part of the initial evaluation of a dyadic infant-caregiver relationship, the therapist begins the assessments with a five minute structured and five minute unstructured play experience between mother/father and child. For infants under 12 months of age, only the unstructured play experience is used. With consent, these sessions are videotaped to be used in intervention if needed.

The following vignette was proposed by Schore to demonstrate the approach of regulatory theory to early assessment and intervention.

> The little boy's mother had been homeless since he was four months, old having left his father due to domestic violence. Mother and son were referred by the onsite childcare program who were concerned about his lack of facial expression and vocalization, and that he appeared to be withdrawn. He seemed to be staring off into space and he did not respond much when his

mother picked him up. During the mother-son-play-situation, the observer noted that the mother was not able to respond to her child in an attuned way. Either she overstimulated him and she controlled his actions rigidly or she didn't realize when he was overtaxed and developed dissociative strategies. He had little to no facial expression, no smile, he had glassy eyes and his movement seemed to be stiffened or eventually collapsing. After this initial observation a member of the assessment team made eye-to-eye contact with the infant, during which he smiled a number of times with the examiner, babbled and seemed to be more active. In the assessment he did not look at his mother during the half hour testing even though she was sitting approximately four feet away. He appeared to stiffen when she picked him up at the end of the testing. Thus the first treatment goal was for the mother to become aware of the infant's thresholds for arousal dysregulation and behavioral disorganization and to reduce her own arousal in order to expand her ability to read her son's nonverbal communication. The second treatment goal was for the mother to recognize her infant's dissociative withdrawal as a cue to not increase but decrease her simulation and give him more interpersonal space. A third treatment goal was to help mother engage in nonintrusive play by following the boy's lead and amplifying his states of regulated positive arousal. The fourth treatment goal then was to have mother in individual psychotherapy as well in a psychoeducational group focused on assertiveness skills, attachment, affect regulation and brain development. Working with clinician/mother video review of sessions, the boy's mother was encouraged to express her feelings and thoughts about what she saw in the video. For parents with unresolved trauma, it is often easier to wonder about what can be seen in a tape when the sound is off as ANS arousal associated with trauma can be easily triggered by sound. The mother had come from a domestic violence relationship with the boy's father and she had also experienced trauma in early childhood and therefore focused on her own trauma during her individual therapy. The attachment impressions witnessed during the play interaction between mother and child were that of childhood disorganization as seen in the boy's use of dissociation to cope with the intense arousal while interacting with the mother which was followed by a body collapse when he could not longer continue the engagement. A disorganized attachment behavior is thought to represent the untenable position of a stressed infant seeking his caregiver for protection and soothing with his attachment system fully activated while at the same time being fearful of the same caregiver, a terrible condition, and being overwhelmed without solutions. Disorganized attachment is a serious childhood indicator for immediate parent infant intervention.

Mother-infant therapeutic intervention for Jonathan and his mother focused on improving both the mother's implicit psychobiological attunement, and Jonathan's ability to respond to her relational signals. This was primarily done with the focus on how mother felt in her body versus what she thought in her mind. As she became more attuned to her own body signals and feelings, assisted by her individual therapy, she began to interact differently with Jonathan. Instead of increasing arousal and blocking Jonathan's bodily based nonverbal communication she learned to match his vocalization with her warm eyes, face, prosody, and touch. The interactive regulation of the dyad's co-created states of dysregulating central and peripheral arousal was a primary focus of the therapeutic intervention: Helping mother play with him while following his lead and giving him a space to explore was a predominant theme for all sessions. As the mother was working through in her individual therapy her complex feelings towards Jonathan's father, she was better able to play with her son using more appropriate voicing and following his lead. This therapy would have continued but mother and son left the child care program and transitioned from homelessness to living with her sister.

The use of regulation theory to guide observation more specifically informs the therapist of risk level. The boy's development was seriously at risk for a vulnerability to a spectrum of later psychopathology and an immediate approach to helping his mother change was needed. His mother however not only came from abuse and trauma herself, she was caring for her son alone. It is well known that transgenerational transmission of attachment trauma is high if no intervention is offered. Although the intervention was too short and the risk still remains, the boy's mother had made progress in becoming more aware of her own body-based cues in apprehending and responding to her child's needs, in reading his bodily-based nonverbal communication, in becoming aware of dissociation, withdrawal, and regulating hyperarousing interactions, and in giving more interpersonal space in the dyadic play.

In his keynote presentation and workshop, Schore offered some thoughts about the unique contributions of regulation theory's integration of biological and physiological domains in constructing more effective models of early pediatric and/or assessment intervention, and prevention. In this approach, the assessment technique is not as important as the assessment process. The interdisciplinary lens of regulation theory can be applied to the therapist's understanding of how one's subjectivity and implicit corporeal self is used in both assessment and treatment. Clinicians can only assess these patterns through their own implicit right brain connections with their patients. This perspective of early assessment and intervention can also be adopted by the pediatrician, frequently the first professional to observe high-risk attachment dyads.

5.2 Addendum to the Conference of the German Association for Pediatricians (2011): integrating the scientific findings of affect regulation and attachment theory in the day-nursery and classroom, by Dr. Eva Rass

At the end of his keynote lecture *Mental Health and Illness* Schore pointed out that in 2011 the pediatrician Jack P. Shonkoff published the essay "Protecting Brains, Not Only Stimulating Minds" in "Education Forum" of the prestigious journal, *Science*. In this article he stressed the one-sidedness of cognitive-linguistic enrichment in early childhood through stimulating and promoting education and cognitive knowledge, yet at the same time neglecting the importance of emotional regulation of the young child's stressful social experiences. I would add that the early childhood field should therefore combine cognitive-linguistic enrichment with greater attention to preventing and/or reducing the consequences of significant emotional adversity on the developing brain. Evidence that executive function and social-emotional self-regulation predict literacy and numerical skills underscores the salience of these capacities for targeted intervention. Teachers realize that competence in the social domain is more important at school entry than knowledge of letters and numbers. Therefore responsive caregiving by the teacher is needed to effectively buffer interpersonal stress, especially for vulnerable toddlers and very young pupils.

In 2006 H. Geddes published *Attachment in the Classroom*. In this remarkable book she described links between children's early experience, emotional well-being, and performance in school. In great detail she worked out the implications of challenging classroom behavior for providers of early care and education. Nowadays it is common for many children to spend more time with professional providers than with their parents in group care (e.g. extended day care), and for many this poses a severe challenge for an immature self-regulating system.

Affect regulation and attachment theory make important contributions to understanding the range of social and emotional difficulties that young children may experience in day care and the entry classroom, and therefore it is important to enhance both the day care providers' and the teachers' response to be more emotionally attuned to their age-appropriate needs. Such understanding would contribute to the emotional health and well-being of all children in institutional care. Children with social-emotional deficits may display problematic behavior in school with the unconscious hope that someone will understand their needs, meaning that the teacher or day care provider might be able to empathically and nonverbally "read" their behavior based on the expression of the child's anxieties. Child care providers and professionals in early education are well placed to take on such a significant task. Without becoming therapists or social workers these professionals can use such insights and understanding to enhance the developing emotional well-being of children by offering skills in supportive and calming affect regulation that, in turn, may increase the young toddler's/child's access to achievement and social inclusion.

Hyperaroused behavior in toddlers can often be associated with tiredness or over stimulation, especially in the day care setting. These toddlers need just as much bodily-based comfort and understanding as irritated-aggressive pupils that experience failure in class or interpersonal conflicts with peers. The teacher should not only be a worker in the field of "culture and education" but also a participant in an emotional and relational dialogue (Rass, 2007, 2010). Although the call for more effective strategies to build parenting capacities is broadly accepted, the unmet, skill-building needs of service providers in these domains are acknowledged less frequently. Studies in Germany (Tausch, 1999; Julius, 2009) pointed to the fact that many members of the educational/social worker field are equipped with insecure attachment styles so that vulnerable children and highly stressed professionals are engaged in dysregulated interactions on a daily basis which may compromise learning and undermine the ability to manage routine challenges and normative life stresses (Schonkoff, 2011, p. 983).

Therefore, the need for greater awareness on how to develop adequate stress buffering capacities and self-regulatory skills for day care and early education workers is needed. These skills portray promising strategies promoting effective learning in a safe atmosphere that helps students feel understood and regulated. The educational field and policy makers need to implement these strategies as well as to formulate evidence-based neurobiologically informed training programs.

References

De Bellis, M. D. (2002). Developmental traumatology: A contributory mechanism for alcohol and substance use disorders. *Psychoneuroendocrinology*, 27, 155–170.

Geddes, H. (2006). *Attachment in the classroom*. London: Worth Publishing.

Gluckman, P. D., & Adler, H. M. (2004). Living with the past: Evolution, development, and patterns of disease. *Science*, 305, 1733–1736.

Helmeke, C., Ovtscharoff, W. Jr., Poeggel, G., & Braun, K. (2001). Juvenile emotional experience alters synaptic inputs on pyramidal neurons in anterior cingulate cortex. *Cerebral Cortex*, 11, 717–727.

Knickmeyer, R. C., Gouttard, S., Kang, C., Evans, D., Wilber, K., Smith, J. K., et al. (2008). A structural MRI study of human brain development from birth to 2 years. *The Journal of Neuroscience*, 28, 12176–12182.

Leckman, J. F., & March, J. S. (2011). Editorial: Developmental neuroscience comes of age. *Journal of Child Psychology*, 52, 333–338.

LeDoux, J. E. (2002). *Synaptic self: How brains become who we are*. New York: Viking.

McGilchrist, I. (2009). *The master and his emissary*. New Haven, CT: Yale University Press.

Rass, E. (2007). Erkenntnisfortschritte in der Psychoanalyse: Implikationen für die Psychotherapie und sozialpädagogische Versorgung von Kindern und Jugendlichen. *Zeitschrift für Sozialpädagogik*, 1 (2007), 51–69.

Rass, E. (2010). Der Lehrer als Beziehungs-und Kulturarbeiter: Bindungssicherheit und Affektregulation im pädagogischen Handlungsfeld. In R. Göppel (Ed.) (2010), *Die Schule als Bildungsort und emotionaler Raum*, 111–124. Opladen: Leske + Budrich.

Schonkoff, J. P. (2011). Protecting brains, not simply stimulating minds. *Science*, 333, 982–983.

Schore, A. N. (2005). Attachment, affect regulation, and the developing right brain: Linking developmental neuroscience to pediatrics. *Pediatrics in Review*, 26(6), 204–217.

Schore, A. N., & Newton, R. (2012). Using regulation theory to guide clinical assessments of mother-infant attachment relationships. In A. N. Schore (Ed.), *The science of the art of psychotherapy*, 383–427. New York: W. W. Norton.

Tausch, R. (1999). Achtung und Einfühlung. *Pädagogik*, 11 (1999), 38–41.

6

AFFECT REGULATION THEORY

Applications to related fields

Schore's body of work over the last three decades is valuable not only to scientists and researchers of human development, but also to the mental health field. The wide range of Schore's theoretical research, psychological and psychiatric knowledge, and clinical wisdom have also added to our knowledge of the deeper mechanisms of the psychotherapy treatment process.

Schore has been relentless in his quest to integrate ongoing research into his developmental models in order to further elaborate the importance of early mother-child bonding not only to optimal and less than optimal right brain development, but also to forge the links between attachment trauma, psychopathogenesis, and psychotherapy. In parallel clinical writings he shows how this bond is expressed in the growth-facilitating patient-therapist working alliance where the same socio-emotional attachment regulatory mechanisms also influence the newly developed neuronal processing and adaptive psychological functions of the patient.

He argues that the interpersonal neurobiological perspective of regulation theory calls for a paradigm shift in models of therapeutic action, beyond the patient's insight of remembering and verbalizing trauma in order to heal and recover from it. The healing is not merely based on explicit psychological and mental reprocessing but more so on the interactively regulated physiological processes implicitly embedded in the emerging safety and trust of the therapeutic relationship. These newly formed circuits therefore override old traumatized neuronal connections and "re-shape" the brain and body, generating neuroplasticity via precise and uniquely tailored treatment helping the patient to perceive not only trauma but self and other differently.

Schore's research serves as an evidenced-based source of affect regulation psychotherapy – an intersubjective emotionally-focused model of clinical intervention which requires not only mastery of various scientific literatures but also self-knowledge and interpersonal skill. This is the central theme of Schore's most recent book *The Science of the Art of Psychotherapy* (2012). He explains that an expert therapist, through clinical experience of working affectively with different types of patients, learns how to flexibly rely less on left brain rational, verbal techniques and to intuitively focus on right brain bodily-based emotional communications within the dynamic therapeutic alliance, thereby reaching, regulating, and neurobiologically impacting the deeper layers of the patient's psyche. This therapeutic intervention has been described in previous chapters. The following chapter will focus on the relevance of Schore's relational psychobiological perspective to the psychotherapeutic as well as to the larger cultural context.

6.1 Clinical social work and regulation theory: implications of interpersonal neurobiological models of attachment

In 2007 Judith and Allan Schore published the essay "Modern Attachment Theory: The Central Role of Affect Regulation in Development and Treatment" in the *Clinical Social Work Journal*. In this article they emphasized the relevance of neurobiologically informed regulation theory which should be incorporated into the core of social work theory, research, and practice. With this emphasis on human development, modern attachment theory shares a common biopsychological perspective with clinical social work. The field of social work was traditionally focused on two core issues: person-in-environment and relationships. This biopsychosocial theoretical orientation encompasses not only psychobiological relational dynamics beginning in infancy, but also individual biological and somatic factors, as well as social and cultural influences which are both internalized and situational. The Schores also pointed out that individual development arises out of the relationship between the brain-mind-body of both infant and caregiver which is held within a culture and environment that either supports, inhibits or even threatens this crucial relationship. One of the key characteristics of a culturally competent social worker is an awareness of the clients pertinent relational beginnings held by the particular social surroundings. Based on this empirical knowledge, the social worker's therapeutic approach with teenage mothers, abused or neglected children, foster or adoptive children, aggressive adolescents, and with people with addictions will assume particular and extended dimensions. The empathic social worker must co-create an attachment relationship with his client, a *sine qua non* for her interventions. Her own inner psychic structure has to be stable yet flexible enough to hold and contain the insecure and disorganized psychic structure of the sometimes hyperaroused or dissociating client with the goal of regulating the patient's stressful, negatively valenced, dysregulated affective states.

Human beings rely intensively on nonverbal channels of communication in their day-to-day emotional, as well as interpersonal changes. Subsequently the social worker who utilizes the theoretical lens of modern attachment theory, interpersonal neurobiology, and affect regulation becomes adept not in a "not talking" but an "emotion-communicating" cure. These advances in clinical intuition can provide interactively regulated corrective emotional experiences that act as a growth-facilitating environment for the client's more complex emotional and relational structures. The expanding knowledge of the various psychological and biological disciplines that underlie development change mechanisms in both early life and in psychotherapy needs to be incorporated into the curriculum of social work studies. Optimal therapeutic and effective relational skills in turn also optimize diversity. The Schores conclude that in terms of the profession of social work's long-held commitment to the broader culture, a clinician informed in modern attachment theory can make important contributions towards not only the client but also the creation of more emotionally intelligent future societies.

6.2 Family law, parenting arrangements, and neuroscience of attachment

In every life of a child there are "normal" and natural separations; birth, kindergarten, school, summer camp with peers etc. These separations are healthy forces of development for becoming independent and mature. In contrast there are "unnatural" separations such as death of beloved persons, moving far away, becoming an adoptive or foster child because of parental inabilities or divorce. The last two phenomena are addressed by the family law system that often has to make critical decisions in "the best interests of the child" concerning parental conflicts about duration of contact as well as access to the child.

In July 2011 these important issues were discussed in an interview between Schore and the attachment researcher Jennifer McIntosh in the *Family Court Review*. McIntosh stressed that professionals in the field of family work need to be aware of recent information about very early development, attachment, and parental (especially maternal) influences on infant brain maturation, and the interpersonal neurobiological perspective of affect regulation theory in order to make scientifically informed legal decisions. When parents of an infant separate and are involved in a divorce dispute, family law has to adequately address who is the primary caregiver. Schore outlined that the primary caregiver is the person who the infant turns to while in distress, meaning the person that the child moved towards in order to seek the external regulation he/she needs at the moment. During early development the primary bond can mostly be observed with the mother and then, in addition to her, the father and others in the second or third year. Females by nature show an enhanced capacity to more effectively implicitly read nonverbal communications, and to empathically resonate with emotional states compared with men. When it comes to reading facial expressions, tone of voice and gestures, women are more able to do so than men. This is why in all human societies young children and old people are often attended to by females. Furthermore, the control center for attachment and the brain's major system of affect regulation (the right orbitofrontal cortex), is generally larger in size in females. In order to co-create a secure attachment, the young child seeks proximity to the primary caregiver, the mother, who must be subjectively perceived as predictable, consistent, and emotionally available. In the first year, and much of the second, separation from the primary caregiver and change in caregiving arrangements are potent stressors of the early developing right brain, and will alter its early maturation. Thus the neurobiology of attachment indicates that joint custody in the first year will have both short- and long-term negative effects on the the developing infant.

As opposed to the soothing arousal reducing quality of the mother the father's arousal amplifying experiences has a different impact on brain development. In the second year, when the toddler's attachment to the father strengthens, the toddler's relationship with a regulating father play is thought to be critical for the child's competent exploration of the physical world and emerging sense of autonomy. The deprivation of the father, especially in the second year impacts the later-developing left hemisphere more so than the right. Considering the neuroscience, the data indicate that weekly paternal visitations in the first year after the separation of the parents would allow the father and the child to begin to know each other, a strong motivator for their forming an attachment bond. These contacts are important also in the second year, when their impact on brain development increases dramatically. If the child is deprived of a sensitive, responsive father in the second year it has an even more negative effect than if the father is absent or less available in the first year.

Additionally, McIntosh asked for Schore's opinion on night-time separations and infant stress. Schore explained that science suggests that the primary caregiver needs to be a constant source included in a nightly bedtime routine as the night-time darkness and aloneness may trigger the attachment system and therefore the primary caregiver should be available, especially in waking-sleep transitions. Other practices may foster future sleep disturbances. Providing an infant "half" of the mother and "half" of the father does not necessarily create a secure attachment with either of them. Two halves do not make a whole, consequently current family law should understand that the stress tolerance level of children is limited.

At the end of the interview Schore summarized the central questions family law has to consider:

- Who can best fill the crucial role of the primary caregiver?
- Who can be intuitively sensitive to the child's emotional needs that are communicated in a nonverbal way?
- Who can act as the psychobiological regulator of the infant's emotional states?
- Can the parents negotiate a solution that is in the best interests of the child's development – if not, can the court help the parents negotiate such a situation via a mandated referral to psychotherapy?
- Are there certain experiences which are so negative to development that it would be better to withdraw the child from a given context?

In the context of Schore's last remarks a presentation from the German attachment researcher Karl-Heinz Brisch during an important conference addressing German family law in (2007) is worth mentioning. In this conference a major focus was on foster children and their contact with thei biological parents who have traumatized them. Brisch referred to the risk associated with the issue of children making their foster parents their primary caregivers, and what is mostly necessary for their psychic recovery. It is crucial that the contact between biological parents and their children be reconsidered, especially in light of the possibility that reactivation of past trauma, which was created by the biological parents, recurs. Schore addressed this as well and expressed that it has to be done without interrupting the developmentally important process which takes course with the foster parents. In German law the legal right of parents frequently may carry more weight than the needs of the child. It was also pointed out that, because of a legally ordered return to the biological family, the positive development processes with the foster parents are interrupted heavily and this may cause a repetitive trauma for the child. Brisch stresses the importance of the biological parents maturing psychologically so that they can fulfill the central demand of becoming a secondary caregiver (psychotherapy may be essential to this process). Both Schore and Brisch emphasized that the family law system needs to be aware of the specific developmental needs of human infancy in order to have a deeper understanding of the early stages of brain/mind/body development upon which to make thoughtful legal decisions concerning the child's future social and emotional well-being, more so than the motivations and needs of one or both parents.

6.3 Ethology: the elephant breakdown

In 2005 Schore and his colleagues published an article in the journal *Nature* on human-induced developmental social trauma in elephants, offering biological data showing "early disruption of attachment can effect the physiology, behavior and culture of animals and human over generations."

Neuroscience has demonstrated that all mammals share an ubiquitous developmental attachment mechanism and a common stress regulating neurophysiology. Elephants are renowned for their close relationships. Young elephants are reared in a matriarchal society embedded in complex layers of extended family. Like females, male socialization begins during infancy with mothers and allomothers. But in adolescence, males leave the natal family to participate in older all-male groups, a period coincident with second major stages of brain reorganization. Young elephants are reared in a matriarchal society, embedded in complex layers of extended family.

Unfortunately, the African elephant population has been decimated through mass deaths caused by human activity (at the time, about 10 million) in the form of poaching, systematic killing to control populations, and habitat loss, which in turn is associated with a social breakdown of the species. Culls and illegal poaching have fragmented normal patterns of social attachment by eliminating the supportive stratum of the matriarch and older female caretakers (allomothers). Calves witnessing culls and those raised by young, inexperienced mothers are displaying symptoms associated with human PTSD – abnormal startle response, depression, unpredictable asocial behavior, and hyper aggression. The critical role of older males in normal social development was clearly demonstrated when researchers reintroduced older bulls to quell the young males' aggression. Hyper aggression and abnormal early periods of sexual activities and hormonal shifts in traumatized males both ceased (Bradshaw, Schore, Brown, Poole, & Moss, 2005).

Psychological trauma affects both human and animals as a legacy of socioemotional, socio-ecological disruptions, and war. Trauma affects society directly through an individual's altered early social experience, and indirectly through social transmission and the collapse of traditional social structures. Long-term studies show that although many individuals survive, they may face a lifelong struggle of behavioral dysfunctions. Their children and families can exhibit similar symptoms – including domestic violence. Trauma can define a culture. The absence of compensatory social structures, such as older generations, can impede recovery.

In a follow-up study in the journal *Ethology*, Bradshaw and Schore (2007) offered "How Elephants are Opening Doors: Developmental Neuroethology, Attachment and Social Context."

They point out that ethology's renewed interest in the developmental context coincides with recent insights from neurobiology and psychology on early attachment. Attachment and social learning are understood as fundamental mechanisms in mammalian development that shape core processes responsible for informing behavior throughout a lifetime. This interdisciplinary convergence is illustrated through the example of abnormal behavior in wild African elephants that has been systematically observed in human-caused altered social contexts. Such disruptions impair normative socially mediated neuroendocrinological development leading to psychobiological dysregulation that expresses as non-normative behavior. Aberrant behavior in wild elephants thus provides a critical field example of what has been established in clinical studies but has been largely absent in wild populations: a concrete link between the effects of human disturbance on social context, and short- and long-term neuroethology. By so doing, it brings attention to the significant change in theories of behavior that has been occurring across disciplines – namely, the merging of psychobiological and ethological perspectives into common, cross-species, human inclusive models.

As perturbing as the data from Africa (and increasingly, Asia) are, the altered behaviors of wild elephants have performed a significant task. They have opened a door that brings ethological, psychological and neurobiological models together to gain deeper insights into the relationships between developmental contexts and behavioral outcomes.

6.4 Gender's influence on the developing brain

In recent decades many adults – probably under the influence of female emancipation – have tended to withdraw from the task of assigning prosocial meaning to gender – especially concerning boys. However, neglecting the gendered needs can be dangerous. The risk of not attending to real differences that exist between males and females can have detrimental consequences, both physical and psychological. It has long been established that males are more vulnerable to externalizing psychopathologies, while females are more so to internalizing psychopathologies. A large body of recent studies document an increased vulnerability of males to autism, early onset schizophrenia, attention deficit hyperactivity disorder (ADHD), and conduct disorders, as well as a recent widespread increase of these disorders in US culture. Allan Schore has suggested that the time is right to address and explore the deeper developmental, neurobiological, and cultural mechanisms that underlie the observation that boys are at risk. Towards that end, he has offered a number of presentations on this topic at conferences in the US, Europe, and Australia during 2016–2017. The first, a keynote address, was delivered on November 5th, 2015 in Santa Fe, New Mexico entitled *The Developmental Neurobiology and Psychology of Boys at Risk*; the second, which was delivered on October 15th, 2016 in Chicago, was: *Boys at Risk. Gender's Influence on the Developing Brain*. The following section gives a summary of these lectures, and elucidates the main themes.

A body of research now clearly shows that the process of cerebral maturation proceeds more rapidly in girls than in boys, a fact that is supported by general evidence of their physical, behavioral, and social-emotional development. This neurobiological mechanism of slower maturation of the developing male compared to female brains is expressed immediately at birth. Gender differences in social responsiveness have been documented within hours of delivery. Male newborns are less responsive to auditory and social stimuli and less able to maintain eye contact, and smile less than female newborns. They also experience greater difficulties in maintaining affective regulation than female newborns. Soon after birth boys display more irritability, crying, facial grimacing, and lability of emotional states. Male newborns show lability of emotional states and also a more rapid building up of arousal and a quicker peak of excitement. They engage in less self-comforting, an adaptive behavior that functions to regulate periods of arousal, tension, excitement, or distress. Schore documents studies indicating that the prenatal and postnatal maturation of boys' autonomic arousal (ANS) and CNS is slower than in the developing female.

These gender differences focus on differences in the rates of social and emotional development, beginning in the earliest stages of life. Due to their greater emotional reactivity and delays in self-regulating their affective states, boys need to rely more on maternal regulatory input than girls, and thus they are more demanding social partners of the primary attachment object, the mother. Girls, who mature more quickly, are less vulnerable to normal interactive stress. These gender differences in emotional expressivity and self-regulation differentially affect the regulatory demands of mothers and sons, as well as mothers and daughters.

Indeed, during infancy, boys show prolonged structural cerebral immaturity in affective processing and stress regulation brain circuits. In his presentation, Schore proposed that the right hemisphere, dominant for processing and regulating emotion, develops more slowly in male than in female infants. Cerebral maturation would be more rapid in girls, as are physical and psychological development, so that the prolonged immaturity of boys would represent a risk for a longer time period. In fact, research now documents that, beginning *in utero,* male and female brains display differential sensitivity towards early life stress. The male's slowly maturing HPA axis during pregnancy is more susceptible than the female's to both external environmental stressors as well as to internal hormonal alterations that accompany these social stressors.

In addition to being more sensitive to normal social stressors, males are also more sensitive to extreme social stressors. Schore cited studies showing that high maternal cortisol in late pregnancy is associated with more difficult behavior during postnatal weeks 1–7. These infants display more crying, fussing, and negative facial expressions, a description of what has been termed "a difficult temperament." The long-held idea that described fixed "inborn" temperament representing genetic factors that are first expressed at birth is incorrect. "Biological" temperament at birth is rather a result of epigenetic mechanisms that have evolved prenatally, and continue to be epigenetically shaped or misshaped by the postpartal social and emotional environment. There is widespread agreement that both prenatal and postnatal maternal–infant factors program the HPA axis and that severe, early life stress, even in pregnancy, permanently impairs the stress regulated system over later stages of the life span, thereby jeopardizing the future mental and physical health of the individual.

Furthermore, in postnatal stages of development and due to an extended period of limbic immaturity, males are more susceptible than females to "relational trauma," especially early abuse and neglect. These most severe forms of early life stress are reflected in documented gender differences in developmental traumatology and in more frequent levels of high-risk disorganized-disoriented insecure attachments in male over female infants. Therefore Schore argued that, due to delayed rates of cerebral maturation in male infants, gender differences must be considered during emotional development and especially in developmental traumatology, which are in turn high-risk factors for later-forming psychiatric disorders. He also suggested that, due to the lack of a national parental leave policy in the US, infants as young as six weeks enter day care, which on the whole is substandard in the US, and that this social stressor to male infants is also associated with an increases in later-forming externalizing psychopathologies in adolescence.

Overall, the central thesis of Schore's work dictates that significant gender differences are seen between male and female social and emotional functions in the earliest stages of development, and that these result not only from differences in sex hormones and social experiences but also from rates of male and female brain maturation, specifically in the early developing right brain. The stress regulating circuits of the male brain mature more slowly than those of the female in the prenatal, perinatal, and postnatal critical periods, and this differential structural maturation is reflected in normal gender differences in right brain attachment functions. Due to this maturational delay, developing males are also more vulnerable over a longer period of time to stressors in the social environment (attachment trauma) and toxins in the physical environment (endocrine disruptors) that negatively impact right brain development. In terms of differences in gender-related psychopathology, the early developmental neuroendocrinological and neurobiological mechanisms that are involved in the increased vulnerability of males to autism, early onset schizo-phrenia, ADHD, and conduct disorders as well as the epigenetic mechanisms can account for the recent widespread increase of these disorders in US culture and beyond.

In 2017, the year following these lectures, Schore published the content in an article entitled "All our sons: The neurobiology and neuroendocrinology of boys at risk" in the *Infant Mental Health Journal*.:

By way of closing remarks, my own understanding of Schore's gender research suggests that due to more advanced emotional adaptability and flexibility, girls – beginning in preschool and kindergarten – show more skills in coping with the social stressors embedded in educational contexts. Therefore an educational gap is widening between girls and boys, especially under less favorable economic cir-cumstances. Due to the increase in males of developmental disabilities, conduct disorders, and ADHD learning disorders many boys across all cultures are struggling educationally, and falling behind females in terms of graduation rates from both high school and college. Indeed, in many countries boys are more likely than girls to repeat a school year, or are placed in special education.

Thus, the education of preschool and kindergarten teachers concerning the social and emotional differences between boys and girls is an absolute necessity. Family policy should be informed about the neurobiology of attachment, and about the fact that the baby boy's need for very early affect regulation cannot be satisfied some weeks after birth by very early day care, now common in many Western cultures. School politics must think about emotional attachment dynamics in the teacher–pupil relationship in the classroom, and not only about cognitively stimulat-ing minds. Without a change in these perspectives, boys will most likely continue to fall behind. As opposed to female emancipation in many countries that has increasingly made it possible for women to achieve professional goals, the failure of males in acquiring equal educational competencies is not only harming their overall life but also is simultaneously presenting problematic situations for women (Rass, 2011a, 2011b).

References

Bradshaw, G. A., & Schore, A. N. (2007). How elephants are opening doors: Developmental neuroethology, attachment and social context. *Ethology*, 113, 426–436.

Bradshaw, G. A., Schore, A. N., Brown, J. L., Poole, J. H., & Moss, C. J. (2005). Elephant breakdown. *Nature*, 433, 807.

Brisch, K.-H. (2007). Bindung und Umgang. In Deutscher Familiengerichtstag (Ed.), *Siebzehnter Deutscher Familiengerichtstag vom 12–15. September in Brühl/Brühler Schriften zum Familienrecht*, Vol. 15, 89–135. Bielefeld: Gieseking.

Rass, E. (2011a). Erziehung heute. Jungen im Abseits–Mädchen im Erfolg. In Gerd-Bodo von Carlsburg (Ed.), *Baltische Stu-dien zur Erziehungs-und Sozialwissenschaft*, Bd. 22, 173–191. Frankfurt: Peter Lang.

Rass, E. (2011b). *Bindung und Sicherheit im Lebenslauf. Psychodynamische Entwicklungs-psychologie*. Stuttgart: Klett-Cotta.

Schore, A. N. (2012). *The science of the art of psychotherapy*. New York/London: Norton.

Schore, A. N. (2017). All our sons: The neurobiology and neuroendocrinology of boys at risk. *Infant Mental Health Journal*, 38, 15–52.

Schore, A. N., & McIntosh, J. (2011). Family law and the neuroscience of attachment, Part 1. *Family Court Review*, 49, 501–512.

Schore, J., & Schore, A. N. (2008). Modern attachment theory: The central role of affect regulation in development and treatment. *Clinical Social Work*, 36, 9–20.

7
CONCLUDING REMARKS

In 1969 John Bowlby wrote: "The truth is that the least-studied phase of human development remains the phase during which a child is acquiring all that makes him most distinctively human. Here is still a continent to conquer" (p. 538). Many years have passed since these significant observations were written. Allan Schore is one of those scientists who has set off to conquer this continent. Over the last three decades he has thoroughly and extensively explored and expanded our knowledge of this fundamental scientific problem, along the way continuously integrating recent evidence from numerous disciplines. Through the lens of his affect regulation theory he has succeeded in identifying the relational origin of the basic neurobiological structures that underlie essential developmental functions, which continue to be expressed over the rest of the life span. Tirelessly – and I would say passionately – he continues to be intensely motivated to educate professionals in the mental health and related fields responsible for social policy. He strives to inform us about the far-reaching consequences of attachment and regulation, both positive and negative, especially during the early years of the life span to the health of the later-developing child, adolescent, and adult.

Meanwhile, important "landscapes" of Bowlby's continent need to be further explored. Not paying attention to this growing body of knowledge is equal to serious neglect. In former times, human misfortune could be thought of as the influence of *force majeure* and sometimes later on the sole influence of genetics. Nowadays, in large part due to Schore's writings, there can be no longer be doubt that it is the adult generation that paves the way for our descendants to develop healthy and stable abilities to master future demands and unpredictable strokes of fate. His work has been an important impetus to the ongoing paradigm shift in our conception of human development, from the primacy of cognition to the primacy of emotion, relationships, and context.

Only time will tell if Schore is a "new Bowlby" or a "new Einstein." Neverthe-less, he belongs to the inner circle of outstanding scientists and intellectual giants. His groundbreaking body of work on the interpersonal neurobiological construct of regulation represents a genuinely novel and creative expansion of not only attach-ment but early human development. The organizing principle that runs throughout all his studies dictates that early childhood is the foundation stone of mental and physical health over all later stages of the life span. Anchored in a solid base of integrated scientific data, a vast storehouse of knowledge across various disciplines, and wisdom, Schore continues to describe, with remarkable precision, the essential relational experiences and developmental processes that shape the arc of human life.

INDEX